1985

STUDIES IN ROMANCE LANGUAGES: 29
John E. Keller, *Editor*

A History of

SPANISH
GOLDEN AGE
DRAMA

Henryk Ziomek

THE UNIVERSITY PRESS OF KENTUCKY

Publication of this book was assisted by a grant from
Research Foundation, Inc., of the University of Georgia.

Scholarly publisher for the Commonwealth,
serving Bellarmine College, Berea College, Centre
College of Kentucky, Eastern Kentucky University,
The Filson Club, Georgetown College, Kentucky
Historical Society, Kentucky State University,
Morehead State University, Murray State University,
Northern Kentucky University, Transylvania University,
University of Kentucky, University of Louisville,
and Western Kentucky University.

Editorial Offices: Lexington, Kentucky 40506-0024

Library of Congress Cataloging in Publication Data
Ziomek, Henryk.
A history of Spanish Golden Age drama.

Bibliography: p.
Includes index.
1. Spanish drama—Classical period, 1500-1700—
History and criticism.   I. Title.
PQ6105.Z56   1984   862'.3'09   83-23309
ISBN 0-8131-1506-X, cloth; -0158-1, paper

Contents

Illustrations

Preface

THEATER IS known to have existed on the Iberian peninsula since its first settlers and invaders arrived. Its origin and development are difficult to determine, but the cradle of Spanish theater is considered to have been in Sagunto, where the Roman ruins of a theater built according to Greek plans suggest Greek influences even before the arrival of the Romans. Classical theater remained alive throughout the Middle Ages but soon had to coexist with the mimes introduced by the Visigoths and the liturgical forms of the Roman Catholic Church. These three forces point to a little-known period during which various dramatic forms were tried, the vernacular gradually took over, and Spanish Renaissance theater developed.

Out of this background one of the true manifestations of Spanish genius—the Golden Age drama, known as the *comedia*—came into existence in the last decades of the sixteenth century and flourished for fifty years. The gradual unfolding of this major genre is not well known to the average English-speaking student of Spanish literature, although many are more knowledgeable about the great playwrights of that period, Lope de Vega and Calderón. A number of high-quality plays by lesser-known authors are less often read, just as the events leading up to that great period are often neglected. The purpose of this volume is to present a comprehensive, chronological account of the development of the Spanish *comedia* through a survey of its dramatists.

To present a picture of fully developed Spanish verse drama as a whole and to place it in its proper perspective requires a review of the elements in the evolution of Spanish theater that brought the *comedia* into existence. The early Spanish drama of the pre-*comedia* period and the Spanish stage are also analyzed. This information is helpful in understanding the hybrid and unique character of the *comedia*.

While the contributions of Lope de Vega's important theatrical precursors are within this work's purview, I naturally emphasize the innovations and additions of Lope de Vega, Calderón de la Barca, and their followers in the maturing of the *comedia*. Thus, through a chronological account rather than a subject-by-subject discussion of themes, characters, and plots, the history of Spanish drama unfolds. In addition to biographical sketches of the important playwrights and analyses of their significant works, brief plot synopses are presented to aid the reader who does not know Spanish, and most Spanish titles and terms are translated into English at their first appearance. Also, while I have attempted to highlight recent research and new approaches, especially those of the last ten years, I have cited secondary sources only in the accompanying notes, while the bibliography is restricted to standard sources for each dramatist's works, some biographies, bibliographical studies when available, and general historical and critical studies.

The vast amount of material to be presented in a limited space has forced me to be selective. Although Lope and Calderón eclipsed all other playwrights of the Golden Age, I have given attention to the supportive contributions of lesser-known playwrights, since inclusive volumes have already been written on the great masters, while their precursors and contemporaries have been neglected.

Since a brief history such as this cannot delve deeply into the excellent critical analyses that have come into existence during the last century, the notes and bibliography provide sources to which the reader can turn for further study. I have relied on the works of the eminent scholars of Spanish Golden Age drama, and acknowledge my gratitude to them for enriching my understanding of the *comedia*.

I wish to express appreciation to Gerald E. Wade and Everett W. Hesse for the benefit of their critical advice, and to David H. Darst and the readers at the University Press of Kentucky for their helpful suggestions in preparing this book. Gratitude is also expressed to the Research Foundation, Inc., at the University of Georgia for financial assistance in publication, and to the University of Georgia, which provided a grant for the typing of the manuscript.

Introduction

THE SPANISH *Siglo de Oro* (Golden Age)—almost two centuries of great cultural intensity—arose out of a rich historical background. A brief review of the origin and early history of the Spanish people provides a fuller understanding of the heterogeneous character of their drama.

The benign climatic conditions, rich resources, and accessible location of the Iberian peninsula attracted invaders from the beginning of time. The earliest record of its aboriginal past is found in the Paleolithic cave paintings, believed to have been made twelve to fourteen thousand years ago, at Altamira in the western Pyrenees. Evidence has also been found of a distinct Neolithic Almerian culture that invaded the southeastern part of the peninsula around 3,000 B.C. Written history records that Iberians coming from North Africa entered the land around 1,000 B.C., and that Celts migrating from Central Europe by way of France invaded the peninsula in the ninth century B.C. and again two centuries later. The subsequent intermingling of these two groups, who settled in the central regions of the peninsula, produced the Celtiberians. During this time the land surrounding the Mediterranean basin came under the control of the ancient civilizations. First among these were the Phoenicians, who established a colony in Cádiz in the eleventh century B.C. Later the Greeks founded other colonies on the eastern seacoast.

In 535 B.C. the Carthaginians militarily took over the peninsula, where they stayed for three centuries. Carthage and Rome clashed for supremacy in the Mediterranean world, and the Carthaginians were expelled in 206 B.C. during the Second Punic War. It took the following two centuries for the Romans to pacify the country and to impose their form of government, language, laws, and religion on the people. In so doing they created on the peninsula one of the most prosperous parts of the Roman Empire.

In 409 A.D., Teutonic invaders—Alans, Vandals, and Suevi—crossed the Pyrenees and created havoc in the land. Nine years later the Visigoths, at the request of Rome, swept down from Toulouse and took control of the entire country, retaining it for nearly three hundred years. Having already been Romanized, the Visigothic kings encouraged the growth of Roman culture, codified Roman and Gothic law, and brought Christianity to the peninsula.

Toward the beginning of the eighth century the Visigothic power weakened under the weight of internal strife; finally a rebellion broke out over the election of a duke, Rodrigo, to the throne. Under the pretext of helping the pretender to the throne, a Moorish leader, Tarik, with his Saracen army invaded the peninsula in 711 A.D. and in seven years, with the help of the Arab Musa and his reinforcement, overtook the entire country except for its northernmost parts. Although Moslem rule was marked by rivalries among various sects of the Mohammedan world, Saracen culture and power in the peninsula attained their peak in the tenth century.

The Christians' nearly eight-centuries-long efforts for reconquest were begun in 718 by Pelayo, a Visigothic chieftain and founder of the kingdom of Asturias. Their progress during the following wartorn centuries was slowed by feudal struggles and political turmoil. The Moslems were not without problems, either. The split of the caliphate into hostile Moorish kingdoms in the eleventh century marked the beginning of the dissolution of their power. Finally the Christians won a decisive battle on the plains of Toledo in 1212, pushing the Moors back to their last strongholds in Granada and the coastal cities around Cádiz. The disunited political division of the peninsula—the Christian crowns of Castile, Aragón, and Portugal, and the Moslem southern kingdoms—was maintained until well into the fifteenth century.

The long crusades against the Moors, with their military raids and migrations, firmly implanted in the Spaniards certain character traits and ways of life. Their militancy inspired the founding of religious military orders, such as those of Santiago, Calatrava, and Alcántara in the twelfth century, which fostered fervor for the holy war against Islam.

The Castilian warriors, who achieved wealth by gaining booty and land, also gained the highest esteem for their courage and honor. As will be shown, these characteristics carried over into the code of behavior in aristocratic Spain for many centuries.

During the last quarter of the fifteenth century Spain entered a new period of military power and wealth. In 1479, when Ferdinand of Aragón and Isabel of Castile married, Christian Spain was united politically and religiously. Soon afterward they consolidated the Aragonese possessions in Italy. In 1492 two other significant historical events occurred that shaped the destiny of Spain. Granada fell to the Spaniards, marking the end of the struggle to reconquer the Iberian peninsula from the Moors; and a Spanish expedition discovered America. Although Moorish culture remained a part of the Spanish heritage, the nation was free now to concentrate its energies on its own evolution and on expansion in the New World.

After the reign of the Catholic monarchs (1474-1504), ending with Isabel's death and Ferdinand's regency (1504-16), Spain continued to be united under the leadership of their grandson, Charles I (1516-56), who was also Emperor Charles V of Austria after 1519. During his reign Spain became a world power, for its position was enhanced by Charles's hereditary possessions in other parts of Europe. In Charles's reign young Spaniards responded to the promises offered by the new age, many of which were to be found in the New World. Their expansive efforts to gain fame and to enhance the prestige of their king, country, and God were not diminished by the realities of death on foreign battlefields or in tropical jungles. Having been under occupation for nearly eight centuries, although decreasingly so as the Moorish presence was gradually reduced, Spaniards responded to their new freedom, and Spain suddenly rose to become not only a unified political entity but also the conqueror of much of the New World, the leader of the Catholic Church, and a major force in European political affairs. The sixteenth century was literally the "Golden Age" of Spain, since the Spanish kings used the gold they obtained from America to support their armies in Europe, to defend the West from the Turks, to battle the German Protestants, and to check the territorial ambitions of the French.

During the sixteenth century many aspects of Spanish life underwent dynamic changes. As a result of the emigrations to America and the consequent growth of commerce and new industries, shifts in population both within and outside of the country created a mobile society with new needs. Spain's military activities in Italy also encouraged the infiltration into Spain of Renaissance culture. Thus, while the country was growing economically and gaining military and political grandeur, its literary men proceeded to blend ideas from the Italian Renaissance with their own medieval ideology, and reflected the period's urge toward concern for the welfare of the individual, a desire for glory or riches, a curiosity about humanistic learning, and increased intellectual activity in all areas.

Intellectual progress was aided by the rapid expansion of printing and by the founding of a number of universities. The university at Alcalá became one of the great centers of learning in the humanities. The court and the nobility encouraged intellectual activity by showing special favor to distinguished scholars, by exempting foreign books from import fees, and by inviting foreign savants to Spain. Large numbers of Spaniards studied abroad and brought back a fresh interest in the major areas of learning.

Under Philip II, who reigned from 1556 to 1598, the new spirit began to show signs of deterioration. This devout monarch, feeling himself the champion of Catholicism in Europe, involved Spain in religious wars in Germany in a vain effort to thwart the spreading influence of the Lutheran Reformation. The elements that had once contributed to the splendor of the *Siglo de Oro* began to work negatively. The economic expansion, which had contributed to growth in the cities and professions, as well as the emigration of many Spaniards to the New World, resulted in depopulation of the rural areas. Inflation raged, there were class struggles, and Spain's isolation from the rest of Europe grew.

The Inquisition, which had begun in 1478 as a control over the heresies against Catholicism, expelled the Moors and Jews who would not convert to Christianity, and thereby deprived the country of two of the most productive segments of its population. The increasing loss of workers in agriculture and industry reduced the food supply and lowered the industrial output. Philip II overburdened his subjects with an inefficient bureaucracy, and the unsuccessful warfare in the

Netherlands and elsewhere contributed to Spain's decline as a world power.

Thus Spain, during a glorious century and more, had risen to heights of political power that were progressively lost after the death of Philip II in 1598. His inexpedient governmental policies were continued throughout the reigns of Philip III, Philip IV, and Charles II, not only diminishing Spain's political position in world affairs but also causing a progressive deterioration in the well-being of the nation and its economic growth.

While Spain was achieving its greatest military and political strength in the sixteenth century, its literary forces were formulating out of a long tradition. It is curious to note, however, that one of Spain's most significant genres, the *comedia*, did not reach its maturity until the following century. Nevertheless, the literary Golden Age probably would not have come about without the greatness of Spain's immediate historical past. Certainly Spain's rich history must be known before the *comedia* can be fully appreciated.

CHAPTER I

The Birth and Development of Spanish National Drama

ALTHOUGH THE Spanish verse drama—the *comedia*—came into existence toward the end of the sixteenth century, its origin as a great art form can be traced not only to the first part of that century, when the Spanish Renaissance influenced the direction of drama, but even to the beginning of dramatic activity on the peninsula. A number of factors and dramatists played important roles in development of the *comedia*.

Little is known about Spanish theater in the Middle Ages. A complete, systematic study of it may never be written because of several problems. Numerous critics have expressed various and contradictory theories in attempting to identify its beginnings. One group of scholars believe that Spanish theater evolved from liturgical and semiliturgical drama, and speculate that it was born, together with poetry, when Spanish literature began. Without making an effort to follow Spanish drama from its Latin beginnings into the vernacular, and discounting a continuity between medieval and Renaissance drama, they emphasize the contribution of the Church to medieval theater. Another theory traces the growth of medieval drama to the continued presence of classical drama on the peninsula, and discounts any evolutionary process.[1] The particular findings of these scholars, nonetheless, contribute to the understanding of early Spanish theater and must be regarded together with newer suppositions.

More recent critics support the theory of a theatrical continuum that sprang from early secular roots, and confirm the coexistence of three distinct dramatic traditions in Spain across the centuries.[2] They trace the beginnings to the Greeks, who brought dramatic art, along with the other arts, to the Iberian peninsula. In Sagunto, near the present city of Valencia, the inhabitants had learned the art of staging plays by the third century B.C., when Lucius Livius Andronicus dramatized theatrical fables 160 years after Sophocles' death. Shortly afterward the Romans introduced anonymous farces called *atellanae* and burlesque improvisations. As the Romans learned more about Greece, dramatic art became important and they built more theaters, whose evidence can be seen in the ancient ruins at Castulo, Mérida, and Bibilis (Calatayud), in which the dramas of Gnaeus Naevius and Lucius Attius, and later the tragedies of Seneca, were staged.

Although classical theater coexisted with and was eventually supplanted by mimetic and liturgical forms between the fourth and twelfth centuries A.D., its continued existence can be documented by the discovery of six comedies written by Hrotsvitha in the tenth century, which were modeled on Terence's works.[3] The Church, cloisters, and universities kept the Latin theatrical tradition alive in the eleventh to thirteenth centuries, when plays were produced in Latin, and later in Spanish as the vernacular took over. As education grew and well-to-do social circles required more sophisticated dramas for their entertainment, the comedies of Plautus and *comedias elegíacas* (elegiac comedies), written in Latin verse but blended with certain Plautine passages in dialogue, came into vogue. At the University of Salamanca, founded in 1243, classical texts used in the teaching of Latin included Roman comedies and tragedies, which the teachers and students also performed, along with imitations of their own in Latin.[4]

Toward the end of the twelfth century appeared an anonymous Latin comedy, *Pamphilus de amore* (*Pamphilus in Love*), which continued to be read until the sixteenth century; it is thought to have influenced the author of the most important Renaissance dramatic work in Spain, *La Celestina*, which will be discussed later. Showing traits of the styles of both Terence and Ovid but erroneously attributed to Ovid, this poem actually has a dramatic structure, having five acts and four characters. In it Pamphilus employs the services of Venus and a crafty old hag to seduce the lovely Galatea.

Despite the Christianization of the peninsula, as a part of the Roman

Empire, in the fourth century A.D., the customary presentations of secular drama continued. When the Roman-educated Visigoths began to rule the country in the fifth century, they enjoyed the existing drama in the amphitheaters and spectacles in the circuses. They later built their own wooden stages. During the next three centuries the Iberian authors wrote farces and mimes in Late Latin for pantomimists and *joculatores* (jugglers). The actors, later called histrions, entertained in their own shows on holy days and at weddings as well as in the circuses, where they exhibited talent in acrobatics and in handling animals, as well as in music and dramatics. Having a pretext to resuscitate classical drama, both authors and actors nonetheless became corrupt, and their drama degenerated into a false orgiastic imitation of ancient classical theater. The spectacles, however, were still widely performed on the streets and in the plazas, while classical drama lost ground.

The dramatic activity of the Visigoths decreased when the Arabs, with their scientific and pragmatic character, invaded the peninsula in 711 and forced the histrions to move northward. Dangerous conditions throughout the period of the Reconquest partly account for the lack of evidence about theatrical activity and the loss of most of the dramatic texts from before 1492. Nonetheless, secular theater in Spain was kept alive into the Late Middle Ages by the jugglers and later the buffoons, who continued the mimetic tradition with *ludi scenici* (scenic entertainments), such as mimes and *juegos de escarnio* (mocking plays). Realistically depicting persons of low station, these short farces presented satirical, obscene, and even sacrilegeous subjects with slapstick humor.[5]

Evidence of the popularity of secular drama can be deduced from the first of the *Siete Partidas*, a collection of laws written under the direction of Alfonso X between 1252 and 1257, which allowed performances of religious but not of secular plays. In this compilation, special legislation is directed against certain *juegos de escarnio* that were being performed in 1252 at the plaza of Zocodover in Toledo, where buffoons disguised as clergymen, and clerics themselves, performed.

Since evidence of the existence of medieval religious drama in Spain is also sparse, speculations about its development must be drawn from the few surviving pieces and archetypes that came from the ritualistic liturgy of the Church. First of these were the tropes—a combination of four or five Latin verses interpolated into the Mass—which came into being between the first and fifth centuries, were set down by St. Gregory around 600 A.D., and developed and flourished until the thirteenth century. Universally used by various cults in Western Europe, they sprang into being out of the necessity to make the Mass more intelligible to the illiterate people, and may indeed have evolved out of the influence of contemporary classical and vernacular drama outside the Church. These antiphonal responses eventually developed into semidramatic dialogues. One of the earliest documented examples came from Valencia in 1432 but is known to have been in use since 1360. Using the Easter theme, "Quem quaeritis in sepulchro?" ("Whom do you seek in the tomb?"), it relates the sorrow of the three Marys at the tomb and their joy when receiving news of Christ's resurrection. Since the dialogue contains many extraliturgical embellishments that are known to have existed in religious ceremony between the eighth and eleventh centuries, it is considered to be the bridge whereby medieval culture made a transition from ritual to representational drama.[6]

Evolving out of an extension of Church liturgy, liturgical plays, soon called *autos* (one-act plays), came into being apart from the Mass but were still attached to the festivities of the church year—Christmas, Epiphany, Easter, and later Corpus Christi Day. Of the numerous anonymous *autos* in the vernacular and belonging to the Christmas and Easter cycles that are known to have existed, only a 147-line fragment of the *Auto* [or *Misterio*] *de los Reyes Magos (The Play of the Three Kings, ca.* 1200) has been preserved.[7] Probably written by a Gascon, this work exhibited dramatic promise and was equal to many works that appeared almost three centuries later. Discovered in about 1785 in the Cathedral of Toledo, this ancient theatrical piece, derived from either the *Officium Stellae* (Liturgy for Epiphany) or *Officium Pastorum* (Liturgy for Christmas Eve), which were used in France at that time, retells the story of the adoration as found in Matthew 2:1-12. Its structure and style show evidence of certain characteristics that continued in the *comedia* of the seventeenth century—the use of three different meters, the arrangement of episodes in climactic order, natural dialogue, swiftness of action, contrasting characters, presentation of action *in medias res*, soliloquies, rhetorical questions, and the use of astrology within the theme.

The first full extant play in Spanish descending from the *Officium Pastorum* belongs to the second half of the fifteenth century. Written by Gómez Manrique (1412-91), this play, *Representación del Nacimiento de Nuestro Señor* (*A Play about the Birth of Our Lord*, 1467-81), is known to have been staged by the nuns of the convent of Calabazanos between 1467 and 1481. Manrique also wrote a passion play [*Lamentaciones*] *fechas para la Semana Santa* (*Lamentations for Holy Week*). A fine example of another late fifteenth-century Christmas piece is an excerpt of *Vita Christi* (*The Life of Christ, ca.* 1480) by Íñigo de Mendoza (1424?-1508?), in which the angel's revelation of the Nativity is presented in the form of a dialogue with four frightened shepherds before they proceed to the manger scene. Not actually intended for the stage, this work contains rustic language and shows the fusion of comic and sacred elements.[8]

Already in the fourteenth century, however, plays dealing with the birth and death of Christ, which were set in churches and in courtyards, found strong competition in the elaborate Corpus Christi festivals in Catalonia and Valencia. Religious bodies and guilds assembled sacred scenes and tableaux, often on Old Testament subjects, which became a part of the moving procession in the streets. Fifty years later this tradition was adopted in other municipal festivals when wagons called *entremeses* or *rocas* were constructed to carry around a city characters dressed as angels and saints, who spoke in dialogues. Different from the *autos*, which were of Castilian origin, these pageants were called miracle plays.[9]

During the fifteenth century, *autos* were also named *misterios* (mystery plays) and *moralidades* (morality plays). The realistic *misterios*, which contained scenes from the lives of Christ and the saints, were later called *autohistorias* and finally evolved into *comedias de santos* (saints' plays) in the Golden Age. In contrast, the *moralidades*, often surrounded with much pageantry, were of allegorical and symbolic character and are considered to have been the origin of the *autos sacramentales* (sacramental plays) that were to evolve.[10]

Considered important among the literary forms that contributed to the creation of drama on the peninsula are certain popular medieval poetic compositions having the structure of disputative dialogues. Although not subject to specific rules, the debates involve two or more characters who argue (occasionally allegorically) about the relative merits of certain ethical problems. A fragment of *Disputa del alma y del cuerpo* (*The Dispute between the Soul and Body*), written toward the end of the twelfth century, depicts an argument between the body and the soul of a dead man, who blame each other for sins he committed in life. This theme continued to receive attention into the seventeenth century, when, for example, Calderón used it in an *auto sacramental*, *El pleito matrimonial del alma y el cuerpo* (*The Matrimonial Dispute between the Soul and the Body*).

Among other similar works is a thirteenth-century piece, *Disputa de Elena y María* (*The Dispute between Helen and Mary*), in which two young ladies argue about the merits of a clergyman and a knight as prospective husbands. Nearly a century later Juan Ruiz (?-1350/51?), in his *Libro de buen amor* (*The Book of Spiritual Love*, 1330-43), interpolated an episode containing an allegorical dispute between Don Carnal (Carnival) and Doña Cuaresma (Lent). After defeating her enemy on Ash Wednesday, Doña Cuaresma is finally forced to flee on Easter Sunday.

The combination of religious, popular, profane, and philosophical truths in drama, which had been popular much earlier elsewhere in Europe, appeared in Spain at the beginning of the fifteenth century in a satirical dialogue, *La danza de la muerte* (*The Dance of Death*). Other semidramatic works later in the century show the influence of the disputative dialogue. *Coplas de Mingo Revulgo* (*The Doggerel of Mingo Revulgo*, *ca.* 1464), containing a censure of Henry IV, presents a dialogue in rustic language between two shepherds, Gil Arrebato and Mingo Revulgo, in which they satirize Henry IV and his minister, Beltrán de la Cueva. *Coplas del Provincial* (*The Doggerel of the Provincial*), which speaks against certain members of Henry IV's court, can be considered the work of several authors but has been attributed to Rodrigo Cota. The poem *Comedieta de Ponza* (*A Play about Ponza*, 1444), dramatic in form, written by Iñigo López de Mendoza, disputatively depicts the naval defeat of the king of Navarre and Aragon in 1435 by the Genoese. Among other poems that show dramatic possibilities are *Diálogo entre el Amor y un viejo* (*The Dialogue between Love and an Old Man*, 1511) and the first *auto* of *Celestina*, which was destined later for the stage.

Several ingredients in the medieval dialogues influenced the development of future Spanish drama. Since the rhetorical exercises ended with the resolution of a conflict between the personages, a dramatic plot evolved together with definite characterization of the people involved. The element of debate also intensifies the conflict and gives a dramatic situation to the characters, who are given the opportunity to express their emotional states. While clashing with their opponents, they display indecision, disharmony, and finally adjustment. These features naturally found their way into later drama.[11]

Secular drama in Spain continued to develop into the fifteenth century despite the objection of the Church and legistlation against it. Evidence from documents reveals that at festivities on New Year's, called The Feast of the Fools, and on saints' days, the lower clergy participated in *farsias* (farces) and other similar types of plays as portions of the Office. At first they were in Latin but later in the vernacular.

During the same period, pageants called *máscaras* (masquerades) were popularly used for royal coronations, weddings, and birthdays as well as for similar festivities in noblemen's homes. These masquerades grew into elaborate representations containing pantomimic songs and burlesque dances. Their productions with masked players often allegorically presented important historical and civic events in the lives of the people. A known writer of these shows, which came to be known as *momos* (mummers' plays), was Gómez Manrique, already mentioned as the author of Christmas pieces.[12]

THE RENAISSANCE AND EARLY SIXTEENTH CENTURY

While Spanish medieval theater generally served as a dramatic ritual or social pastime rather than a literary art, the concept of dramatic art in its full complexity was rediscovered during the Renaissance. Spaniards traveling to Italy brought back the Italian *novelle* (short novels) and *comedias humanísticas*, which flourished in Italy as early as the fourteenth century. Becoming popular in Spain, these Italian literary forms influenced the maturation of the Spanish language and promoted new interest in theater. When the Italian theatrical troupes came to Spain in the middle of the sixteenth century with their well advanced dramatic art, they persuaded the Spaniards to imitate aspects of their style, to modify their calendar for the performances of plays, to modernize the stage, and to introduce women as members of the cast. During this time Spanish grandees also began to follow the example of Italian dukes by becoming patrons of dramatists.[13]

The Italian humanistic plays influenced the writing of similar works, such as Carlos Verardi's *Historia Baetica* (Andalusian Story, 1492); written in Latin, it has a Spanish subject. The genre was taken to a brilliant form in the vernacular with the appearance of one of the most exceptional works in Spanish literature, *Comedia* (later *Tragicomedia*) *de Calisto y Melibea* (*Tragicomedy of Calisto and Melibea*), which generally became known as *Celestina*, after the name of its central character.

Based on both medieval and Renaissance models and morals, the first known edition of *Celestina* was thought to have been published in 1499 by Fadrique de Basilea in Burgos. In 1951, however, Francisco Vindel disclosed that the final page of what was thought to be the first edition is actually a modern facsimile, since the paper on which it was printed was manufactured in the eighteenth century.[14] Thus an edition published in Toledo in 1500 by Pedro Hagenbach (?) is now thought to have been one of the earliest. It contains sixteen acts together with short summaries of the action, and a letter in which the author acknowledges having taken his first act entirely from an *auto* by an unknown author in Salamanca. The playwright of the longer work is discreetly revealed as Fernando de Rojas (1465?-1541) in acrostic verses at the beginning. Another edition, dated 1501 in Seville, also contains sixteen acts, but in an edition of 1502 many additions were interpolated, including five more acts.

Celestina (*or La Celestina* in later editions) relates the tragic love story of a young couple, Calisto and Melibea, who, unbeknownst to the latter's parents, are aided in the love affair by their servants and an old go-between, Celestina. Their illicit affair comes to a tragic end when Calisto fatally falls from the garden wall while attempting to assist his servants, and the desperate Melibea hurls herself from a tower to join her lover in death. The dramatic conflict arises from differences between the idealistic and realistic worlds. The two planes of life are maintained throughout the work in an irreconcilable position; moreover, the poetic

world of the lovers stands in opposition to the base, carnal realism of
Celestina and the servants. Morality, pessimism, renunciation, and lack
of freedom are typical medieval themes, whereas the unrestrained enjoyment of love and the concept of beauty are ideals belonging to the
Renaissance.[15]

Despite its heterogeneous form, having both dramatic and novelistic
elements, *La Celestina* directly contributed to the evolution of the
comedia. Certainly the first persons to attempt playwriting afterward
were well aware of its existence, since three anonymous imitations soon
appeared—the *comedias Tebaida* (written before 1504) and *Serafina*,
which was about a woman disguised as a man, and *Hipólita*, a festive
play; the latter two were published in Valencia in 1521. Numerous other
continuations and adaptations of the original drama can be perceived
in later works, such as Juan del Encina's *Egloga de Fileno y Zambardo*
(*The Play of Fileno and Zambardo*), Gil Vicente's *Barca do Inferno* (*Boat
of Hell*), and the plays of Lucas Fernández, Bartolomé de Torres Naharro, Lope de Rueda, Juan de la Cueva, and Lope de Vega.[16]

The first Spanish dramatist to come under the influence of the
Renaissance, especially in the use of Latin comedy through Italian imitations, was Juan del Encina (1468?-1529?). Often called the father
of secular theater in Spain, he inherited all the medieval concepts of
his past and became, at the same time, a pioneer of the Renaissance.[17]
His plays, known as *églogas* (eclogues), were presented in the privacy
of the palace of the Duke of Alba and Cardinal Arborea in Rome. He
is credited with giving Spanish drama popular, realistic, and national
inspiration.

Encina's career as a playwright had three periods. At first he was a
simple inheritor of the medieval mystery play, as can be seen in his
Egloga de los pastores (*The Play of the Shepherds*, 1492). Depicting
the joy of the shepherds at the birth of Christ and their departure for
Bethlehem, this play was typical of the mystery plays of his time. *Egloga
de las grandes lluvias* (*The Play of the Great Rains*) marks the beginning of his second period, when the ingredient of ridicule, coming from
the *juegos de escarnio*, can be found. In his farcical *Auto del Repelón*
(*The Hair-Pulling Skit*), Encina produces humorous dialogue between
two shepherds who joke about how they became victims in a clash with

some students from Salamanca. Their vulgarity and rustic language in *sayagués* (a dialect spoken in Sayago in the province of Zamora) were to become a model for the speech of the comic characters in the *paso* (skit) and the *graciosos* (comic characters) of the *comedia*.[18]

In his third phase, represented by *Egloga de Plácida y Vitoriano*, Encina made marked use of Italian influences. The most ambitious of his works, this drama exalts neopagan love. Offended by Vitoriano's disdain, Plácida commits suicide. When Vitoriano tries to take his life, he is stopped by Venus, who brings Plácida back to life with the help of Mercury. Thought to be the forerunner of Torres Naharro's *Comedia Himenea* (*The Play of Hymen*) and Lope de Rueda's *Los engañados* (*The Easily Deceived*), this play is subdivided with the use of songs. These Spanish poets' adaptations of fifteenth-century Italian reworkings of Latin comedies give evidence of the marked progress of Spanish drama in the early sixteenth century.

Encina's pupil, imitator, and rival was Lucas Fernández (1474-1542), whose *Farsas y églogas al modo y estilo pastoril y castellano* (*Farces and Eclogues in the Pastoral and Castilian Style*, 1514) is made up of five secular and three religious plays. Lacking divisions into acts and scenes, these plays are enlivened with the inclusion of dances and songs. Although these secular pieces possess little action and the delineations of the characters are weak, they contain certain germs that suggest motives of love and honor.[19]

Another early sixteenth-century playwright who wrote secular drama was Bartolomé de Torres Naharro (1485?-1530?).[20] Many of his dramatic pieces have Plautine titles. Eight of them, written between 1503 and 1520, deal with events and manners of that period and were directed toward mixed audiences of the lower and upper classes. Among those of interest are three works. *Comedia Soldadesca* (*Military Comedy*, 1510) a play in five acts, reveals the dissolution of its action in a series of dialogues. Probably paralleling the author's own experiences as a soldier, it presents a Spanish braggart captain who is recruiting soldiers in Italy for the pope's service. The lively action in *Comedia Tinellaria* (*The Servants' Mess Hall*, 1516) is saturated with a farcical spirit. In it the playwright exposes the corruption he saw in Rome by satirizing conditions in the lives of the servants of the cardinal of San Iano. And *Come-*

dia Trofea (Triumphant Comedy, 1514) uncovers immorality within the nobility and clergy.

Torres Naharro's *Comedia Himenea (The Play of Hymen)* is considered the best Spanish dramatic work before the *comedia*. A reworking of the plot of *La Celestina*, the story ends happily when the brother, defending his family's honor, induces the suitor of his sister to marry her. Because of the elements of love and intrigue in the plot, the dramatic motive of feminine honor, the introduction of *graciosos*, and the natural, humorous dialogue, this play could be considered the first *comedia de capa y espada* (cloak-and-sword play). Another of Torres Naharro's social plays, *Comedia Serafina (Seraphic Comedy*, 1508-09) has similar features; it is about a young man who marries the former fiancée of his married brother in order to provide a happy ending.

Torres Naharro's importance as a critic is revealed in the dramatic theories he laid down in the prologue to his *Propalladia (First Fruits of Pallas)*, a collection of eight plays that was published in Naples in 1517. In this work he classifies dramas in two groups: realistic plays dealing with customs, and imaginative plays of intrigue. Among other dramatic precepts, he advocates the classical division into five *jornadas* (acts or resting places), adherence to verisimilitude, limitation of the number of characters to between six and twelve, and the observance of decorum.

Gil Vicente (1453-1537) was another early sixteenth-century playwright who paid more attention to secular theater than did his immediate predecessors. He wrote over forty pieces, sixteen in his native Portuguese, eleven in Castilian, and the remainder in both languages.[21] Many of these works are pastoral eclogues with lively dialogues and plots containing a variety of new situations.

Vicente's works can be classified into four groups. Among the devotional works, which include *Auto pastoril castellano (A Castilian Pastoral Play*, 1502) and *Auto de San Martín* (1504), his *Auto da Mofina Mendes (The Play of the Luckless Miss Mendes*, 1534) fuses the pastoral theme of the Nativity with a folkloric subject about a shepherdess who sees her illusions broken when she breaks her jug. *Auto de la sibila Casandra (The Play of the Sibyl, Cassandra*, 1512), which was derived from the *Ordo prophetarum (The Procession of the Prophets)*, combines mythological, biblical, Christian, and pagan elements; Casandra, the Trojan prophetess, rejects the advances of Solomon to become the Virgin in whom the Son of God will become incarnate. Within the use of a biblical source Vicente also reflects his love for country life in his *Auto de los Reyes Magos* (*The Play of the Three Kings*, 1503). Included in his group of devout works are a trilogy, *Barcas* (*The Ships*, 1517-19), written on the medieval subject of the Dance of Death, and *Auto da Feira* (*The Play of the Fair*, 1528), which contains anticlerical nuances of Erasmian thought.

Among Vicente's comedies are *Comedia de Rubena* (1521) and *Comedia del viudo* (*The Play of the Widower*, 1521). In the latter work Rosvel, prince of Huxonia, falls in love with both Paula and Melicia, daughters of a recently widowed merchant from Burgos. The young man's brother soon arrives in the city in search of him. The crown prince of Portugal finally decides for Rosvel which daughter he should marry, and the play ends happily with a double wedding involving both pairs of siblings. This play reflects the literary tradition of courtly love and presents two portraitures of marriage in the widower and the godfather.

The first dramatizations of the books of chivalry to appear in Spanish theater are Vicente's tragicomedies *Don Duardos* (1522), which is based on *Primaleón* (1512) by Francisco Vázquez, and *Amadís de Gaula* (1523?), an adaptation of a book by the same title that was published in 1508 by Rodríguez de Montalvo. Both plays distort the heroism typical of knights-errant and display a ludicrous representation of the chivalresque ideal. The farcical plays for which Vicente is best known are *Farsa de Inés Pereira* (1523) and *Farsa dos Físicos* (*The Farce of the Doctors*, *ca.* 1512). He used greater variety in the choice of themes than his predecessors, increased the number of characters in his plays, and demonstrated a delicate lyricism that was to reverberate later in the plays of Lope de Vega.

In the middle of the sixteenth century Spanish secular theater continued to display steady growth. The Italian theatrical companies of Muzio and others performed widely in Spain and exerted much influence. Italian reworkings of Latin comedies, which had started with Encina, continued in popularity and reached a peak in the works of Lope de Rueda (*ca.* 1505-65). The first to commercialize theater in Spain by bringing it directly to the masses, Rueda started as an actor in the Italian troupe of Muzio. He later became the manager of a traveling company and finally a dramatist before staging his own plays in the marketplaces and taverns in the major cities of Spain.

As a dramatist Rueda paid tribute to the reigning Italian drama. His full-length plays *Eufemia*, *Los engañados* (*The Easily Deceived*), *Armelina*, and *Medora*, which were written in prose and published sometime around 1538, are adaptations from various Italian sources. The slowly moving plots that he borrowed, however, serve only as frameworks to support witty dialogue. The primitive humor, provoked by minor characters, such as a Negress, a Moor, and a Biscayan, is achieved through the use of their particular dialects.

Rueda's real talent is evident in his prose interludes, or *pasos*, a genre later perfected by Cervantes and Quiñones de Benavente. These skits were presented between the scenes of longer plays to provide comic relief. Of Rueda's ten *pasos*, the best is *Las aceitunas* (*The Olives*, 1548), in which a family of farmers argue about the price of olives as soon as the trees have been planted. Its simple and lively plot is told in a racy, natural language that is similar to that spoken by the servants in *La Celestina*.

Not intended for courtly audiences of academic circles, Rueda's plays were written in prose rather than verse and indicated the direction drama was to take in the time of Cervantes and Lope de Vega. Departing from the Celestinesque dialogue of the lower classes and influenced by Latin comedy (which was generally believed at that time to have been written in prose), Rueda brought to the stage the colloquial speech of his contemporaries—their proverbs and malapropisms. In introducing Spanish popular realism in his one-act plays, Rueda was among the first to break away from Renaissance themes and other influences that Spanish playwrights had been slavishly following.

Among Rueda's followers were Alejo Venegas del Busto (1495?-1554?), Vasco Díaz Tanco (1496?-1573?), Luis de Miranda (*ca.* 1510-65), Juan de Timoneda (1520-83), Francisco Sánchez de las Brozas (1523-1601), Juan de Mal Lara (1524-71), Pedro Simón de Abril (1530?-95), and Francisco de Avendaño (fl. 1551). In this group also belongs an actor in Rueda's company, Alonso de la Vega (*ca.* 1510-65), whose three plays clearly show Italian influence. His *Tragedia Serafina* ends with the suicide of the protagonists; *Comedia Tholomea* is based on the device of mistaken identity; and the best of the three, *La duquesa de la rosa* (*The Duchess of the Rose*), is about a princess saved by a paladin.

Juan de Timoneda, more a propagator of drama and a bookseller than a playwright, published three plays in 1559.[22] His *Amphitrión* and *Los Menennnos* were the first translations of Plautus's plays into Spanish and *Cornelia* was a reworking of Ariosto's *Il Negromante* (*The Necromancer*). Under his anagram, Joan Diamonte, Timoneda issued six other plays in verse which are less important.

Despite the growing popularity of secular theater in Spain, religious theater also remained active. Medieval influences in literature lasted longer in Spain than elsewhere in Europe because the Spainards did not entirely reject their Gothic past. Thus the tradition of the early Nativity and Passion plays and the tableaux for Corpus Christi Day continued well into the sixteenth century with the active cultivation of the *auto sacramental*. Having developed out of the various earlier representations, especially the morality plays, the *auto sacramental* made use of allegory and theological symbolism to explain the meaning of the Eucharist. Considered to be among the first of such works are Lucas Fernández's *Auto de la Pasión* (*Passion Play*, 1502), Gil Vicente's already mentioned *Auto pastoril castellano* (1502), and *Farsa sacramental* (1520) by Hernán López de Yanguas (*ca.* 1487-1545), which is the first play known to have been written for Corpus Christi Day.

One of the major writers who contributed greatly to the evolution of the *auto sacramental* was Diego Sánchez de Badajoz (?-1552).[23] His *Farsas*, *alegorías*, and *moralidades*, written between 1525 and 1547 and published posthumously in *Recopilación en metro* (1554), are based on the Bible, hagiographies, and religious dogma. Outstanding among his twenty-eight *autos* are *Farsas del Santísimo Sacramento*, *Farsa de Santa Susaña*, *Farsa del herrero* (*Farce of the Blacksmith*), and *Danza de los pecados* (*The Dance of Sins*).

The direction that the *auto* took can be observed in many of the sixteenth-century religious plays.[24] *Tragedia llamada Josefina* (*The Tragedy of Joseph*, 1535), published in 1546, by Micael de Carvajal

(1501?-1576), is one of the earliest with a tragic outcome. *Auto de Caín y Abel* (1562?) by Jaime Ferruz (1517-94) is actually a well-developed tragedy in miniature; and *El robo de Digma* (*The Theft of Digma*), attributed to Lope de Rueda, contains a *bobo* (a comic character foreshadowing the *gracioso*). The six-act *Historia de la gloriosa Santa Orosia* (*The History of the Glorious Saint Orosia, ca.* 1550?) by Bartolomé Paláu (1525-?) is the first tragic hagiographic play that dramatizes an important historical event—the defeat of King Rodrigo at the hands of the Moors—and is the forerunner of the *comedias de santos*. In Paláu's Easter play, *Victoria Christi* (1569), the elements of the earlier morality and mystery plays are fused. The best Easter piece in Spain during that period, *Auto que trata primeramente cómo el ánima de Christo descendió al infierno* (*The Play about Christ's Descent to Hell*, 1549), was composed by Juan de Pedraza, who also wrote *Farsa llamada Dança de la Muerte* (*The Farce of the Dance of Death*, 1551). Sebastián de Horozco (1510?-80) experimented with a mixture of religious and traditional elements in his *Representación de la historia evangélica del capítulo nono de San Juan* (*An Evangelical History of the Ninth Chapter of St. John*), *Representación de la parábola de San Mateo a los veinte capítulos de su sagrado Evangelio* (*Parable of the Holy Gospel in the Twentieth Chapter of St. Matthew*, 1548), and *Representación de la famosa historia de Ruth*.[25] The anonymous writer of *Auto de los hierros de Adán* (*A Play about Adam's Chains*) was the first to include a portrayal of Adam, along with other symbolic characters, in a Corpus Christi play, a tradition that was to develop in the interpretations of Timoneda and later writers in the Golden Age.

During the latter part of the sixteenth century, when the moving processions on Corpus Christi Day were adopted for other municipal festivals, increased importance was given to the *autos sacramentales* at the expense of the Nativity and Passion plays. One of the better known writers of Corpus plays was Juan de Timoneda,[26] whose *Ternario Sacramental* (1578) contains six *autos*. *Oveja perdida* (*Lost Lamb*) in this group demonstrates the dramatic power and lyric atmosphere that are characteristic of his style. The quality of Timoneda's plays surpasses that of earlier anonymous works, since he incorporates the new artistic tendencies of his day into his works.

As religious drama progressively declined toward the end of the six-teenth century, some serious Spanish playwrights turned to imitating classical tragedy, which had been brought to Spain earlier. Between 1572 and 1582 experimentation with classical drama reached a peak. Al-though these early attempts at tragedy were sporadic and met with lit-tle success, the elements of tragic pathos in these honor and legendary plays were to become important ingredients in the new *comedia* that was developing.

The first group of tragedians included Carvajal, Ferruz, and Paláu, whose *autos*, as already mentioned, occasionally had tragic outcomes. To the second group belong Juan Pastor, Juan Cirne, Alonso de la Vega, and Hernán Pérez de Oliva; these writers cultivated tragedy more closely in the classical style. A third group of authors, who focused their at-tention on Spanish themes, were Jerónimo Bermúdez, Cristóbal de Virués, Andrés Rey de Artieda, Juan de la Cueva, Lupercio Leonardo de Argensola, Miguel de Cervantes, Lobo Lasso de la Vega.

The first work to come from the second group was Juan Pastor's *Far-sa de Lucrecia: Tragedia de la castidad de Lucrecia (The Farce of Lucretia: A Tragedy on the Chastity of Lucretia* (1528). Having no divisions into acts and scenes, this play has little in common with its successors as far as form is concerned. Juan Cirne's *Tragedia de los amores de Eneas y de la reyna Dido (Tragedy of the Love between Aeneas and Queen Dido*, 1536) has five acts, and *Tragedia Serafina* by Alonso de la Vega is a pseudo-pastoral tragedy in eight scenes based on the mythological story of Pyramus and Thisbe.

The first real secular composer of tragedy in Spain, Fernán Pérez de Oliva (1494-1531?),[27] made free translations in prose of the Latin ver-sions of Sophocles' *Electra—La venganza de Agamenón (Agamemnon's Revenge*, 1528)—and of Euripides' *Hecuba—Hecuba triste (Hecuba's Melancholy)*. He also made a translation of Plautus's comedy *Am-phitryon*. Pérez de Oliva sought to show in his plays that the Spanish language was sufficiently mature for serious literature. In order to render classical tragedy more intelligible for Spaniards he did not adhere closely to the original works, lessened the importance of the chorus, and re-placed the Greek religious ethic with that of Christianity. Although the precedent for tragedy that Oliva set did not affect popular theater for more than four decades, the dramatic circles of universities responded. Classical tragedies and comedies and their imitations were presented at the University of Salamanca beginning in 1538, and soon afterward in the Jesuit schools as well.

The first tragedian in the third group, Jerónimo Bermúdez (1530?-99?), called himself the first author of Spanish tragedy. A Galician and a Dominican friar, he acclimatized classical tragedy to Spain. Although he lacked inspiration and dramatic skill, he is known for having introduced Spanish legendary and historical themes in place of those from classical sources. Bermúdez followed, however, the dramatic style of Seneca, whose tragedies had become known in Spain after Antonio Vilaragut, a Spanish dramatist of the fourteenth century, freely translated eight of his ten plays into Valencian and later into Castilian.

Bermúdez adapted the tragedy *Inés de Castro* (written sometime between 1533 and 1567) by the Portuguese Antonio Ferreira, two works of his own that were published in 1577: *Nise lastimosa (Suffering Nise)*, which had five acts and made use of two choruses, and *Nise laureada (Nise Rewarded)*, its sequel. The historical-legendary basis for these plays is the romantic love of Inés de Castro and a Portuguese crown prince, which ended with her cruel death in 1355.

The classicism of Bermúdez was gradually relaxed in the tragic plays of his immediate successors. The most important of them, Cristóbal de Virués (1550-1610), is considered to have held a pivotal position in the evolution of the *comedia* because he fused classical precepts with the sensibilities of his time and was one of the first playwrights to reduce the genre to three acts.[28] Written between 1570 and 1590 but not published until 1609, his five plays contain shocking scenes, present the unexpected, reflect the artificial language of the court, and cultivate the theme of self-determination.[29] *Elisa Dido*, his only play to have five acts and a chorus, is the closest of his works to classical concepts; nevertheless the dramatist rejected the fatalistic wheel of fortune when he fused classicism with seventeenth-century Christianity. *Elisa Dido* is derived from Justin's *Historiae Philippicae* and Virgil's *Aeneid*.

Although the intrigues in Virués's four other plays can be found in Roman tragedy, they are composed in a so-called "new style," having three acts, prologues, and epilogues, and lacking choruses. *La gran Semíramis* (*The Great Semiramis*), whose plot was also taken from Justin's history, covers a period of twenty-two years and is a dramatization of evil personified. It treats a queen's ascent to power and her eventual fall because of selfish ambition, but the play's action is shaped less by fortune than by the will of the feminine protagonist. In this play Virués regarded each of the three acts as a separate dramatic situation. The meeting of Semíramis and Nino is the concern of the first, the reign of Semíramis dominates the second, and the vengeance of Ninias is contained in the third. This innovation was to be adopted by Virués's successors.

In *La cruel Casandra* Virués abandoned ancient history and presented a cruel woman who plots against a prince and princess in Leon. Upon sacrificing her brother, Casandra pays the penalty for her deed with her death. Although some critics have called Virués inexpert for creating an incoherent, obscure plot with exaggerated passions, he has recently been praised for his ability to present the absurdities of court life in his own day and to portray a character who is driven by her own self-confidence.[30]

In *Atila furioso* (*Furious Attila*) Virués achieved the height of mental distress. After numerous scenes containing bloodshed, the protagonist, Flaminia, finally poisons Attila, who in turn strangles her to death. Although the influence of Seneca's *Hercules Furens* and *Hercules Oetaeus* is evident, Virués emphasizes the adverse characteristic of fortune and presents a shift in the characters' opinion that human will, not the whims of fortune, shapes life's triumphs.[31]

Virués's last drama, *La infelice Marcela* (*The Unfortunate Marcela*), less filled with horror, is based on the story of Isabel in the cantos of Ariosto's *Orlando Furioso*. Concerned with the conflicts of socially inferior but more dynamic individuals, the play approaches the romantic comedy that was to become so popular in Spain. In it Virués commingles noble and plebeian characters, introduces the *romance* form of versification, uses verse forms that conform to the dramatic situation, and invents a plot dealing with honor. Since all these elements were to be essential in the *comedia* that was to emerge, Virués holds an important position in the transitional period of Spanish drama.

Andrés Rey de Artieda (1544-1613), also a classical dramatist, made extensive use of national themes. For this reason he could be classified with the nationalistic group of dramatists who were headed by Juan de la Cueva.[32] The only extant tragedy by Artieda, *Los amantes* (*The Lovers*, 1581), follows a national legend about the lovers of Teruel. This work anticipated those of Yagüe de Salas, Tirso de Molina, and Pérez de Montalbán. Its four acts contain none of the bloodshed and horror that appeared in the works of earlier playwrights. In fact, his characterizations are the opposite of those of Virués. Artieda's preoccupation with psychology is seen in the excellently portrayed internal struggles of his characters. Their development and the play's dénouement are determined not by external incidents but by the characters themselves. The tragedy concentrates on the theme of fatal love. Having earlier secured the promise of his fiancée Sigura to wait for him, Marcilla unexpectedly returns to Teruel after seven years to find that she has been married to someone else against her will. In a tragic outcome, Marcilla dies first, followed by Sigura. The basic feature of this love conflict is the expiatory deaths as the solution to the lovers' unlucky struggle. In this play Artieda augments the dramatic tone with motives of passionate love and honor, which were to prevail in the *comedia*.

Although the quality in other plays by Artieda—*Los encantos de Merlin* (*The Enchantments of Merlin*) and *El príncipe vicioso* (*The Vicious Prince*)—do not approach that of *Los amantes*, they helped secure for the playwright a place among Lope de Vega's predecessors.

THE IMMEDIATE PRECURSORS OF THE *COMEDIA*

The most important dramatist in the transitional period between early Spanish drama and the *comedia* was Juan de la Cueva (1550?-1610). He was born in Seville, then spent three years in Mexico, from 1574 to 1577, before returning to Spain. After staging his first play in 1579, Cueva continued to be theatrically active until 1581. Unfortunately his creative activity later in his life is unknown. A tragic author in some of his plays, like Virués, Cueva laid important foundations for the emerging dramatic form. He decisively influenced the formation of the Spanish theater by adding national themes to the tragic plays that were becoming accepted, and by giving it more social and political importance.[33]

Cueva's fourteen dramatic works were first published in Seville in 1588. Among these extant plays are four dramas of classical antiquity: *Ayax Telamón*, *Libertad de Roma por Mucio Scévola* (*The Deliverance of Rome by Mucius Scaevola*), *Virginia y Apio Claudio*, and *Príncipe tirano* (*The Tyrant Prince*). These plays are divided into four *jornadas* (acts) and are written in octaves, *redondillas* (roundelays), and tercets. Cueva drew the stories of his plays from Virgil's *Aeneid* and the thirteenth book of Ovid's *Metamorphoses*, but he digressed from the classical precepts of drama and was inconsistent in the development of his plots. Furthermore, Cueva substituted for the fatalistic concepts of classical tragedy those pertaining to divine providence and free will. For example, in *Ayax Telamón* the protagonists lose their tragic postures when they quarrel and insult each other.

As a dramatist Cueva was an uneven but extraordinary improvisor. His wild dramatic conceptions display vigorous and emotional scenes. He is known for having definitely established strophic flexibility through the intermingling of various Spanish and Italianate verse forms—a practice that previously had been only sporadically experimented with. Another contribution of his to Spanish drama—the use of national legends—opened the way for the dramatization of material from the *romancero* (the Spanish anthology of ballads) and the Spanish chronicles in historico-legendary plays that were to follow. Cueva's objective portrayal of popularly known historical characters from the collection of old Spanish ballads can be seen in such plays as *Los siete Infantes de Lara* (*The Seven Princes of Lara*), *La muerte del rey don Sancho y reto de Zamora* (*The Death of King Sancho and the Challenge of Zamora*), and *La libertad de España por Bernardo del Carpio* (*The Liberation of Spain by Bernardo del Carpio*). Although these plays show the early playwright's deficiencies in stage art, they became popular because of his novel idea of employing traditional ballads.

Cueva also brought contemporary subjects to the Spanish stage, such as the sacking of Rome in *El saco de Roma*. Furthermore, the popular theme of honor was used in his novelesque play *El infamador* (*The Defamer*, 1581?), whose protagonist Leucino sketchily presents himself as a seducer of women, thus anticipating for the first time in Spanish drama the character of Don Juan in Tirso de Molina's *El burlador de Sevilla* (*The Trickster of Seville*). Using mythological material and a Sevillian background, Cueva intermingles various dramatic traditions in his play; he also echoes Rojas's Celestina in his portrayal of a go-between, Teodora. Other novelesque plays by Cueva are *El viejo enamorado* (*The Old Man in Love*), *El degollado* (*The Beheaded Man*), *El tutor* (*The Guardian*), and *La constancia de Arcelina* (*Arcelina's Constancy*).

In imitation of Horace's *Art of Poetry*, the third section of Cueva's *El ejemplar poético* (*The Poet's Guide*, 1606)[34] exposes his dramatic theories, thus anticipating Lope de Vega's dramatic treatise by three years. Without attempting to defend his own plays, he claims he was the first to use kings in comic plays, which he divides into *jornadas*, as Torres Naharro did, and he reduces the number of acts from five to four. Cueva nevertheless made a noteworthy contribution to the development of the *comedia*, especially in his use of various verse forms.

A lesser-known dramatist who anticipated Lope de Vega's theater was Diego López de Castro. The rigid style of his best-known four-act play, *Tragedia de Marco Antonio y Cleopatra* (1582),[35] mixes comic and tragic elements.

Lupercio Leonardo de Argensola (1559-1613), another composer of tragedy who wrote between 1581 and 1585, experienced little success. His *Filis* (which has been lost), *Alejandra*, and *Isabela* are not highly regarded, although Cervantes praised them. Using the conflict between the Christians and the Moors for the historical background of *Isabela*, the playwright dealt in Senecan-Italian style with the passionate love of a Moorish king, Alboacén, for a Christian lady, Isabela. The action in this romantic tragedy is broken, since Isabela dies as a martyr before the play ends, thus denying the opportunity for the plot to end with a logical catastrophe.

Alejandra is inferior to *Isabela* because of the irregular structure of its plot and the unusual brutality of its characters. The double plot, which deals with a prince's revenge for his father's death and the jealousy of a king who kills his wife, combines the themes of Shakespeare's *Hamlet* and *Othello*. The fervent moralizing tone in Argensola's tragedies was directed toward the intellectual minority in Spain.[36]

An important contributor to the development of drama before Lope de Vega was Miguel de Cervantes (1547-1616). As a dramatist Cervantes was not an innovator but seems to have been influenced by the classicists Virués and Argensola. In his first period of dramatic production (1580-87) he wrote between twenty and thirty plays in verse, from which have survived two four-act dramas: *Los tratos de Argel* (*The Treatments in Algiers*) and *El cerco de Numancia* (*The Siege of Numancia*).[37] The first play, in which the dramatist transfers to the stage his personal experiences during his five-year Algerian captivity, recounts an exotic story about two Christian lovers who are captured by some Moorish pirates but are finally ransomed.

Cervantes' most impressive play, *El cerco de Numancia*, is based on the tragic fate of the Celtiberians, who were besieged in the ancient city of Numancia in 133-134 B.C. by the Romans and who perished after many years of resistance. The lofty conception of this play, with its rhetorical style, collective hero, and patriotic theme of collective suicide, makes it the greatest sixteenth-century Spanish tragedy. The sources that Cervantes probably used for the account of this heroic historical incident are Florián de Ocampo's *Crónica general de España* (1541) and a Spanish ballad, "De cómo Cipión destruyó a Numancia" ("How Scipio Destroyed Numancia"), which contains a fragment of the story.[38] Despite the grandeur of its theme, the tragedy, written in several verse forms, has shortcomings, such as overly episodic and slow-moving action and the involvement of forty-three characters. But the foreign Romantics—Goethe, Bouterweck, Shelley, and Schlegel—were impressed by its grandiose conception and pathetic quality, and called it a masterpiece of dramatic art.

When Cervantes returned to playwriting toward the end of his life, continued at first in the old style and utilized material from his military experiences and captivity in North Africa in *Los baños de Argel* (*The Turkish Prisons in Algiers*), *El gallardo español* (*The Gallant Spaniard*), and *La gran sultana* (*The Grand Sultaness*). The rest of his later plays approach the "new style" of the *comedia* and have three acts. They include *El rufián dichoso* (*The Blessed Scoundrel*), a dramatization of the life of a saint who started as a ruffian, and several plays that were in-

Miguel de Cervantes Saavedra (1547-1616)

fluenced by the Italian *novelle*—*La entretenida* (*The Entertaining Comedy*), *El laberinto de amor* (*Love's Labyrinth*),[39] *La casa de los celos* (*The House of Jealousy*), and *Pedro de Urdemalas* (*Peter, the Artful Dodger*). The overly episodic and occasionally rigid features of Cervantes' plays show that he lacked poetic talent in the dialogue form,[40] although he contributed to the evolution of the *comedia* by including patriotic themes and contemporary national events.

Cervantes is more famous as the author of the greatest Spanish novel, *Don Quixote*, but he is also known in the dramatic world for being an *entremesista* (writer of interludes, or *entremeses*)[41] of first rank. With his unusual talent for giving vitality to the language, he created in his interludes superb combinations of prose and dramatic *costumbrista* (folkloric) spirit. Surpassing the rough style of Rueda's *pasos*, he created in his interludes (two in verse and six in prose) true masterpieces of satirical irony. Their themes encompass a variety of experiences in lower-class society: (1) preoccupation with purity of blood in *Retablo de las maravillas* (*The Wonder Show*); (2) the tricking of a greedy prostitute by two cheaters in *El fingido vizcaíno* (*The Basque Impostor*); (3) the consolation and advice of some hoodlums to their recently widowed friend in the verse interlude *El rufián viudo* (*The Pimp Who Lost His Moll*); (4) unfaithfulness in marriage and cuckold husbands in *La cueva de Salamanca* (*The Cave of Salamanca*), again in verse, and *El viejo celoso* (*The Jealous Old Husband*); (5) the insolubility of marriage in *El juez de los divorcios* (*The Divorce Judge*); (6) competition between a soldier and a rustic sacristan for a maiden's heart in *La guarda cuidadosa* (*The Careful Guard*); and (7) prejudice and ignorance in *La elección de los alcaldes de Daganzo* (*The Election of the Councilmen in Daganzo*). These interludes show that Cervantes had the ingenious ability to turn farcical material into serious matter.

Gabriel Lobo Lasso de la Vega (1559-1615), who was born twelve years after Cervantes, was more successful in freeing himself from the classical rules of drama, and replaced the long narrations characteristic of Virués's style with successive presentations of epic episodes. In his two tragedies published in 1587, *La honra de Dido, restaurada* (*The Restored Honor of Dido*) and *La destrucción de Constantinopla*, Lobo Lasso de la Vega tried to adapt epic stories with lyrical incidents to the dramatic form. The first tragedy, with its episodes about the destruction of Carthage, are reminiscent of those in Cervantes' *Numancia*.[42]

One of the last playwrights at the turn of the sixteenth century to exert certain influence on the dramatists of the *comedia* was Cristóbal de Morales. His works are worthy of mention in part because Lope de Vega may have used a number of them, including the title of one, as models for his own plays. Morales' legendary-mythological dramas are *El Caballero de Olmedo* (*The Knight of Olmedo*, ca. 1606), *La Estrella de Monserrate*, and *Dido y Eneas*. His fictional plays, *El legítimo bastardo* (*The Legitimate Bastard*) and *El peligro de venganza* (*The Danger of Vengeance*), are based on subjects from Italian *novelle*. And his religious works are *El renegado del cielo* (*The Renegade of Heaven*) and *Renegado, rey y mártir* (*Renegade, King and Martyr*).[43]

THE SPANISH STAGE IN THE LATE
SIXTEENTH AND EARLY SEVENTEENTH CENTURIES

Although theatrical spectacles were still being crudely staged in the yards of inns and public squares and were performed by itinerate groups of actors, even after 1560,[44] theatrical companies had been established in most of the important Spanish cities by the second half of the sixteenth century. As we have already noted, the tradition of *tableaux* and miracle plays led to the evolution of *entremeses* and *rocas* in Valencia and the Catalonian cities. One of the most famous of several playhouses in Valencia after 1566 was the Corral de la Olivera.

The establishment of a commercial theater in Seville was linked to the name of Lope de Rueda, who wrote and directed *autos* and plays of Italian influence until his death in 1565. Theater in Seville continued to develop, especially in the 1570s under the influence of the Italian impresario Alberto Ganassa, who was also active elsewhere in Spain. In this Andalusian city Cueva's plays were performed between 1579 and 1581 in the open-air theaters named Las Ataranzas, Doña Elvira, Don Juan, and Las Higueras. Meanwhile, playhouses in other Spanish cities were becoming known before the turn of the century: the Corral de la Longaniza in Valladolid, the Mesón de la Fruta in Toledo, the Corral del Carbón in Granada, a theater that staged its plays in the hospital yard in Zamora, and other *corrales* (open-air theaters) in Barcelona and Zaragoza.[45]

When in 1561 Spain's capital was moved to Madrid, which was soon converted into a royal court, the unusual growth in population and affluence made that city the theatrical capital by 1585. Already in 1565 the citizens, observing the profitable earnings of the theatrical managers, founded a charitable institution called the Cofradía de la Sagrada Pasión (Brotherhood of the Sacred Passion), whose purpose was to sublet *corrales* where companies could perform their plays. The players received a share of the profits and the rest went to a hospital for poor women.

At first the brotherhood rented a lot on Calle del Sol, which was owned by Valdivieso, and built a temporary wooden platform on which they staged their plays in the open air. They established two other locations on Calle del Príncipe—one, owned by Isabel de Pacheco, came to be known as the Corral de la Pacheca, and the other was owned by N. Burguillos. Another lot they used on Calle del Lobo was owned by Cristóbal de la Puente. Not all of the open-air theaters functioned at the same time, and in 1567 another institution, the Cofradía de la Soledad, founded a hospital for abandoned children near La Puerta del Sol and took control of the *corral* owned by Burguillos. After 1574 the profits of the theaters in Madrid were divided three ways—two-thirds went to the Cofradía de la Sagrada Pasión, and one-third went to the Cofradía de la Soledad. Supervised somewhat loosely by the City Council in Madrid, the brotherhoods enjoyed a certain freedom in the management of their *corrales* until stricter administrative regulations were enacted in 1615 and 1638.[46]

The yards of houses and the vacant lots in which the *corrales* were established later became fixed theaters. The plays were staged in the rear of the lot or in front of the house on a *tablado* (platform) so that the facade of the house served as the play's backdrop; in later years a curtain with more elaborate scenery was added. Changes in scenery were left to the imagination of the spectators, who were kept informed by the actors that a shift in setting had occurred.

The players made their entrances and exits from the doors of two *vestuarios* (dressing rooms) built at the back of the stage, one on each side. Movable curtains covered the space between them and could be opened suddenly to achieve a dramatic effect, such as the unexpected appearance of a king or a dead body. Actors occasionally used the upper level of the balconies to effect a descent from a wall or mountain. *Tramoyas* (stage machinery) served to raise angels; opened trap doors through which flames could penetrate carried out the punishment of sinners; and a *palenque* (ramp) joining the pit with the stage made it possible for animals to be brought on stage. At the front of the stage the *paños* (draperies) could be used by the actors as lurking places from which to spy. The actors wore contemporary dress, and some pieces of furniture and hand props—such as letters, jewelry, pictures, crosses, chains, muskets, and daggers—were used.

Before each performance street criers and posters plastered over the walls of buildings on the most frequented nearby streets announced the new attraction. When the play was presented most of the audience stood in the *platea* (yard), having gained admission by buying one *boleto* (ticket). Called the *mosqueteros* (standees, literally "musketeers"), they noisily threatened the actors whenever they became dissatisfied. Members of the charitable institutions rented boxes or rooms, called *desvanes*, in the upper stories of the facing houses. They were leased for larger sums to the privileged classes, who could view the performances from the windows and also watch the spectators below through the *celosías* (slatted shutters). The rooms just above the ground level, called *aposentos* or *palcos*, were also rented. Those who could afford two tickets were given seats either in boxes formed from the *ventanas* (windows) of the adjoining buildings or in rows of seats, called *gradas*, which were installed in a semicircle below the *aposentos*. Far to the rear, a closed-off upper section called a *corredor de las mujeres* or *cazuela* (gallery for women) was set apart for peasant women, while the more illustrious women had reserved seats in the balconies of the houses facing the *corral* or sat with their male escorts in the boxes. During certain intermissions vendors sold refreshments, the most popular being *aloja* (a mixture of water, honey, and spices).

Music, which was a part of each performance, was provided at first by one or more guitarists, who sang from behind the stage. Later, concerts by notable musicians, who sang and played guitars, trumpets, hornpipes, and kettledrums, were given. Their music served to welcome the actors and to quiet the audience.

A prescribed order of musical entertainment was followed during the production of a full-length play. Preceding the first act either preliminary music was sung and played or one of three joyful, lascivious dances—an *escarramán*, *zarabanda*, or *chacona*—was performed to the accompaniment of music. Next a *loa* (a monologue or dialogue spoken by one or two principal members of the cast, who sought the good will of the audience) was recited. Two *entremeses* (farces in verse) or other light farcical pieces were staged between the two acts of the *comedia*, and the whole spectacle ended with a *baile* (a dance mixed with a monologue or dialogue, accompanied by song, castanets, and guitar) while the men in the audience flirted with the women.[47]

At first the performances took place on Sunday afternoons or on holidays only, but in time they were also presented on Tuesdays and Thursdays except during Lent. Having a duration of about two hours, they started at two or three o'clock, depending on the time of year. During the Lenten recess new theatrical companies were formed, and the new season was inaugurated each year on Easter Sunday.

Since the *corral* lacked a roof, inclement weather could bring a performance to a sudden end. But in 1574 the Italian company of Alberto Ganassa improved the Corral de La Pacheca by putting a roof over the stage and covering the pàtio with a *toldo* (awning) to shade the audience from the sun.

Toward the end of the sixteenth century and at the beginning of the seventeenth, numerous *corrales* in Valencia, Toledo, Seville, Madrid, and other Spanish cities progressively grew into permanent theaters. Among the most famous were the *corrales* on Calle de la Cruz (founded in 1574) and Príncipe Street in Madrid, which became permanent in 1579 and 1583. After 1584 they remained as the only public theaters in Madrid. These two playhouses continued to exist, with certain modifications, for 165 years, until about 1744, when they were torn down and replaced by new theaters called *coliseos*. In fact, the Teatro Español today stands on the original site of the Corral del Príncipe.[48] Court theaters in which both professional actors and courtiers performed, were also established to produce festive spectacles. One of the first to become popular, in 1607, was a *corral* that performed on a patio at the Royal Palace in Madrid. In the 1620s court theaters likewise became active at Aranjuez and the old Alcázar. In 1640 the royal family continued to be entertained at the Coliseo Theater in the Buen Retiro, where Cosme Lotti, a Florentine landscape architect who had been brought to Spain by Philip IV, is known to have designed the elaborate stage decorations.

While the theater was developing as a modern institution, certain practices affecting those in the theatrical profession were changing. At first most dramatists sold their plays to the managers of theatrical groups, who managed to retain relatively good profits because they paid their actors modest and varied salaries. The managers, however, often altered the manuscripts, wore them out through use, or lost them. In addition, because there were no copyright laws, lesser-known writers stole other authors' plays, often copying them with errors and making handsome profits. Thus, out of defense, renowned dramatists turned to publishing their plays in *partes* (collections, each containing twelve plays) before offering them for sale or after retrieving them from theatrical managers or actors.

Soon after the establishment of permanent commercial theaters and the prolific production of plays, local religious authorities pressed for the preservation of good morals, while theologians began to voice negative criticisms. Theaters often gained reputations as houses of corruption and their players as licentious persons. For these reasons the king was often forced to issue decrees concerning the conditions under which plays could be staged or banned. Certain circumstantial events also placed restraints on performances. For example, Philip II ordered the theaters closed after the death of his daughter Catherine in 1597, and again in 1598, when a council of theologians urged the prohibition of plays for moral reasons, but Philip III, a partisan of the theater, revoked the decree in 1599. Later suspensions, the longest being from 1646 to 1649, occurred when the deaths of Spanish royal persons were commemorated. Although clergymen attacked the theater on moral grounds, other groups sanctioned and fought for its existence since it was a source of income for the city's hospitals. The brotherhoods were always successful ultimately in inducing the kings to reopen the theaters.[49]

Public passion for the theater grew to enormous proportions in the first half of the seventeenth century. With the immense popularity of the new dramatic form, the *comedia*, the number of dramatists and players greatly increased. During the first third of the century, approximately a hundred theatrical managers were active, each of whom staged from twenty to forty plays yearly. Often a play was given only one or a few performances. There was great competition among the theatrical companies to perform in Madrid and other important Spanish cities. Since the production of a full-length play required five to eight players, there must have been over two thousand actors at the height of the Spanish Golden Age.[50]

CONCLUSION

Theatrical activity on the Iberian peninsula from the early days of its settlement provided the fertile ground out of which the drama of the Golden Age grew. The coexistence of various dramatic traditions coming from Roman, mimetic, and liturgical roots contributed to the forms, principles, and character of the Spanish *comedia* that were being formulated. Classical drama, having influenced theatrical activity into the Middle Ages, continued to be emulated by many of the early Spanish playwrights of secular drama and tragedies, who in turn played a part in the evolution of the *comedia* with their own innovations. The mockery plays and medieval dialogues that grew out of the vernacular gave Spanish drama the particular character for which it became famous. And the medieval liturgical plays, together with the later mystery and morality plays, not only laid the ground for the saints' plays and *autos sacramentales* that were to become a part of the new drama, but also provided ingredients that would be used in secular drama.

The circumstances of staging in these three traditions, moreover, contributed to the character and development of the *comedia*. The early playwrights found a medium for their works on the Spanish stage, which moved from crude beginnings in the streets, churches, and courtyards to the private residences of the kings and noblemen, and finally to the open-air and permanent theaters. The formulative period of Spanish drama contained a brilliance of its own and must be taken into consideration when studying Spanish drama of the Golden Age.

CHAPTER II

Lope de Vega and the Formation of the *Comedia*

IN THE LAST quarter of the sixteenth century two trends in Spanish theater became evident: the popular, represented by Lope de Rueda and Juan de la Cueva, and the classical, headed by Cristóbal de Virués, Lupercio Leonardo de Argensola, and Miguel de Cervantes. In the period beginning in the 1580s, Spanish theater underwent a change that was to affect its development in the following century.[1] The foundation for the new drama was laid by the early dramatists, but its form was definitely fixed by Lope de Vega (1562-1635), one of the greatest geniuses the dramatic world has known.

Lope de Vega was born in 1562 shortly after his father, who made a living as a craftsman in gold filigree, and his mother arrived in Madrid from Asturias. According to his biographer, Pérez de Montalbán, Lope was dictating poetry before he could write and succeeded in translating Claudius Claudianus's Latin poem *De raptu Proserpinae* (*The Rape of Proserpina*) at the age of five. During his precocious childhood he studied Spanish and Latin with the writer Vicente Espinel for two years.

From 1574 to 1576, Lope de Vega attended the Jesuit Theatine college in Madrid, where he received instruction in grammar, rhetoric, singing, dancing, and fencing. He may also have taken part in school plays there, having already written his first play, *El verdadero amante* (*The True Lover*), at the age of twelve. After leaving the Jesuit school, where he had been caught in an amorous escapade, Lope was employed in the household of Gerónimo Manrique, bishop of Avila, where he probably began to compose his early plays. From 1576 to 1578 the poet also studied at the University of Alcalá de Henares, where he acquired a vast knowledge of literature, especially that of the classical writers whose learned theses he later displayed in his own plays.

After his father's death in 1578, Lope left the service of Bishop Manrique and became the secretary to Pedro Dávila, Marquis of Las Navas, and may also have studied at the University of Salamanca in 1580. Shortly after establishing his career as a dramatist in 1583, Lope had an affair with Elena Osorio, the married daughter of a leading theatrical manager. In the same year, he enlisted in Alvaro de Bazán's naval expedition to put down a rebellion in the Azores.

Upon his return two months later Lope de Vega and his juvenile companions roamed the streets of Madrid in pursuit of women, challenging all fathers, brothers, and lovers in their way. Their brawls occasionally resulted in arrest and detainment. He also continued his affair with Elena Osorio, the "Filis" of his pastoral ballads and the heroine of *La Dorotea* (1632). Her father, Jerónimo Velázquez, staged some of Lope's plays but, together with his family, vigorously opposed the love affair. Their opposition motivated the poet to write violent libels against the family, which eventually resulted in his arrest in 1588 and banishment from Madrid to Valencia for eight years.

Lope de Vega quickly broke the terms of his sentence and returned to Madrid, where he abducted and later married by proxy the seventeen-year-old Isabel de Urbina, the "Belisa" in his poems and his play *Las bizarrías de Belisa* (*The Gallantries of Belisa*). Soon after his marriage in 1588 he volunteered to join the Spanish Armada, an experience which he recorded in *La Dragontea* (*The Green Dragon*, 1598), an epic poem about Sir Francis Drake.

Returning in 1589 from the ill-fated expedition, in which his brother had been shot, Lope moved to Valencia with his wife to fulfill the terms of his exile. After becoming prominent among the Valencian dramatists, he entered the service of the Marquis of Malpica in Toledo for several months. Soon afterward, in 1590, he moved to Alba de Tormes to become the secretary of Antonio, the Duke of Alba. The following five years of domestic life marked his most productive period as a poet. It came to an end, however, when his wife and daughter Teodora died in 1594; his second daughter, Antonia, died two years later.

When Jerónimo Velázquez, the father of Elena Osorio, pardoned

Lope de Vega (1562-1635)

Lope de Vega in 1595, the recently widowed poet left the Duke of Alba and returned to Madrid in 1596. He immediately had an affair with Antonia Trillo de Armenta and cultivated another passionate love for an actor's wife, Micaela Luján, the "Camila Lucinda" in many of his poems. After marrying Juana de Guardo, the daughter of a rich butcher, in 1598, he divided his time in Toledo, Seville, and Madrid between his legitimate home and that of Micaela, who bore him five children. He also traveled to Valencia again with the Marquis of Sarriá to attend a royal double wedding.

By the time Juana died in 1613, the poet had already instigated love affairs with Jerónima de Burgos and Lucía Salcedo. In his early fifties, however, the poet experienced a religious crisis and sought refuge in the Church. After a period of initiation in a tertiary order, he took the orders of priesthood in 1614. During this time Lope's prestige as the highest among Spanish authors enabled him to deal with his noble patrons on equal terms. In particular, the Duke of Sessa, his last Maecenas, became also his personal friend. His fame, spreading abroad, brought foreign visitors to his door, including papal envoys with special compliments. In 1627 Pope Urban VIII bestowed on him an honorary doctorate in theology and the cross of the Order of St. John of Jerusalem at the Collegium Sapientiae, which explains the poet's titles of "Doctor" and "Frey."

Although the poet made a serious attempt to bring order to his chaotic life, he continued his profane writing and amorous behavior. Some time around 1616 he met and fell in love with a businessman's wife, Marta de Nevares, who became the "Amarilis" and "Marcia Leonarda" in his poetry. A cultivated woman, Marta shared the intellectual interests of the poet. After the death of Marta's husband in 1620, the lovers still could not marry because of Lope's vow of celibacy; nonetheless, Marta in 1617 gave birth out of wedlock to their daughter, Antonia Clara.

The last years of Lope de Vega's life were unhappy, despite the honors he received from the king and the pope. His popularity declined because of the influx of younger dramatists. Furthermore, he was sorrowed by Marta's becoming blind in 1626 and by her insanity and death in 1628. The elopement of Antonia Clara and other domestic calamities seriously broke his health, and he died on August 27, 1635. His death was officially mourned by high dignitaries of the Church and the nobility, while the populace swarmed the streets. About two hundred authors contributed to necrological volumes that were published in Madrid and Venice. During his lifetime Lope de Vega acquired an almost mythical reputation. "Es de Lope" ("It is by Lope") became synonymous with perfection, and Cervantes' epithet, "the prodigy [*monstruo*] of nature," earned for him universal fame.

THE DRAMATIC ART OF LOPE DE VEGA

The *comedia*, although not technically the creation of Lope de Vega, owes to him its definitive form. In his lifetime the poet succeeded in developing a new type of drama which disregarded the pseudo-Aristotelian precepts that were being propagated in Spain. In Lope's hands the term *comedia* came to mean any type of full-length play, whether comedy or tragedy. The term is still used with that connotation. By modifying and enriching the drama of his predecessors, Lope de Vega allowed the dramatic form to assimilate new features. Within the narrow framework of the existing dramatic structure he incorporated a variety of material from ancient mythology, the Bible, the lives of saints, ancient history, medieval legends, Spanish history, the subjects of Italian novelists, and Spanish life in the seventeenth century. He created realistic character types whose language was appropriate to their stations. According to the seventeenth-century Valencian playwright Ricardo de Turia, "the *comedia* performed in Spain is not really comedy but rather tragicomedy, a mixture consisting of the comic and tragic. Illustrious characters, noble actions, horror, and compassion are derived from tragedy; whereas, comedy usually also provides examples of humorous personal situations and witticism. Spaniards do not regard this blending to be inappropriate since, in nature and in poetry, persons in high and low stations often confront and deal with each other."[2]

The mixed form of the *comedia* was condemned, however, by the academically-minded Spanish writers, such as Cristóbal Suárez de Figueroa (1571?-1644) in *El passagero* (*The Passenger*), Francisco Cascales (1564-1642) in *Tablas poéticas* (*Poetic Lists*, 1617), Alonso

López Pinciano (1547-1627) in *Filosofía antigua poética* (*Ancient Theory of Poetry*, 1596),[3] and Pedro Torres Rámila (1583-1642) in a satirical libel, *Spongia* (*Sponge*, 1617).[4] These writers advocated a return to the well-defined distinctions between comedy and tragedy. Their objections apparently fell on deaf ears. Lope de Vega and his successors used the terms *tragicomedia* and *tragedia* when they designated a form for a particular play, but in general they also referred to a play as a *comedia*.[5]

The new theater was also criticized on aesthetic grounds by the supporters of classical drama, who advocated Aristotelian theory. Ignorant of Greek drama and scarcely acquainted with Aristotle's *Poetics*, however, the Spanish critics lacked a true concept of classicism, since they relied on Italian interpretations of Aristotle which erroneously praised him for imposing the three unities. Actually, Aristotle's concern for unity was of an internal nature and was much more philosophical. He may have pointed to the existence of the unity of time when citing the practices of playwrights before him and when comparing tragedy with epic poetry, but he never mentioned the unity of place, even though the nature of Greek drama necessitated it. Furthermore, when he used the term "action" it was in the sense of "conflict."[6] Nonetheless, the insistence of older playwrights on preservation of the unities was ignored by the new dramatists, who thought the lapse of time could be of indefinite duration and the place of action did not have to be confined to one setting.[7]

As the innovator of a dramatic form that was unmercifully attacked, Lope de Vega rose to his own defense by writing *Arte nuevo de hacer comedias en este tiempo* (*The New Art of Playwriting in This Age*, 1609).[8] In his treatise he defies established classical rules and supports popular Spanish tradition. Occasionally, however, he sympathizes with the classicists and belittles the masses. Lope de Vega did not derive his ideas of imitating reality and natural dialogue directly from Aristotle's *Poetics* but from the Italian dramatic treatises, such as Francisco Rebortello d'Udine's *De comoedia* and Aelius Donatus's *De tragoedia et comoedia*, which Lope paraphrased. More interested in the function of *comedia* than in its form, he declares that all of the 483 plays he has written thus far, except for six, were written against classical rules, and announces that his new type of dramatic art will be based on a compromise between the classicists and the taste of the masses. In the choice of subject matter, grave and humorous situations should exist side by side, since both produce the versatility that is found in nature. A mixture of these elements is essential to please the audience. He also argues that a play's action, which is often broken when he switches the plots, becomes more real when the unities of time and place are ignored.

Regarding poetic form within the dramatic genre, Lope advocates the use of the known Spanish and Italian meters of his day. In the matter of versification, however, he refuses to admit that the long Italian verse has an advantage over the Castilian octosyllabic verse. Unfortunately, because of his fear of criticism from the Italians, the poet retains the use of some of the prevalent mannerisms and empty, pompous phraseologies. In passages in which he does not attempt to imitate the Latins or Italians, his language flows more clearly. Recommending that different verse forms be chosen in order to differentiate between the episodes and to harmonize with particular dramatic situations, he lays down rules for the five most favored verse forms. The *décima*, ten octosyllabic lines, rhyming a b b a a c c d d c, is recommended as appropriate for plaintive speeches, expressions of dissatisfaction, and grievances. (This meter in some ways is actually a combination of two *quintillas*, with a pause after the fourth line.) The sonnet, reserved for monologues, is considered appropriate for moments of suspense. The *romance* (ballad meter), having an indefinite number of octosyllabic lines with assonance in the evenly numbered lines, is deemed proper for narration, description, light dialogue, and development. Tercets— stanzas having three hendecasyllabic (eleven-syllable) lines linked by rhyme, A B A, B C B, etc.—are suited for serious matters. The *redondilla*, a quatrain of octosyllabic lines with consonantal rhyme, a b b a, is to be used in animated conversations, love scenes, and quarrels. Finally, the royal octave, consisting of six hendecasyllables with alternate rhyme, followed by a rhyming couplet (*A B A B A B C C*), is to be employed in serious narrations and for special effects.

Other verse forms not cited by Lope de Vega in his *Arte nuevo* were also more or less commonly employed during the Spanish Golden Age. The *quintilla*, a stanza of five octosyllabic lines with two rhymes, provided no more than two lines with the same rhyme come in succession, was used to express feeling and emotion rather than action. The *silva*, an unlimited grouping of hendecasyllables and heptasyllables, freely arranged, and rhymed with no fixed stanza structure, was appropriate for soliloquies, emotional narration, and passages containing descriptions. Less common were: (1) the *lira*, a group of verses containing lines with seven and eleven syllables, whose rhyme schemes are *a B a b B* and *a B a b c C*; (2) the *verso suelto*, an eleven-syllable blank verse without rhyme, except that it usually ends in a rhyming couplet; and (3) the *pareado*, a hendecasyllable verse form (which can be mixed with heptasyllable lines) whose lines rhyme in pairs. Occasionally minor strophic lyrical compositions, such as the *copla*, *letrilla*, *canción*, *romancillo*, and *estribillo*, which are of irregular length and have no fixed rhyme scheme, were employed to summarize the problem of the play and were meant to be sung.

Since Spaniards had a passion for poetic language on the stage, Lope de Vega and his followers strove for poetic excellence by making use of the metrical forms known in their time. They blended the native Spanish meters harmoniously with the Italian ones. The musical quality of Spanish poetry may be attributed in large part to the rhythmic flexibility that was available in the large variety of meters they used. The traditional stanzas in Spain, which had been transmitted from the Middle Ages, mostly contained eight- and occasionally six-syllable lines; these included the *romance*, *redondilla*, *quintilla*, and *décima*. The imported Italian strophes were the eleven- and seven-syllable lines—the sonnet, royal octave, tercets, *silva*, *lira*, *sueltos*, and *pareados*. When analyzing the structure of each line, one counts not feet but syllables, since the structure of Spanish versification depends on a fixed number of syllables within each line.

The three most important Spanish verses were: (1) *Verso llano* (paroxytonic, ending flat), in which the accent falls on the next-to-last syllable, ending the verse open or flat; e.g., *La/ ra/ zón/ va/ de/ ven/ ci/ da* (8). The stress in this eight-syllable line is on the seventh syllable. (2) *Verso agudo* (oxytonic, ending sharp), in which the accent falls on the last syllable, ending the verse sharply with a silent beat; e.g., *Los/ re/ yes/ han/ de/ que/ rer* (7 + 1 = 8). To seven existing syllables a silent beat is added, and the accent falls on the seventh syllable. (3) *Verso esdrú-*

julo (proparoxytonic), in which the stress is not on the usually accented next to last syllable but on the one preceding it; e.g., *Des/de/ las/ to/rres/ de/ Cór/do/ba* (9 - 1 = 8).

In addition, certain poetic devices helped to determine the number of syllables in a verse: syneresis, dieresis, synalepha, and hiatus. These devices allowed the poets to maneuver the character of vowels by making them strong or weak, and to abbreviate or lengthen their lines with the use of diphthongs and triphthongs. Since the pattern of accents in Spanish versification is not rigidly set, the rhythmic arrangement of the syllables within each line can be determined by the poet. In order to achieve a certain harmony, the stressed syllables may be alternated with the unstressed ones; however, there must always be a stress on the last syllable or the next-to-last, or on the third from the end.[9]

As the exponent of a new dramatic form, Lope de Vega rejected most of the Aristotelian precepts, since his audiences expected him to disregard classical rules and was pleased when he adopted Renaissance ideas about moral truth. Although his plays are expansive rather than compact, they seldom contain obscure conceits and allegories, except for some of his later plays in which he approached baroque tendencies by employing varied stylistic effects, such as chiaroscuro and symbolism. Relying on expressive words, images, metaphors, and tropes to convey human sentiments, he developed an expository style that was meant to reflect life more or less accurately.

Lope's ideas regarding life are to a degree reflected in the behavior and attitudes of his many characters. The dialogues, commentaries, and action in each play usually approximate the portrayal of real persons in their natural conditions of life in regard to age, sex, and profession. While his dramatis personae represent dramatic stereotypes in the traditional groups—the *caballero* (gentleman) or *galán* (young cavalier) and the *dama* (lady), the *gracioso* (a comic character who is the servant of the *galán*), and the *criada* (the lady's maid)—they display a variety of human impulses along with the ideas, beliefs, and sentiments that existed in seventeenth-century Spanish society. Usually the kings, peasants, soldiers, and musicians, as minor characters, provide the veracity that is needed in the special circumstances of each play. Indicating in his *Arte nuevo* that each character should speak with appropriate diction, the playwright insists that *graciosos* should talk like clowns and kings should be solemn. Women should be treated with decorum, even when they appear disguised as men, and lovers should convincingly show their affection or passion. It is also important that soliloquies be acted out well, and actors should dress in contemporary Spanish attire.

Dramatic intrigue is often developed through the use of the *galán* and *dama*. The typical traits of the cavalier are valor, audacity, generosity, and idealism, whereas those of the *dama* are beauty, passion, and constancy. The *galán* is usually a patient, persistent adorer and often an amusing, semirepentant, although at times somewhat wicked, lover. Portrayed at first as avid for adventure and as the conqueror of female hearts, he reveals during the action of the play that he is likely to be dependent on his loyal and quick-witted servant.

Other *caballeros* who are portrayed as fathers, husbands, or brothers represent authoritarian power over their womenfolk and defend the social order in the family, since they jealously oversee the love affairs of a daughter, wife, or sister. If the family honor is stained by a "wayward" female, they are compelled to seek vengeance.

The typical *dama* is not always depicted as relying entirely on chance to solve her problems. At times she takes matters into her own hands without depending on her *criada* to carry out her intrigues. The character of the *dama* is likely to be more carefully drawn than that of the other characters. Endowed with wit and initiative, she is successful in choosing her own consort in marriage.

In some of Lope's plays of intrigue a *dama*, after being deserted by her *galán*, disguises herself as a man in order to pursue him and win him back; e.g., Leonarda in *La prueba de los amigos* (*The Test of Friendship*). This theatrical device was borrowed from the Italian *novelle*. When men are occasionally disguised as women, it is usually a *gracioso*, who appears episodically to flirt humorously with a man. The device of reversing the sex of a character contributes to the mistaken identity technique.

Lope de Vega also portrayed virtuous women, who, with the characteristics of Roman matrons, are capable of resisting the advances of a king; e.g., Queen Isabel in *El rey sin reino* (*The King without a Kingdom*). Reminiscent of the great heroines of antiquity, some female characters act more bravely than men and challenge tyrants in civil strife and war, for example, Laurencia in *Fuenteovejuna* (*The Sheep Well*). Others resent man's advantageous position in society and scorn their inconstancy—Casandra in *El castigo sin venganza* (*Punishment without Revenge*). Lope's presentation of queens showed some of them as more ambitious than their historical counterparts, such as Etelfrida in *La imperial de Otón* (*The Imperial Crown of Otón*).

The conventional omission of the mother in the *comedia* can be attributed to the fact that motherhood was highly revered in Spanish society. The mothers who occasionally appear in Lope de Vega's plays are from the upper classes and display the virtues of piety, humility, and love.

The *gracioso*, an indispensable character in the *comedia*, stands out for his comic characteristics. Evolving from the Latin slave in Roman comedy and the shepherd and servant in early Spanish drama, the *gracioso* emerged as a stock figure in the hands of Lope de Vega. This comic character is ingenious, indiscreet, and presumptuous. Often fond of proverbs and believing himself to be a polyglot, he can be a grumbler, a braggart, anxious for money, an inoffensive liar, a coward, and a gambler. It is possible for him to possess simultaneously the reputation of a drunkard and that of a loyal servant and advisor. Although the butt of constant jibes, he displays the virtues of friendship, loyalty, and truth, and attacks the ignoble traits of slander and lying.

As the confidential advisor to his master, the *gracioso* is unconditionally loyal. His active role in the plot development perhaps reveals Lope's democratic attitude concerning the social relationship between a master and his servant. In his plays the servant, who more or less directly influences the plot and may maneuver the intrigue, is endowed with the practical intelligence that enables him to help his young master turn his dreams into reality. Since the *gracioso* also parodies the behavior and speech of the *galán* and marries the *criada*, sharp contrasts between the materialistic and idealistic worlds are constantly present. While exposing the differences between the social classes, the *gracioso* provides comic relief. His satirical presentation of the customs of Madrid and the provinces supplies information about the classes and dialects of seventeenth-century Spain.

Although the *criada* is the counterpart of the *gracioso*, she occupies a discreet position as the soubrette within the *comedia* and usually plays only a minor part in the development of the intrigue. Possessing none of the ostentatious qualities of the *gracioso*, she covers up her lady's love affairs and is a submissive advisor.

The roles of magnates or kings in the *comedias* are not always the same. When the king appears as a passive character, exerting no influence on the action, he plays a supportive role, either as a father or as the highest authority, who gives consent for marriages and verdicts in civil cases. He often acts as the *deus ex machina* to bring about a happy resolution. In plays in which the monarch actively participates in the action, his personal relationships support the principle that the king is the source of all laws. In these plays the presence of the monarch underlines concepts regarding the divine right of kings and exalts the position that kingship represents the highest dignity. Young rulers occasionally appear elsewhere as leading characters, usually when involved in love intrigues. Causing at first confusion and unhappiness, they reform in time to change the outcome of the play to the satisfaction of all concerned.

The peasants or villagers act collectively as if they were living in a large rural family. Their simple environment is described in the scenes presenting festive celebrations, but when their peaceful life is threatened by a tyrant, they rise up with force to regain justice. Contrary to the usual practice of presenting the natural speech of people, peasants occasionally assume the posture of educated persons, as, for example, at the beginning of *Fuenteovejuna*, where they discuss the concept of love in neo-Platonic terms. The peasants as well as the musicians are remnants of the chorus in classical tragedy, but their role in the *comedia* is usually less important, since their main purpose (except in the plays in which they carry the major roles) is to contribute to the general entertainment with popular Spanish songs and dances.

Other character types appear in accordance with the needs of a particular play. Soldiers, who usually appear in military plays, fulfill only functional roles. In comedies of manners the occasional stereotyped figure of the *indiano* presents a greedy, disreputable adventurer who, having just returned from America with great wealth, lacks any signs of nobility, especially the virtue of honesty. In the mythological and novelesque plays, especially, characters in the guises of giants, dragons, monsters, and fauns appear, together with *salvajes* (savage men), who have been drawn from primitive men, barbarians, Indians from the New World, Guanches (natives from the Canary Islands), and savages out of mythology, folklore, legends, and books of chivalry. Neither totally bestial nor genuinely noble but a blend of the two, *salvajes* sometimes even rise to become protagonists, such as Ursón in Lope de Vega's *El nacimiento de Ursón y Valentín* (*The Birth of Orson and Valentine*) and Segismundo in Calderón's *La vida es sueño* (*Life Is a Dream*).[10]

According to Lope de Vega, the typical plot of a three-act play consists of the exposition, the *enredo* (entanglement or complication), and the *desenlace* (dénouement). The exposition, which characteristically is condensed to about a hundred lines at the beginning of the first act, acquaints the spectators with the place and time of action, the nature of the subject matter, and the main characters. The playwright often makes use of the *relación* (flashback) device to provide information about the events that happened before the time of the play. The *enredo* (the ascending part of the action, during which intrigue and suspense are sustained) consists of a series of connected episodes that complicate one or two plots. The cohesive structure of each episode, in itself, is developed in three stages: prefiguration, activation, and recapitulation. After a climax is reached toward the end of the third act, when the problem is solved, a dénouement, or *desenlace*, promptly brings the play to an end. From another viewpoint, the evolution of a plot emerges out of a protagonist's decision to solve a problem, and the resulting conflict with other characters. After an initial disagreement arises, a clash of the two opposing forces provides the suspense. The dramatic action moves toward a resolution until the protagonist's premise is proved or disproved.[11]

The recurring themes of honor, love, patriotism, and religion are woven into most of Lope de Vega's plays. They also usually underline parental authority and deal with morality. The family as an entity often plays a major role in portraying the meaning of honor. When the reputation of a family is threatened by a secret amorous intrigue or a love game, its integrity must be restored. If a father is not available to solve the honor problem, a brother or uncle must rise to the occasion; sometimes a young lady will even pursue her offender and restore her own sullied honor by whatever means are necessary.

Aside from certain incidents in Lope's life, a variety of reflections on Spanish thought and life can be found in his *comedias*. Independent of classical theater, his plays served, although less than perfectly in many ways, as a mirror of Spanish manners.[12] Whereas the Italian Renaissance revived Greek tragedy and Latin comedy, the Spanish authors developed their theater with an orientation more toward national interests and likings.

Lope and his contemporaries drew material from history, tradition, and folklore in order to satisfy popular demands. Although ancient, medieval, and Renaissance pasts were represented in their plays, allusions to the Golden Age were clearly evident. Furthermore, they focused on producing dramas with entertaining action, rather than introspective plays with character studies, such as those of Shakespeare, Racine, and Molière. Lope de Vega established the *comedia* by using various aspects of Spanish history and culture together with the idiosyncrasies of Spanish society; thus he produced entertaining showpieces that contain some moral instruction.

LOPE'S *COMEDIAS*

One of the greatest literary improvisers, Lope de Vega wrote with extraordinary facility. His literary production—three novels, four long stories, nine verse epics, three didactic poems, numerous occasional poems, and about three thousand sonnets—is small compared to his staggering output of dramatic works. Having written the vast majority of his plays in haste at the request of theatrical directors, he did not hesitate to confess that more than a hundred of his *comedias* had taken only twenty-four hours to pass from his mind to the theater. His plays were admittedly written more for the ears of spectators than for readers; nevertheless, many of his dramas were carefully planned and elaborated.

According to his own account, Lope's plays numbered 230 by 1604. By 1609 the number had risen to 500, by 1618 to 800, by 1620 to 900, by 1625 to 1,070, and by 1632 to 1,500. Lope's admirer, Montalbán (in *Fama Posthuma*, 1636), has credited him with some 1,800 plays and 400 *autos sacramentales*, though this figure is probably somewhat exaggerated.[13] From this total count, about 600 plays are known by their titles in the cataloguing in Lope's *El peregrino en su patria* (*The Pilgrim in His Homeland*). Of these the manuscripts or printed texts of over 440 plays, over 40 *autos*, and a few *entremeses* are extant. Although many holographs of Lope's plays are in existence in various libraries, most that have survived were mutilated before they were published because Lope sold them to theatrical managers, who altered them as they liked. Booksellers also bought written-out parts from actors and notes from spectators who had written the plays down from memory. Since these plays cannot be regarded as authentic, their defects cannot necessarily be blamed on Lope. Lope was also attributed as author of numerous plays that he probably did not write.

During and after the time Lope wrote his plays, publishers printed them as *sueltas* (single editions) or in *partes*. Between 1604 and 1647 his *comedias* were published in twenty-five *partes*, fourteen of which (the ninth through the twenty-second) were printed under his supervision at irregular intervals between 1617 and 1625. About two dozen of his plays became the most popular, often reappearing on the stage and in print.

A study of this vast production is a difficult task. Although some dated autograph manuscripts exist, the chronology of a large number of his plays has been difficult to establish. Morley and Bruerton have attempted, and with recognized success, to solve the problems regarding the dating of his plays.[14] This they did by examining the poetic structure of his dated manuscripts, and thus they were able to assign approximate dates to the undated plays. By arranging the plays in their proper sequence, these scholars provided a basis for subsequent research on Lope's drama.

In his youth Lope de Vega wrote eclogues and pastoral and allegorical morality plays. His earliest preserved play, *Los hechos de Garcilaso de la Vega y el moro Tarfe* (*The Exploits of Garcilaso de la Vega and the Moor Tarfe*, written between 1579 and 1583),[15] is a youthful reverie about military honors. He emerged as a serious playwright in 1587 with the beginnings of his prolific theatrical activity, which lasted for almost half a century until his death in 1635. His plays may be classified according to subject, but there is often overlapping between groups.

The Heroic-Honor Plays. In Lope de Vega's repertory the heroic plays excel. They are differentiated from his other plays in that their themes, drawn from history, national annals, and current events, possess a grave tone and include more royal and aristocratic characters. Having scenarios set in a milieu familiar to his audiences, they display nationalistic and democratic ideals. The playwright identified himself with the heroic protagonist early in his career with *El hijo venturoso* (*The Fortunate Son*) and *El hijo de Reduán* (*The Son of Reduán*), both from 1588-95.

At the peak of his career Lope wrote a series of rural heroic-honor dramas whose plots on subjects of love are interwoven with themes pertaining to history. These rural *comedias* combine historical, pastoral, and romance modes while idealizing the communal life of peasants. Outstanding among them is *Fuenteovejuna* (*The Sheep Well*, 1612-14), which deals with a stirring period in Spanish history, the War of Succession, fought between 1474 and 1476.[16] The play is set in the period when Ferdinand and Isabel were attempting to integrate their kingdoms and to preserve them from depredation by the Portuguese and the military Order of Calatrava. In the first act of the play the new grandmaster of the order, Rodrigo Téllez Girón, and his advisor, Commander Fernán Gómez de Guzmán, with their armed forces, capture Ciudad Real and hold it for Portugal, which claimed this part of Spain for its queen, Juana "la Beltraneja."

After returning home to Fuenteovejuna in southern Spain, the victorious Commander Gómez, who is the overlord of the town, mistreats the villagers and unsuccessfully pursues Laurencia, the mayor's daughter. When the Catholic sovereigns recapture Cuidad Real, Gómez must leave the village with his army, and the peasants are happy to see him go.

The defeated commander returns on the wedding day of Laurencia and Frondoso, who had earlier saved her from being abducted. Gómez demands the bride for himself, but her father refuses to let her be carried off. The enraged tyrant imprisons the groom with the order that he be hanged later, and puts the bride in the citadel. His cruel career comes to an end after Laurencia escapes and inspires the townspeople to kill their overlord. Upon hearing the details of the uprising, the king pardons the villagers of the murder and makes Fuenteovejuna a protectorate of the crown. Frondoso is released from prison, and the happy couple are finally reunited.

Using for his source the ballads about Fuenteovejuna found in the *Chrónica de las tres órdenes y cauallerías de Santiago, Calatrava y Alcántara* (*Chronicle of the Three Religious and Military Orders of Santiago, Calatrava, and Alcántara,* 1572) by Francisco Rades y Andrada, Lope de Vega composed this play in accordance with metaphysical theories of his day, which spoke of the Platonic obligation of the poet to reconstruct chaotic historical incidents, to "correct" and "reform." Depicting parallel turbulence in four separate strata—lovers who are forcefully separated, oppressed peasants in the village, the irresponsible nobility and their civil war in Ciudad Real, and the Catholic kings who are seeking to establish a democratic monarchy—the poet brings each of them from violence finally to love and justice. Despite the wide range of activities, abrupt shifts of scene, and occasional interruptions in the play, the macro-microcosmic relationship between the levels serves to unite the play and reinforce its epic character. In the first two acts the forces of violence are paralleled in the acts of treason and sedition by the noblemen, then in Téllez Girón's brutal punishment of the city for its resistance, and again on the personal level when the commander attempts to violate the maiden in the village. In the last act, the fall of the commander makes possible harmonious order: first in the realization of the lovers' hopes, then in the monarchs' victory; and finally in the forgiveness of the townspeople for avenging their injustice by beheading their tyrant[17]

In this play Lope de Vega's use of the people of the village as the collective protagonist is fully developed. A few predecessors in the use of a collective hero can be found in Aeschylus's *Persians* (fifth century B.C.) and Cervantes' *Numancia* (1585). Whereas earlier Spanish playwrights treated the people as lowly, Lope de Vega made use of the masses to underline the theme that rebellion against tyranny is justifiable and to symbolize idealistically the process through which Spain became unified.

Lope de Vega broke another precedent in Spainish literature by endowing his heroine with unusual powers of leadership.[18] Lacking at first the courage to resist the commander's outrageous demands, the men of the village forget about their fears when Laurencia inspires them to behave like warriors equal in rank to noblemen. Later she extols the peasants for restoring the disrupted harmony in their community, and Frondoso exclaims that their social love has moved them to act unselfishly. In the light of recent metatheatrical theories, both Laurencia, from an individual point of view, and the villagers, from a collective perspective, can be called "metagonists," since they adopt new roles in their specific situation and seem to surrogate the playwright's function.[19] Lope de Vega no doubt chose these particular historical incidents to dramatize because he admired the role-playing characteristics of the peasants in Fuenteovejuna.

In his portraiture of characters, customs, and milieu in this play, Lope used the contrivance of dichotomy. The passive peasants become responsible citizens as a result of their struggle; likewise, the most timid among them, Mengo, emerges as the town hero, and the formerly courteous *comendador* becomes repugnant. Contrasts can be found between the realistic and idealistic portrayals of some characters, such as in the lusty, exuberant behavior of the commander as opposed to the idyllic love of the peasant couple. Opposing viewpoints about governing are also exposed—those of a military-religious order and of the Catholic monarchs—when the commander exhibits a negative aspect of leadership, while Ferdinand and Isabel display an enlightened philosophy regarding the rights of the people in relation to government.

The versification in *Fuenteovejuna* is consistent with Lope's theories as expressed in his *Arte nuevo*. Employing seven verse forms to fit the moods, characters, and situations in the play, he uses the traditional octosyllabic verse forms more frequently than the Italianate seven- or eleven-syllable lines. The poetic language, which displays richness in imagery, racy dialogue, and vivid narratives, contributes to the excellence for which this drama is known, and the binary structure, which proceeds from disorder to order restored, provides the basis by which the play can be studied from the semiotic critical approach.[20]

Together with the play just discussed, *Peribáñez y el comendador de Ocaña* (*Peribáñez and the Commander of Ocaña*, 1605-12) and *Los comendadores de Córdoba* (*The Knight-Commanders of Cordova*, 1598), which will be classified as an honor-vengeance play and discussed later, are considered to be the first in a long series of Lope's plays that depict oppressed but rich peasants who rebel against their tyrannical overlords.

Peribáñez resembles *Fuenteovejuna* in subject matter and stylistic structure. Whereas *Fuenteovejuna* is drawn from history and deals with collective vengeance, *Peribáñez* is based on an excerpt from a popular ballad and is concerned with an individual's honor. The main plot has as its protagonist a well-to-do peasant, Peribáñez, who protects the honor of his wife, Casilda, by killing her assailant, the commander of Ocaña, and the two servants who have betrayed Peribáñez—Inés and Luján. In the surprising outcome of the play, the king declares that the murder was justified although the victim was of the nobility, and Peribáñez is made a nobleman in a knighting ceremony. An important element in this play's theme is the ritualistic restoration of damaged honor.[21] The secondary action pertains to the historical events when King Henry III (reigned 1390-1406) is preparing for war against the Moors.

A study of this *comedia* uncovers the playwright's sensitivity to the cultural developments and social problems of his time. By depicting two worlds—that of the unassuming Peribáñez, who is attached to country life, and that of the refined *comendador*, who represents courtier life—the poet presents colorful contrasts characteristic of the Renaissance. Through the new obligations that Peribáñez assumes while ascending into a higher social class, the poet is also able to compare simple, virtuous country habits with the intricate, corrupt attitudes of the aristocracy. By idealizing rural life and giving rustic characters the traits of noblemen, he attempts to describe and justify the rapid growth of the Spanish middle class. Because of its closely knit plot and simple, unobstructing action and fine versification, *Peribáñez* is regarded as a model of poetic creation.[22]

Since these heroic plays dealing with vital situations intrigued the Spaniards, Lope continued to write on similar subjects. Another well-known work in this group is *El mejor alcalde, el rey* (*The King Is the Best Judge*, 1620-23), whose simple plot was inspired by a tale attributed to the twelfth-century King Alfonso VII and contained in the fourth part of the *Crónica General*. The play deals with two young villagers, Sancho and Elvira, who invite the Infanzón, or liege lord, Don Tello, to their wedding. Captivated by Elvira's beauty, Tello carries her off for himself. When Sancho implores the king for justice, Alfonso VII sends Tello a letter of reprimand and orders him to return the bride to the groom. Tello haughtily disobeys the royal order, and the monarch, disguised as an *alcalde* (mayor), personally goes to the town with other judges to administer the law. After the king is told about Elvira's dishonor and is mocked by Tello, he reveals his true identity and obliges the nobleman to marry Elvira. After the wedding Don Tello is beheaded and the bride inherits half of his estate and marries Sancho. The thematic content of this play reveals the dramatist's conception that human justice must be satisfied on both the civic and the personal level, and that marriage should be based on mutual love. One of the most frequently staged and printed among the classical plays of the Spanish Golden Age, *El mejor alcalde, el rey* has also appealed to foreign audiences, as can be witnessed by its translation into many other languages.

Another play, almost identical to *El mejor alcalde, el rey*, is *El rey don Pedro en Madrid y el infanzón de Illescas* (*King Peter in Madrid and the Liege Lord of Illescas*, 1618?), whose authorship has been attributed also to Tirso de Molina.[23] The romantic story in this *comedia* deals with the dissipated life of the Infanzón don Tello García. While traveling incognito, King Pedro I (reigned 1350-69) meets two peasant women, Elvira and her maid Ginesa, who report that they have been seduced by the Infanzón and his servant, Cordero. Still disguised as a traveler, the monarch visits Tello García, who treats him with scorn. When the victims bring their case to court, Tello García is summoned before the king. In the courtroom scene the king first hurriedly tries four cases before hearing the women's complaints. After he sentences the Infanzón and his servant to death, the women implore the king to save the men's lives, and the monarch absolves them on condition that they will marry the women.

Although the play's theme is the recovery of lost honor, its motif underlines King Pedro's human qualities and judicious attitude toward his vassals. The change of his first historical appelation, "el Cruel," for the later "el Justiciero" perhaps stresses the progression of Pedro's character as he matured from a romantic young man to a just ruler. King Pedro's play-within-a-play appearance as a nobleman was yet another dramatic technique of which the poet availed himself to display the authentic king's fondness for entering into the life around him. Although the story about the historical king is taken from an early period of his reign, there are numerous semiotic references to his death at the hand of his brother: the repeated use of the phrase *ser piedra* ("to become stone"); the appearance before Pedro of the ghost of a murdered priest, who exposes the Carthusian concept of *memento mori* ("remember that you must die"); and the night visits to the king of his half brother, Henry II of Trastamara (1369-79), who is friendly but, among other deeds, returns to the king a dagger he happens to have found. These foreboding suggestions give the play an additional dimension, since Spaniards in the seventeenth century and others in later generations were well versed about the life of Peter the Cruel.[24]

In numerous other *comedias* in the cycle of heroic-honor plays, Lope de Vega showed great interest in Pedro I. These include *La niña de plata* (*The Stunning Beauty*, 1610-12), *Audiencias del rey Don Pedro* (*The Royal Hearings of King Pedro*, 1613-20); *Lo cierto por lo dudoso* (*The Finding of Truth through Doubting*, 1620-24), and *La carbonera* (*The Charcoal-Burner Girl*, 1623-26).

The playwright wrote another series of heroic plays about unrestrained young kings. Among them are *Fuerza lastimosa* (*Pitiful Power*, 1595-1603), *Servir con mala estrella* (*To Serve with Bad Luck*, 1604-08), *La batalla del honor* (*The Battle of Honor*, 1608), and *El poder en el discreto* (*The Power in Being Discreet*, 1623). Outstanding in this group is *La Estrella de Sevilla* (*The Star of Seville*, 1623?), which until 1920 was considered to be Lope's work but whose authorship has since been called into question.[25] This play was neglected until the Romantic period, since its unflattering portrayal of a king was unpalatable to seventeenth-century Spaniards. When Cándido María Trigueros recast the longer version of the play in 1800, entitling it *Sancho Ortiz de las Roelas*, interest in the play was revived. Subsequent editions follow his adaptation, and abridged versions have been translated into English, French, German, Italian, and Polish.

An interesting play with tragic import, *La Estrella* is historically based on the first days after Sancho IV (the Brave) became king of Spain in 1284. Although the plot is purely fictional, the play contains the local color of that period in the resplendent capital at Seville, which was also a major Spanish port. The play opens with the king's entry into the city. He is immediately attracted by Estrella's beauty and begins to scheme with the assistance of his unscrupulous minister, Arias, to seduce her. After learning that she is the younger sister of Busto Tavera, the king informs Busto that he wishes to find a suitable husband for Estrella and give her a dowry. During Busto's absence, Estrella's slave maid consents to lead the king to her lady's boudoir in exchange for her freedom. When the monarch attempts to enter Estrella's room, Busto unexpectedly returns and forbids the king's entrance.

Complications deepen when the furious king, influenced by Arias to avenge his dishonor, instructs Estrella's fiancé, Sancho Ortiz, to slay an enemy of the state. Upon reading the king's letter and learning the true identity of the victim, Ortiz is forced to make an agonizing choice between love and duty. Deciding to obey the king, Ortiz kills his future brother-in-law, thus dishonoring Estrella and her family. Ortiz is imprisoned, since neither he nor the king reveals who gave the order to kill Busto. Although Estrella is then permitted by the king to judge the killer of her brother, she goes in disguise to the prison and offers her fiancé freedom and forgiveness. She later declares to the king that she cannot marry Ortiz because the murder would hang over them too heavily. At the end of the play the problems are resolved unsatisfactorily, since Ortiz goes voluntarily into exile and the king promises to give Estrella in marriage to another partner; however, it is presumed that she chooses to enter a convent.

The dramatic and swift-moving action in *La Estrella* provides substantial suspense, and the episodes unfold with the inevitability of fate. Although the play lacks a subplot, which could have been used to develop the dramatic action more fully, the friendship of Busto and Sancho and the love between Busto and his sister are motives that reinforce the theme.

The play's theme, dealing with notions of chivalrous loyalty to a king, concerns a young ruler who chooses to disregard the social requirements of his monarchical position and succumb to his personal desires. The conflict created by the impulsive monarch points to the inconsistencies in the prevailing Spanish concept that a man's honor cannot be violated—not even by a king—and that the supreme authority of a sovereign requires all his subjects to be servile. The dilemma the king faces, his human weaknesses, and his final admission of wrong-doing reveal the playwright's doubts about the divine right of kings. The truculent conduct of the monarch, furthermore, shows the dramatist's intent to parallel the historical figure of Sancho the Brave and probably also to make contemporary inferences.

The polymetric versification in *La Estrella de Sevilla* possesses unusual grace. Occasionally, however, inconsistencies occur because of missing verses and the inclusion of assonance in the rhymed strophes. Elsewhere, the spontaneous poetic language sometimes becomes affected with euphuistic metaphors and comparisons.

Plays with Themes of Honor and Vengeance. One of the most interesting aspects of the *comedia*, the motif of vengeance, is usually precipitated by an honor problem. The sentiment of honor as portrayed in Spanish Golden Age drama cannot, however, be called exclusively a Hispanic phenomenon, since it had been a part of chivalresque and courtier behavior in Western European medieval and Renaissance cultures. Reflected also in the laws since the time of the Visigoths and the Moors in Spain, the concept of honor appeared in various forms early in Spanish dramatic literature—a father's honor in *La Celestina*, a brother's honor in Torres Naharro's *Comedia Himenea*, and national honor in Cervantes' *El cerco de Numancia*—before becoming a prominent motif in Lope de Vega's plays.

Among the customs pertaining to survival within a village community in a feudal society, the authority of a man as the head of his family unit was of prime importance. The early outside cultural influences, together with the qualities of courage and honor that were esteemed in the early Castilian warriors, ingrained in the Spaniard a driving responsibility to defend his family name and personal honor. Since his reputation was his highest priority, vengeance was required if his honor should be stained. One of the most serious disgraces he could suffer was an offense against his wife or daughter. Any insult had to be quickly avenged; otherwise his prestige and that of his family would remain tarnished. Likewise, in accordance with law as early as the Visigoths, the punishment of an erring woman was a swift death at the hands of a father or brother. Condemnation to live out her life in a convent was a later alternative. A husband's cruelty in putting an unfaithful wife to death by bleeding was a remnant of chivalresque practices. A gentleman's honorable behavior, furthermore, assimilated qualities of a courtier during the Italian Renaissance.

Two distinct divisions within the theme of honor can be discerned. One is related to the immanence of manliness and the other is concerned whith social reputation. The first deals with a nobleman's personal esteem and self-affirmation, which is based on the fact that he is an old Christian. In the second, the problems of conjugal honor as viewed by the public are treated casuistically, and each honor-vengeance play contains a distinct and individual solution.[26]

During Lope de Vega's time, the public was zealously fond of dramas whose actions revolved around themes of honor. To the Spaniard, the discussion of honor had to include certain prescribed components. Just as love cannot exist without jealousy, dishonor could not subsist without revenge. Although the honor problem exists in the conflicts of a large number of *comedias*, the application of the sacrosanct principles of *pundonor* (the code of honor) was linked dogmatically to the sacrament of marriage. Adultery was punished by death, much like the cutting off of the erring hand to save the rest of the body in Hebraic law. Thus an adulterous wife had to be sacrificed for the preservation of a man's honor. The code of honor, furthermore, upheld the importance of silence, secrecy, prudence, and intrigue.

A number of Lope de Vega's plays that deal with some aspect of honor, even those ending happily, display his compliance with the fundamental principles of honor. The tragedy for probably his earliest honor play, *Los comendadores de Córdoba* (*The Knight-Commanders of Cordova*), was inspired by an Andalusian ballad. In defense of his conjugal honor, an outraged alderman in Cordova, Fernán Alonso, kills his adulterous wife, her two knight-lovers, and even his own servants and the animals on his land, in order to destroy all the witnesses to the dishonor. In his frenzy the wronged husband expresses the exaggerated Spanish idea of honor, as Lope interpreted it, as man's highest value. The brutal motives pertaining to lust and blood, the spontaneous action, and the lively dialogue made this drama exceptionally popular with the Spanish audience. This play anticipates the characteristics this genre was to take; nonetheless, in later honor plays vengeance is often sought on mere suspicion of a female's wrongdoing.

The plot in *El médico de su honra* (*The Surgeon of His Honor*)[27] centers around a husband's suspicion of adultery. The Infante Enrique falls in love with a married woman, Doña Mayor, who resists his advances. Although her husband, Jacinto, knows she is innocent, he feels obliged to erase any suspicions of dishonor and hires a barber to bleed her to death. King Pedro el Cruel accepts Jacinto's explication and offers to him the hand of Margarita. The play ends with preparations for the wedding and for the burial of Doña Mayor. Calderón later used the same title and theme for one of his most famous plays. Although Lope's play excels for its spontaneous action and simplicity of versification, Calderón's became more famous because the love conflict in his play was more logically developed.

In another Lopean drama on the theme of vengeance for dishonor, *El alcalde de Zalamea* (*The Mayor of Zalamea*), it is not the women but their seducers who are punished. The plot is based on a story that circulated in Spain in 1580 after the Spanish army went to Portugal to unite that country with the Spanish crown. Two captains in a military troop stay overnight in Zalamea and seduce the two daughters of the town's mayor. In order to vindicate his stained honor, the mayor requests the officers to marry his daughters; when they refuse, they are hanged. In this work the playwright again expressed his sympathy for a municipality that was struggling for freedom against the nobility. This worthy play by Lope was soon forgotten because Calderón's drama by the same title, written soon afterward, rendered a more masterful interpretation of the subject.

In *Las paces de los reyes y judía de Toledo* (*The Reconciliation of the Royal Couple and the Jewess of Toledo*, 1610-12), the legendary love of Alfonso VIII (reigned 1158-1214) is unfolded. According to sources in the chronicles, the Jewess Rachel of Toledo was put to death by vengeful Spanish noblemen because the king was so enamored of her that he neglected his official duties. To gain dramatic interest, the poet makes the jealous queen, Leonor, responsible for Rachel's death. After the Jewess dies, the king repents before the queen and they are reconciled. Although the unity of action is broken by the historical lapse of time between the first and second acts, the play's superb poetic quality and its intriguing treatment of romantic love contributed to its success in Spain and abroad. Later dramatists—Mira de Amescua, Diamante, and Grillparzer (an Austrian)—were inspired to write on the same subject.

In *El castigo sin venganza* (*Punishment without Revenge*, 1631), Lope illustrated the carrying out of vengeance to an extreme to demonstrate how shallow the principles of honor could become. Based on a dramatic story from an Italian *novella* by Bandello,[28] the play raises the question of the wisdom of matrimonial matches which go against the natural love between two young people. At the suggestion of the town councilors, a middle-aged libertine, the Duke of Ferrara, marries a young noblewoman, Casandra. After the duke learns that his new wife has seduced his illegitimate son, Federico, he imposes a severe punishment. In a darkened room he ties Casandra to a chair and covers her with a pall so that she cannot move or speak. Then he orders his son to enter the room and kill the "conspirator" there. Obeying, Federico realizes too late what he has done. Meanwhile, the duke calls the guards to kill the assassin, which they do.

Although the duke makes reference to the biblical account of the incestuous love between Amnon and Tamar, the playwright was probably recalling in this play the love of Prince Carlos (the weakling son of Philip II) for his stepmother, Isabel of Valois. He may also have been alluding to the dissolute life of Philip IV of Lope's time, since the play was not staged for some time after its premiere.

Written in the poet's later years, *El castigo sin venganza* is considered to be the most perfect of his dramas of honor because of the complexity of circumstances within the action. Its title alludes to the coldness with which a man seeks to restore his honor. Instead of seeking public vengeance, the duke inflicts a private one, using first his son, who caused the injury, and then the palace guards. The ironic suggestion that there is "punishment without revenge" is not fulfilled in the way that might be expected. Casandra avenges herself against a wandering husband, who has married her without love, by engaging in an affair with his illegitimate son; but she pays the price of death for her mistake. The consequences of the duke's cruel actions, moreover, prove him to be the loser because he destroys credibility with his own people, who wanted him to preserve his dynasty.

In an age when plays about cuckoldry contained ludicrous incidents and ended comically, Lope chose to change the usual stock characters into passionate beings who spontaneously bring about the tragic outcome. He succeeded in dramatizing the notions popular in Spain about honor and the virtue of vengeance. The duke's Machiavellian action to restore his damaged honor through the instigation of barbaric crimes and to preserve his image as a just ruler is in exact contradiction to Christian justice based on forgiveness. It has been suggested, furthermore, that since the duke seems to accept responsibility for the role he imitates, Lope made him appear to have taken over his own function as the playwright and he can therefore be called a "metagonist."[29]

Each of Lope's numerous other honor plays dealing with adulterous love, real or imagined, provides a different set of circumstances for this theme. In *El castigo del discreto* (*The Punishment of the Discreet*, 1598-1601), the husband, while pretending to be his wife's lover, gives the real lover an exemplary beating when he makes his appearance. In *Las ferias de Madrid* (*The Fair of Madrid*, 1585-89), a father kills his son-in-law so that his adulterous daughter can marry her lover. In *La locura por la honra* (*Madness Caused by Honor*, 1610-12), a husband murders his adulterous wife, since he does not dare to challenge his rival, a crown prince.

A vengeance play not concerned with a jealous husband's honor is *El bastardo Mudarra* (*The Bastard Mudarra*, 1612). Based on a twelfth-century version of an epic about the seven princes of Lara and on elements from an old ballad and tradition, this play centers around betrayal and vengeance in one of the most interesting sagas to come from the tenth century. During the wedding festivities of Doña Lambra, one of her servants is killed during a petty quarrel by the youngest of seven brothers. Affronted by this incident that has marred her wedding, she seeks revenge by betraying the brothers' father, Gonzalo

Bustos, to the Moors. When the brothers attempt to free their father from prison in Córdoba, they are betrayed by Ruy Velázquez, their uncle and Lambra's husband. The seven are beheaded by the Moors, who send their heads to the imprisoned father. Years later, an illegitimate son of Bustos by a Moorish princess, Arlaja, avenges the deaths of his half brothers by killing Velázquez and burning Lambra at the stake. This intriguing play, whose subject had already been used by Cueva, can be compared for its treatment of tragedy with Sophocles' *Electra* and Shakespeare's *King Lear*.

Plays on Spanish History. Lope de Vega's predilection for writing military and historical plays can be seen throughout his long career. For these plays he drew largely on chronicles and recorded history. Using the medieval chronicles, he put on the stage stories about a variety of Spanish kings and historical or legendary events from the time of Pelayo to his own. He was skillful in popularizing the old epics, even though his historico-epic plays are not always to be trusted for detailed historical accuracy.

A wide range of historical events can be found in Lope's plays, but since a complete list that would include both major and minor themes would be endless, I shall deal only with several from different periods of history. In *La amistad pagada* (*Friendship Repaid*, 1604) Lope depicted the war between the ancient Cantabrians and their Roman conquerors. *Comedia de Bamba* (*The Play of King Bamba*, 1598) reenacts the anarchy that caused the disintegration of the Gothic monarchy. In *El último godo* (*The Last Goth*, 1599-1603) the death of Rodrigo and the Moslem victory are shown. In *El casamiento en la muerte* (*The Wedding in Death*, 1597) and *Las mocedades de Bernardo del Carpio* (*The Youthful Deeds of Bernardo del Carpio*, 1599-1608), the legendary Spanish hero is dramatized. As previously indicated, the princes of Lara appear in a play about vengeance, *El bastardo Mudarra*, and the Cid is personified in *Las almenas de Toro* (*The Merlons of Toro*, 1610-13). *Las famosas asturianas* (*The Famous Asturian Women*, 1610-12) is based on the legendary account of the annual Christian gift of one hundred maidens to the Moslems, and its discontinuance.

Sancho the Great of Navarra (reigned 1000-1035) emerges as a protagonist in *El testimonio vengado* (*Testimony Avenged*, 1596-1603).

Presenting in this play the clashing personalities of the medieval king's sons, Don García and Don Ramiro, the dramatist alludes to the sociopolitical conflict that existed in the late fifteenth century. Alfonso VIII appears in the previously mentioned *Las paces de los reyes* (*The Reconciliation of the Royal Couple*) and in *La corona merecida* (*The Deserved Crown*, 1603), and Enrique III is depicted in *Porfiar hasta morir* (*To Persist until Death*, 1624-28) and *El hidalgo Bencerraje* (*The Moorish Nobleman*, 1605-06). The excesses of the nobility during the reign of Ferdinand of Aragón (1492) are portrayed in *La inocente sangre* (*The Innocent Blood*, 1604-08) and *El galán de la Membrilla* (*The Gallant of Membrilla*, 1615).

The theme of *El mejor mozo de España* (*Spain's Fairest Son*, 1610-11) is the unification of Spain under Isabel and Ferdinand. The wars between the Christians and Moors and the civil wars of the Moslems are reflected in several plays, including *Ramírez de Arellano* (1604-08) and *Las cuentas del Gran Capitán* (*The Accounts of the Great Captain's Exploits*, 1614-19). Spain's participation in the discovery and conquest of America is observed in *El Nuevo mundo descubierto* (*The Discovery of the New World*, 1598-1603). Events that occurred during the time of Emperor Charles V are represented in *El cerco de Viena por Carlos V* (*The Siege of Vienna by Charles V*, 1598-1603), and *Carlos V en Francia* (*Charles V in France*, 1604). Spain's imperial military deeds abroad are also depicted in *La Santa Liga* (*The Holy League*, 1595-1603) and *El asalto de Mastrique por el Príncipe de Parma* (*The Assault of Mastrique by the Prince of Parma*, 1600-1606).

Since the theater was a channel for information and a means of arousing patriotism, Lope also made use of events from his own time. Thus he chose to give an account of a victorious battle in Flanders that was won by Don Gonzalo de Córdoba, the brother of the Duke of Sessa (his patron) in *La nueua victoria de don Gonzalo de Cordoua* (*The New Victory of Gonzalo de Cordoua*, 1622). While many other historical plays by Lope de Vega are extant, many of those listed in his *El peregrino en su patria* have presumably been lost.

Plays Based on Popular Ballads. Toward the end of the sixteenth century popular ballads, some of which had their origin in long medieval epics, became a major branch of Spanish literature and achieved deserved status as serious literature. Handed down by oral tradition, they were first printed in single editions and were later included in the *Cancionero de romances* (before 1550), the *Primera parte de la Silva de varios romances* (1550), and the widely-known *Romancero general* (1600). As a young lyric poet, Lope de Vega imitated the popular balladry in his verses; many of them are found in the *Romancero general*. He was also the most brilliant of the Spanish poets to use fragments of these ballads as sources for dramatic works. Since the old ballads were well known and appealed to the Spaniards, the interpolation of portions of unfinished ballads within the plays was popularly accepted.[30]

Like *Fuenteovejuna* and *Peribáñez*, discussed above, *El caballero de Olmedo* (*The Knight from Olmedo*, 1622) is a *comedia* based on a portion of a popular ballad. Also resembling a play of manners with a love intrigue, *El caballero de Olmedo* begins innocently as a gentleman, Alonso, seeks to gain the hand of a beautiful lady, Inés. He secures the aid of Fabia (a Celestina-like go-between) and his squire, who goes in disguise to Inés's house to teach her Latin. They are successful in persuading the young lady to choose Alonso over two other suitors, Rodrigo and Fernando, and a private meeting between Inés and Alonso is arranged. The two rivals jealously spy on them, however, and hatred continues to grow in Rodrigo's heart, even after Alonso saves his life during a bullfight. A fatalistic mood is introduced in act 3 when Alonso travels to his parents' home in Olmedo and hears a peasant singing "Que de noche le mataron" ("At Night They Killed Him"). Like a ghost, the peasant disappears quickly after warning Alonso to turn back. Resolved to continue, however, Alonso walks into the path of his rivals, who fight with him before Rodrigo's servant fatally shoots Alonso.

Lope de Vega based this play's action, together with Rodrigo's jealousy and scorn for his rival, on a ballad pertaining to the time of Juan II (reigned 1406-54). The song in the third act can be traced to a Castilian folksong whose story symbolically makes use of a goldfinch and a hawk to suggest Alonso's character and to give foreboding warnings of his death.[31] The dramatist was also influenced by *La Celestina* and probably by an earlier play of the same title by Cristóbal de Morales, though both playwrights may have obtained their stories independently from oral tradition.

The dramatic technique in *El caballero de Olmedo* attains a high level of expression, and the poetic language possesses both grace and melody. Numerous contrasting elements—romantic love and ironical death, and idle jests and portentous presages that can be found in the bullfight and the ghostly appearance—contribute to give this play the popularity it attained in the Golden Age.

As a matter of interest, Lope de Vega's fondness for presenting ghosts on the stage can be observed in, among other plays, *El marqués de las Navas* (1624). In this vengeance play he dramatized a contemporary tale about a nobleman, Leonardo from Toledo, who, after abandoning his mistress Feliciana and their illegitimate daughter, arrives in Madrid to marry another woman and finds death at the hands of the marquis of Navas. At the end of the play Leonardo's ghost appears before the marquis, asking him to arrange for Feliciana's marriage to a suitable partner, which the marquis does.

Plays about Foreign History. Although the great master, as we have already seen, used Spanish history in many of his plays, he also wrote several historical plays about foreign events. The best known of those dealing with Portuguese history, which was the most frequently used, are *El príncipe perfecto* (*The Perfect Prince*, 1616), *El duque de Viseo* (*The Duke of Viseo*, 1608-09), *La discreta venganza* (*The Discreet Vengeance*, 1620), *El guante de doña Blanca* (*The Glove of Doña Blanca*, 1630-34), and *El más galán portugués* (*The Greatest Portuguese Gallant*, 1610-12). In these and other plays on foreign historical matters, Lope did not feel constrained to follow history carefully; Spain's seventeenth-century milieu is much in evidence.

Spanish local color is also prevalent in his dramas on ancient history, such as *El esclavo de Roma* (*The Slave of Rome*, 1596-1603), *El honrado hermano* (*The Honest Brother*, 1598-1600), *Roma abrasada* (*Rome in Ashes*, 1598-1600), *Las grandezas de Alejandro* (*The Great Deeds of Alexander*, 1604-8), and *Contra valor no hay desdicha y primero rey de Persia* (*Bravery Conquers Everything and the First King of Persia*, 1625-30). The protagonists in these plays—Androcles, Horatius, Nero, Alexander, and Xerxes—have the personalities of Spanish kings and nobles rather than those of ancient rulers.

During the reign of Charles V historical works and epic poems ex-

alting the Spanish Habsburg dynasty began to appear. Under this influence Lope de Vega rendered homage to the Spanish representatives
of the Austrian dynasty. The best-known of these plays are *La Imperial
de Otón* (*The Imperial Crown of Otón*, 1595-1601) and *El rey sin reino*
(*The King without a Kingdom*, 1599-1612). Both plays are concerned
with dynastic disputes in Central and Eastern Europe.

In *La imperial de Otón*, Lope dramatizes the election of a Habsburg,
Rudolph I (1273), to the throne of the Holy Roman Empire.[32] The
play deals with the tragic story of one of the pretenders, Otón (historically, Ottokar II of Bohemia, 1230-78), who, under the influence of his
ambitious wife, Etelfrida, seeks to regain the throne. The Spanish
pretender to the throne, Alfonso X, is represented by his ambassador,
Juan of Toledo. No doubt Alfonso's claims to the imperial crown
motivated Lope to write this play, whose theme is ambition that destroys
an otherwise successful king.

The detailed historical facts in this play, which are provided
sporadically in long monologues, point to the fact that the playwright
had not yet fully developed his skill in weaving historical material evenly
into the fabric of a plot. The amorous subplot suggested in the first
act is left unfinished; thus the opportunity to end the play in the fashion
of a *comedia de capa y espada* is also missed.

The historical setting for the first two acts of *El rey sin reino*, which
is also concerned with dynastic disputes in central Europe, is the four-
year period 1440-44, when the rule in Hungary of Wladislaus Jagellon
of Poland was challenged by the Austrian Habsburgs, who wanted to
place the posthumously born son of Albert on the throne.[33] The events
presented in the last act took place thirteen years later, when Matthias
Hunyadi, the younger son of a famous general, finally became the
Hungarian king. For the play Lope followed the complicated historical
facts with surprising accuracy, but he displayed the ability to achieve
dramatic unity by giving the impression that the space of time between
the murder of Lasslo Hunyadi, the older son of the general, who was
the people's favorite, and the young Austrian king's mysterious death
was only two days, when historically eight months lapsed between the
two deaths.

Lope's ability to condense the complicated affairs of other Hungarian

and Polish royal families within the confines of a play can be seen in
La reina Juana de Nápoles (*The Queen of Naples*, 1597-1603) and *La
corona de Hungría* (*The Crown of Hungary*, 1623). The historical
background for *El gran duque de Moscovia* (1606), moreover, centers
around Russian and Polish affairs. After Tsar Ivan the Terrible died in
1584, he was succeeded by his sickly older son, Fedor, who was over-
thrown and murdered by his brother-in-law, Boris Godunov in 1591.
Rumors that Ivan's younger son, Demetrius (who was presumed also
to have been murdered) was living in Poland, spread when Boris's firm
rule became unpopular during a famine. In a bloody uprising Boris
was killed and the alleged Demetrius was crowned as tsar in 1605. The
new ruler's popularity lasted only eleven months, however, because he
married a Polish princess; he was killed during an insurrection in 1606
and was succeeded by Vasily Shuisky.

Since Lope's play ends showing Demetrius alive and the master of
the empire, he presumably wrote the play before news of Demetrius's
tragic end reached Spain.[34] His most probable source was a Spanish
translation of an account of the events by Antonio Possevino, who had
been a special envoy of Pope Gregory XIII to mediate peace between
Russia and Poland in 1581 and who returned to Venice in 1605.[35]

The characters in these and other early historical plays, except for
La corona de Hungría, are not as fully delineated as those in the
playwright's later works. The protagonists do not undergo a change of
character, as is true in his more mature plays. Instead of creating a strong
protagonist in each play, who would appear throughout the action, Lope
de Vega gave importance to each of the several personages as they would
appear in a historical source. Thus, in his early career he placed more
emphasis on history than on character development.

"Comedias de costumbres" and Novelesque Plays. Social conventions,
Spanish habits, and traditional practices are a part of most of Lope de
Vega's plays. A number of his plays are *comedias de costumbres* (comedies of manners), which depict stereotyped characters in the colorful
milieu of seventeenth-century Spanish country, city, or court life. The
young protagonists in these plays are mostly pleasure-seeking, selfish
noblemen.

Some of his comedies of manners have subjects that glorify idyllic life, such as *El villano en su rincón* (*The Peasant's House Is His Castle*, 1614-1616), which reflects an admiration for country life and thus repeats the *beatus ille* theme in Horace's work. In this play the country life of an old, rich peasant, Juan Labrador, is set against the burdensome requirements of high society. Living on a farm near Paris, "John Farmer" enjoys a life of patriarchal independence. After accepting a royal invitation to live at the court for a while, the peasant concludes that he does not need the king as much as the king needs him. Labrador remains convinced of the superiority of rural existence and even expresses fear that court life will corrupt him. Nevertheless, his rivalrous opposition turns into genuine friendship for the king, and as the play closes the peasant becomes the king's steward and the monarch promises to become God's steward. Thus both live up to their roles in a monarchical society. One of Lope's most ambitious works, *El villano en su rincón* contains a characteristic theme of the *comedia*—admiration for country life. Within the other theme, pertaining to glorification of royalty, however, the dramatist found opportunity to discuss the merits of parental duties, civic obligations, and honesty.[36]

Another idyllic *comedia de costumbres*, in two parts, is *Los Tellos de Meneses* (*The Telloses of Meneses*, 1625-30), which depicts the domestic and patriarchal side of life within the Spanish nobility, as opposed to their military life.

A comedy of manners dealing with city life is *La prueba de los amigos* (*The Test of Friendship*, 1604). This play exemplifies the wide range of sources from which Lope de Vega drew for his subjects, plots, and dramatic devices. He was indebted to Boiardo's *Il Timone* for the play's dramatic framework and theme, to the biblical parable about the prodigal son for its subject, and to the tone of *La Celestina* for its situation. The characters can be compared to those in the apologues in *El conde Lucanor* (*Count Lucanor*, 1335) by the Infante Juan Manuel, while the dramatic devices of mistaken identity and the *deus ex machina* technique were borrowed from the Roman comedy of Terence and Plautus. The play's main action centers around Feliciano, who dissolutely squanders his inheritance on his friends only to find that all of them abandon him when he runs out of money, except his fiancée, Leonarda, and his servant, Galindo.

A number of *comedias de costumbres* were derived from Italian *novelle* and Byzantine and chivalresque stories. The poet drew upon a novel by Bandello for a macabre *comedia*, *La difunta pleitada* (*The Disputed Deceased*, 1593-95), in which a recently married woman who falls into a coma, is buried alive. Her lover brings her back to life and makes plans to marry her. During the wedding the first husband recognizes her, claims her, and takes her away. *Castelvines y Monteses* (1606-12) follows another novel by Bandello, which was also used by Shakespeare in writing *Romeo and Juliet*. The Spanish play, however, ends happily with the marriage of the lovers and peace between the quarrelling families.

Sources from Boccaccio are evident in several plays. *El halcón de Federico* (*Federico's Hawk*, 1601-05) is about a poor nobleman who, through constancy, wins the affections of a lady. A picaresque play, *El anzuelo de Fenisa* (*Fenisa's Lure*, 1604-06), depicts a beautiful courtesan who makes a fortune by taking advantage of rich businessman, but she loses all she gains when a Spaniard cheats her. *La discreta enamorada* (*The Discreet Girl in Love*, 1606) contains an amorous intrigue in which a young lady marries her lover even though her mother wants her to marry his father. In *Los ramilletes de Madrid* (*The Flowers of Madrid*, 1615) and *No son todos ruiseñores* (*Not All Are Nightingales*, 1630) the lovers, disguised as gardeners, serve in their fiancées' households and marry them after all obstacles are removed.

Those plays based on Giraldi Cinthio's novels possess more of a moralizing tone than those based on Bandello. They are *El hijo venturoso* (*The Happy Son*, 1588-95), *El favor agradecido* (*Recovered Grace*, 1593), *Piadoso veneciano* (*The Pious Venetian*, 1599-1608), and *La discordia en los casados* (*Discord between the Married Couple*, 1611). Influence from a Byzantine novel can be observed in *Los tres diamantes* (*Three Diamonds*, 1599-1603) and *La doncella Teodora* (*The Maiden Theodora*, 1610-12).

Lope de Vega drew little from his own life experiences in developing the plots for his plays. In addition to borrowing from the sultry tales in Italian *novelle*, he repeatedly brought to dramatic life the medieval romantic, chivalresque stories coming from European literature. His novelesque plays dealing with the Carolingian theme are derived from the Italian current rather than the French. Based on exaltation of the virtues of honor, Platonic love, and the sentiment of Christian chivalry, his chivalresque plays are *El nacimiento de Ursón y Valentín* (*The Birth of Orson and Valentine*, 1588-95), *Los celos de Rodamonte* (*The Jealousy of Rodamonte*, 1595?), *El marqués de Mantua* (*The Marquis of Mantua*, 1596), *Las pobrezas de Reinaldo* (*The Hardships of Reinaldo*, 1599), *La mocedad de Roldán* (*The Youth of Roldán*, 1599-1603), *Los palacios de Galiana* (*The Palaces of Galiana*, 1602), and *El premio de la hermosura* (*The Reward of Beauty*, 1609-20).

Cloak-and-Sword Plays. From the beginning of the sixteenth century, romantic plays evolved out of a period of elaborate artistic workmanship, but they were not called *comedias de capa y espada* (cloak-and-sword plays) until the time of Lope de Vega. Beginning generally as superficial, declamatory plays, they finally attained the character of the specific dramatic genre of which Lope de Vega was especially fond. These remarkably popular plays acquired their name from the dress of the gallant gentlemen of seventeenth-century aristocratic and middle-class life who were portrayed. The outdoor garment of these cavaliers became an impressive theatrical costume, since it could be swung about to express passion, and the sword became an indispensable stage property not only for theatrical duels but also for the actor to fling out occasionally when emphasizing an issue.

The complicated amorous intrigues and adventures in these plays are centered around questions of honor, jealousy, and revenge. While the main plots present the ingenious schemes of *galanes* or *damas*, their actions are paralleled by the adventures of their *graciosos* or *criadas* and other sets of characters. They often carry out their plans through the use of confusing disguises and skirmishes. Frequently the plots become entangled with complicated love triangles, which are usually happily resolved in the end with the reunion of the estranged lovers and double or triple weddings. The confusion they create, however, does not go so far as to endanger the reputation of the women involved; thus the *comedias de capa y espada* are considered to be antithetical to the honor dramas. Given the opportunity to invert accepted social behavior and manners in these amusing plays of fantasy, the playwrights used it to assess the social mores of their day without fear of being censured.

The cloak-and-sword plays can be divided into various subgroupings. Most of Lope de Vega's are *comedias de costumbres* (plays of customs), in which he invented plots out of his immense imagination and personal life experiences. Other cloak-and-sword plays are dramas of high intrigue, and a few contain novelesque plots and characters, resembling comedies of manners.

Some of Lope's plays which could be classified as *comedias de costumbres* present settings from Spanish summer festivals. In *Santiago el verde* (*St. James the Lesser*, 1615), the plot, in which Celia and García dishonestly attempt to foil the amorous pursuits of their friends Teodora and Rodrigo, is woven around May Day celebrations at the Manzanares River in Madrid. In *La noche de San Juan* (*The Midsummer Night*, 1631), which was written in one day, the circumstantial amorous adventures in the meager plot provide a framework to display the festivity, with its elaborate costuming, of the magic night on June 24 when young ladies, looking for independence and gaiety, fall in love and find their husbands. Similarly, *El arenal de Sevilla* (*The Riverside at Seville*, 1603) displays the colorful, exotic milieu of that busy Andalusian port, as a group of young Sevillians enjoys an outdoor festivity.

Lope de Vega's most successful *comedia de capa y espada* dealing with customs is *Amar sin saber a quién* (*To Fall in Love with an Unknown*, 1620-21). Excelling in disguises, adventures, love affairs, and honor, its plot starts with the imprisonment of its protagonist, Juan, who is mistakenly accused of murdering a famous fencer, Pedro. The true killer, Fernando, asks his sister, Leonarda, to visit the imprisoned man with financial aid. Although she sends her maid with a letter, Juan falls in love with Leonarda, whom he has never seen. After Juan's innocence is proved, Leonarda marries him. The conceptual title of this unusually complicated play, which suggests the subtle idea that the imagination can create love, is reflected in the chivalric conduct and discrete actions of the characters.

A play incorporating Moorish customs, in which Lope made extensive use of the play-within-the-play technique, is *El Argel fingido y renegado de amor* (*The Renegade of Love and His Make-Believe Algiers*, 1599).[37] In it Rosardo attempts to steal Flérida from her fiancé, Leonido, while Flérida's brother, Aureliano, pursues Flavia, who is in love with Manfredo, Leonido's brother. After Flérida spurns the wealthy Rosardo, he announces his plans to join some Moorish pirates from Algiers, but actually builds a fictitious Moorish fortress on a nearby island and populates it with his servants, whom he calls his pirates. The play-within-the-play continues when Leonido and Manfredo, disguised as monks, gain entrance to the fortress. Each character attempts to alter the events in his newly acquired identity until Rosardo abandons his disguise. Although Rosardo has manipulated a favorable dénouement in his fictitious play, it works to his disadvantage in real life, since the other players' love for each other is strengthened and his own for Flérida is destroyed. The play ends as Manfredo is restored to Flavia and Leonido wins Flérida.

Lope wrote a number of *comedias de enredo* (plays of high intrigue) whose protagonists are women of strong character: *La moza de cántaro* (*The Girl with the Jug*, 1625), *La dama boba* (*Miss Simpleton*, 1613), and *El acero de Madrid* (*The Iron Tonic of Madrid*, 1610). The most outstanding among these, *The Girl with the Jug*, portrays a pretty young noblewoman, María, who kills a man who has dishonored her old father, then escapes the law by moving to Madrid in the guise of a peasant girl. While María works as a kitchen maid, a gentleman, Juan, falls in love with her, but they cannot marry until she is pardoned and her identity is happily revealed. Although this play's action tells the story of love and marriage in a popular setting, its theme is the restoration of an gentleman's familial honor.

La dama boba, an entertaining drawing room comedy, illustrates the love game, or *jeux d'amour*, of a simple young lady, Finea, who acquires the ability to manipulate her suitors and cleverly outwits the intelligence of her sister and rival, Nise. Although Finea's naiveté stands out at first in contrast to Nise's affected superiority, Finea is gradually transformed by love into an intelligent young lady and wins Laurencio. While the distinct characteristics of the men in the play remain unchanged—the pragmatist Laurencio appears to be seeking a rich dowry, while Liseo regards intelligence and character in a woman as more desirable, and Otavio, the practical father, desires only his daughters' happiness—Finea seems to surrogate the playwright's original intent for her. Assuming responsibility for her changing role, she influences the direction of the plot, thereby giving this comical and colorful *comedia* the qualities of a metaplay.

In the third of these plays, *El acero de Madrid*, Belisa teaches her lover, Lisardo, to use his servant, Beltrán, to deceive her father, Prudencio, by disguising himself as a doctor who will prescribe iron water and long walks for her. The two lovers are able to enjoy some solitude together, when a friend of Lisardo seduces Belisa's chaperone, Teodora. Her father's opposition to the marriage is overcome when Belisa's pregnancy is revealed. Teodora is punished, and the illicit behavior of the couple is rewarded. Despite the social obstacles regarding womanhood in Spain, Belisa, the protagonist in the play, also cleverly succeeds in manipulating the outcome to her liking.

A call for improvement in the social position of women, especially for giving them the liberty to choose their own husbands, is evident in several of Lope's *comedias de costumbres* that include high intrigue. They are *La viuda valenciana* (*The Widow from Valencia*, 1604), *La mal casada* (*The Mismatched Wife*, 1610-15), *La vengadora de las mujeres* (*The Women's Avenger*, 1620), *Por la puente, Juana* (*Across the Bridge, Joan*, 1624-25), *La boba para los otros y discreta para sí* (*Foolish for the Others and Smart for Herself*, 1630), and *La hermosa fea* (*The Beautiful Ugly Woman*, 1630-32).

La mal casada satirizes the subject of marriage arrangements. Lucrecia cannot marry the lover of her choice, since her mother insists that she marry an old, rich man. After his death, Lucrecia is forced again, for reasons of inheritance, to marry his crippled nephew. Finally, after obtaining permission to have her second marriage annulled, she contracts the marriage of her choice. Lucrecia's vitality and resourcefulness in the face of almost insurmountable obstacles contribute to make her a living and colorful character. Lope's ability to portray her persistence, patience, and hope shows his sensitivity to the antifeminist social barriers of his time.

Los melindres de Belisa (*Belisa's Extravagances*, 1608) is a dramatic exposition of the psychology of two different kinds of women in love. Belisa and her mother are presented as capricious in their relationships to their suitors, as opposed to the passionate Celia, who is in love with Felisardo. Lope, who is known to have been making reference to his first wife, reveals in the eccentric life-style of Belisa his own view that love, being the principal object of life, should be treated sincerely and as a sacred sentiment, not as a game. In the sudden dénouement, the play ends abruptly without a logical conclusion. In probably the last of his plays, which is also about Belisa, *Las bizarrías de Belisa* (*Belisa's Gallantries*, 1634), the disguised Belisa pursues a lover, whose life she saves twice, before finally marrying him.

El perro del hortelano (*The Dog in the Manger*, 1613), falling somewhere between a play of manners and a play of high intrigue, is based on a novelesque source.[38] The title derives from a fable and the play's solution is farcical. Focusing on the true nature of love, it affirms the right of young people to disregard class structures when falling in love. Countess Diana Belflor not only prevents her secretary, Teodoro, who comes from a peasant family, from marrying her maid, Marcela, but also resists his affection for her because of their social differences. Before a solution is found, Diana behaves like the churlish dog in the popular fable, which, unable to eat his own food, prevents others from eating theirs. Teodoro's *gracioso*, Tristán, finally fabricates a Byzantine story about the noble lineage of his master. Thus, when public opinion is satisfied, the high-born heroine and her employee happily marry. In a sense, Tristán takes over the role of the playwright as his ruse diminishes the love-honor conflict and solves the play's problem. In this play, and also in *El maestro de danzar* (*The Ballet Teacher*, 1594), Lope relies on the vagaries of love and focuses on the social problems of class inequities when young people fall in love.

As we have seen, Lope de Vega's cloak-and-sword plays contain strong yet charming characterizations of women, while the *galanes*, who are clever in speech but slow to solve their problems, depend upon their *graciosos'* schemes and realistic, albeit comical, attitudes toward money, food, and the opposite sex.

Pastoral Plays. Bucolic literature, having come from the Italian Renaissance eclogue, had been in vogue in Spain for some time before Lope de Vega began his career. Evidence of the idyllic genre was first seen in Juan del Encina's pastoral plays and Garcilaso de la Vega's eclogues, and later in Jorge de Montemayor's novel, *La Diana*. Among the Italian pastoral plays popular in sixteenth-century Spain was a tragicomedy, *Pastor Fido* (*Shepherd Fido*, 1585), by Giovanni Battista Guarini (1538-1612).

Lope de Vega made his dramatic debut with a pastoral play, *El verdadero amante* (*The True Lover*, 1574-75), at the age of twelve. Originally in four acts, the play's action centers on Amaranta's false accusation that her lover, Jacinto, killed her husband. After the truth is revealed, the two lovers can marry. After making improvements in this piece some time later, the playwright included it in a collection of his plays. Lope's second play, *La pastoral de Jacinto* (*The Pastoral of Jacinto*, 1595-1600), in which a shepherd is cross with himself because his rival has outwitted him, contains autobiographical inferences. *La Arcadia* (1610-15), based on the plot of a pastoral novel of the same title, contains numerous historical situations in which appear authentic figures from the court of the Duke of Alba and the poet himself. Autobiographical elements are also seen in *Los amores de Albanio y de Ismenia* (*The Love of Albanio and Ysmenia*, 1591-95) and *Belardo el furioso* (*The Furious Belardo*, 1586-95), whose main character also resembles the Fernando in Lope's dramatic novel, *La Dorotea*.

Another pastoral eclogue by Lope is a short piece of some seven hundred lines, *La selva sin Amor* (*The Loveless Woods*, 1629). In the opening prologue Venus rebukes her son Amor (Cupid) for wasting his time in hunting and for being inattentive to his business as the god of love. She sends him to the banks of the Manzanares—the place of Philip's court—where she has heard there is no love, and instructs him to set the forest on fire. Upon his arrival, Amor finds two shepherdesses who are rejecting their swains. They immediately declare war on Amor because he tyrannically threatens their freedom and reveals his plans to burn down their world. A happy dénouement is attained when Amor's arrows change their hearts.

This eclogue became famous, since the entire text was used as the libretto for the first operatic work in the Spanish language. Although no longer in existence, the music may have been composed by two musicians in the royal chapel, Mateo Romero and his assistant, Carlos Patiño. Most of the words were set for solo voices, although the work also contained a trio, a duet, and a final chorus. When it was first performed toward the end of 1629 in the royal palace for a festivity in honor of

Philip IV, another innovation perhaps in musical history—at least in Spain—occurred. The orchestra was placed in a pit below the stage where it was hidden from view. The stage decorations and elaborate machinery for this musical production were designed by the famous Cosme Lotti.

Although Lope's pastoral plays may lack original and sustained intrigues, they display lyric beauty and superb versification.

Plays on Mythological Subjects. The mythological plays that Lope de Vega wrote during the later part of his life, at the height of the baroque period, did not follow the line of direction that had been cultivated in the universities immediately before his time. Using different sources and themes, he based his courtly, decorative musical dramas on classical mythology, often drawn from Ovid's *Metamorphoses*, and wrote in accordance with Renaissance aesthetic poetic rules, closely following classical versification.[39] Since they were commissioned as entertainments for court celebrations, these spectacles are interspersed with casual compliments to the royalty. Occasionally members of the royal family were given small parts to play. Since the composition and versification in these works approached lyric opera, the players were required to be musically talented. The elaborate baroque staging also called for complicated scenic machinery to carry out such effects as lifting gods in chariots into the clouds, changing a god into a blossoming branch, and *deus ex machina* endings.

Of the numerous mythological plays that Lope wrote, only eight have been preserved. The most esteemed out of these is *Adonis y Venus* (1598-1603), a play inspired by an ancient myth that Ovid had used. It deals with the ill-fated, unrequited love of Venus for Adonis, who turns a deaf ear to her warnings and is killed by a boar in a hunt. Possessing an especially musical character with its classical heptasyllabic lines, this play was commissioned by Philip III and was performed by a royal cast—the crown prince, his two sisters, and their ladies-in-waiting. Its staging required complicated technical means to carry out the unusual theatrical effects that were required. The mythological, religious, and secular plays that required stage machinery to accomplish the desired effects were sometimes also called *comedias de teatro*, *comedias de cuerpo*, or *comedias de ruido* (situation plays).

Among Lope's other mythological plays, *El vellocino de oro* (*The*

Golden Fleece, 1620) deals with the Jason myth. Performed first in Aranjuez to celebrate Philip IV's birthday, it too required an elaborate setting and called for unusual acoustic effects. In *El laberinto de Creta* (*The Labyrinth of Crete*, 1612-15), which is concerned with the exploits of Theseus, the mythical feminine characters, who are disguised as men, much in the style of a cloak-and-sword play, perform a Castilian dance and sing Spanish ballads. *Las mujeres sin hombres* (*Women without Men*, 1613-18), *El Perseo* (*Perseus*, 1611), *El marido más firme* (*The Loyal Husband*, 1617-21), and *La bella Aurora* (*The Beautiful Aurora*, 1620-25) treat respectively the myths of the Amazons, Perseus, Orpheus, and Aurora.

Lope's last extant mythological play, *El Amor enamorado* (*Cupid in Love*, 1630), combines two closely integrated plots on mythological and pastoral subjects. Its central story about Febo's passion for Dafne and her disdain of him because of Cupido's arrows is taken again from Ovid's *Metamorphoses*.[40] While the play's essential theme of love involves hatred, pride, and vengeance, Dafne's narcissism is the force that gives rise to the dramatic conflict. In the amorous games among the contesting gods, the defeated one uses love as a weapon of revenge.

Typical of this genre, Lope's mythological plays appear to the modern reader to be somewhat cold and tedious; furthermore, their stories misrepresent the ancient ideals of the mythological world. But they display lyric beauty, a rich variety of situations, innovative mechanical and decorative devices, and clever romantic transformations of mythological stories.

Religious Plays. The numerous religious plays by Lope de Vega comprise various categories, including biblical, hagiographic, legendary, sacramental, and morality. Church celebrations and saints' days encouraged the proliferation of this genre in the Golden Age. By the time of his mature period Lope had composed several three-act biblical pieces. *La creación del mundo* (*The Creation of the World*, 1631-35) is based on Genesis, with its theme of original sin. *La hermosa Ester* (*The Beautiful Esther*, 1610) is about the deliverance of the Jewish people from Egypt. Other plays deal with the histories of Jacob and Tobias. Borrowing from Eastern religion, Lope wrote *Barlaán y Josafat* (*Barlaam and Josaphat*, 1611), which is based on the early life of Buddha.

The lives of saints provided him with topics for many other religious plays. His dramatized hagiographies are a mixture of religious, secular, allegorical, and popular elements.[41] One of the best, even though its structure is dramatically weak, is *El divino africano* (*The Divine African*, 1610), which deals with the life of St. Augustine. The first two acts closely follow the life of the saint, according to his *Confessions*. The scenes in the third act kaleidoscopically present various events that took place during his final stay in Africa, and were taken from the episodic *Flos Sanctorum* (*Lives of the Saints*), which deals with the effects of conversion. The play contains a series of visions that appealed to the seventeenth-century Spanish public, who were familiar with mysticism and especially enjoyed Augustinian iconography.

Among many other *comedias de santos* are *San Angel Carmelita* (*St. Angel Carmelite*, 1604?), *San Isidro de Madrid* (*St. Isidore of Madrid*, 1604-06), *Lo fingido verdadero* or *El mejor representante* (*The Deceptive Truth* or *The Best Actor*, 1608), *San Diego de Alcalá* (*St. James of Alcalá*, 1613), and *San Nicolás de Tolentino* (*St. Nicholas of Tolento*, 1614). Most interesting among these plays, *Lo fingido verdadero* retells the martyrdom of San Ginés, a Roman actor who, while playing the role of a Christian at the request of Emperor Dioclecian, was converted to the faith he was at first only enacting. Displaying a theocentric view of life together with notions that the world is a theater, this play reflects baroque preoccupation with the illusory aspects of life. The metatheatrical structure, furthermore, reveals Lope's own view about the theatrical experience.[42]

Outstanding among Lope's works based on traditional pious legends are *El capellán de la Virgen* (*The Chaplain of the Blessed Virgin*, 1615), which dramatizes the Toledan legend about San Ildefonso, and *La buena guarda* (*The Good Custodian*, 1610), which deals with a medieval Marian legend. *La fianza satisfecha* (*The Outrageous Saint* or *The Satisfied Bond*, 1612-15) is about a sadistic libertine who is suddenly converted in old age and dies a martyr. The theme of divine and human mercy is discussed, since Leonido, after leading the life of a savage sinner, repents and purifies himself in order to satisfy the terms of the guarantee for God's forgiveness through the crucified Savior. In this play Lope expresses the irony in the relationship between Christian Providence and free will. Instead of being punished for his crimes, Leonido is converted through the compassionate intervention of Divine Providence.[43] The dramatic technique used in this play's structure anticipated Tirso de Molina's *El condenado por desconfiado* (*The Man Condemned for Little Faith*) and *El burlador de Sevilla* (*The Trickster of Seville*).

Lope de Vega has won recognition for his artistic contribution to the development of the religious *auto*. Although his earlier works reflect the literary tradition that he inherited and merely blend morality and mystery plays with eucharistic elements, his later *autos* show how he perfected the genre. The most admired of Lope's more than forty sacramental and morality plays[44] is *La siega* (*The Harvest*, 1621-35). Alluding to the biblical parable about the wheat and the tare, it is built around the love of Esposa (allegorically, the Church) for Señor de la Heredad (Christ). After failing to seduce Esposa, Envidia (Envy) and Soberbia (Pride) wound her by prophesying that her husband (Christ) will die and her children (faithful believers) will suffer persecution. Since Esposa represents good seeds and a field of wheat, Envidia and Soberbia try again to hurt her by sowing the seeds of weeds in her garden. A sudden dénouement reveals that three of the four weeds that mature, each representing a different religion, are converted; only the Hebraic one remains unchanged.

Other outstanding religious plays by Lope are *El viaje del alma* (*The Soul's Journey*, 1585), *El tirano castigado* (*The Punished Tyrant*), *El hijo pródigo* (*The Prodigal Son*—a morality play written toward the end of the sixteenth century), and *La locura por la honra* (*Foolishness Because of Honor*). The last is a religious drama of honor in which a demon attempts to seduce Blanca (allegorically, the Soul), the wife of the Lord. Based on the parable of the vineyard, *El heredero del cielo* (*The Heir of Heaven*) is about a farmer who sends three shepherds to collect rent from a congregation of Hebrew people. After the three die at the hands of the debtors, the farmer finally sends his son, whom they also kill and hang on a cross.

The eucharistic allegory of the morality play *La maya* (*The May Pageant*, 1585) is taken from a popular custom from the festive days of May, when an elegantly dressed girl sits on a table and begs for money. The play's theme of hunger is personified by two abstract characters, Gula (Gluttony) and Cuerpo (Body), who are constantly seeking food. When consecrated bread is offered in Holy Communion to Gluttony, he enjoys only the corporal substance of it without recognizing its sacramental significance.

Although Lope's sacramental plays lack a systematic arrangement of symbolism and content, their temporal content and the inclusion of amorous and rustic poetry from popular songs contribute to the religious sentiment they have inspired. These spontaneous, lyrical works stand between the earlier *autos sacramentales* and those of Valdivieso and Calderón, who explored intellectual and theological concepts more thoroughly.

CONCLUSION

Lope de Vega's total dramatic output represents a prodigious achievement. He created a vigorous, inventive theater of action by blending preexisting dramatic conventions with the popular elements of his own time. Possessing the skill to contrive intricate plots and love adventures, he fascinated the world with his characterizations of women. His ability to create vivid dialogue, intense situations, poetic diction that is almost free of stylistic abuses, and flowing versification stands as a precedent in the history of Spanish dramatic literature. Lope's poetic penetration of the world on the stage served as a model for his contemporaries and a legion of dramatic poets who followed. Perhaps only Tirso de Molina excelled him in the study of character and irony, Alarcón in the blending of ethical values with the aesthetic, and Calderón in dramatic structure. No one, however, reached his immense power of creation in the vast world of human actions. The innumerable poets who succeeded the master inherited a rich dramatic treasury.

CHAPTER III

The Proliferation of the Comedia: Lope de Vega's Contemporaries

IN THE TIME of Lope de Vega, the public's passion for the theater made possible the unusual growth of the *comedia*. Their deeply infused attraction for theatrical entertainment, which was supported by the government and the Church, became in part an artistic substitute for their interest in the politically declining Spain. Since the Spaniards looked upon playwriting as a profitable art that could be easily acquired, a large number of gifted poets tried their talents in it. In the prolific period that followed, over one hundred dramatists contributed several thousand short and full-length plays, of which nearly 2,000 are still in existence. Comparable in quality to ancient classical, French neoclassical, and Elizabethan dramatic literatures, Spanish Golden Age drama exceeded them in output.

In order to facilitate their study, scholars of Spanish drama have divided the Golden Age into the Lopean and Calderonian cycles. This chapter will be concerned with the close followers of Lope de Vega's dramatic art: the dramatists in the Valencian group, as well as Tirso de Molina, Juan Ruiz de Alarcón, Antonio Mira de Amescua, Luis Vélez lesser-known playwrights. Following in their master's footsteps, these dramatists changed little of substance in the Lopean formula. Each, however, had certain characteristics peculiar to his art.

THE VALENCIAN GROUP

A center of late sixteenth- and seventeenth-century Spanish dramatists, second only to that in Madrid, sprang up in Valencia, out of which came Rey de Artieda, Cristóbal de Virués, Francisco A. Tárrega, Gaspar de Aguilar, Miguel Beneyto, Carlos Boyl, Ricardo del Turia, and the most renowned, Guillén de Castro. These writers are considered to be partially precursors of the *comedia*, since they exerted a certain influence on Lope de Vega, but they also followed him and benefited from his art.[1] Since the Levantine city was already a cultural center and had an active theater when Lope de Vega lived there for short periods of time to fulfill the terms of his exile, the master's mutual friendship with the Valencian playwrights not only influenced their work but also contributed to Lope's success in Valencia.

The oldest among the Valencians, Francisco Agustín Tárrega (1554?-1602), in 1591 founded the Academia de los Nocturnos (Literary Society of the Night Revelers), whose members included other dramatists and poets in that city.[2] Having made his debut as a playwright in 1576, Tárrega is considered to belong to both the pre-Lopeans and the Lopean cycle. His heroic drama *El cerco de Pavía* (*The Siege of Pavía*, written before 1602) and several others of his well-developed plays display the main characteristics within the Spanish *comedia*. *La duquesa constante* (*The Constant Duchess*, 1576?), *El Prado de Valencia* (*The Meadow of Valencia*, 1590-91?), and *La enemiga favorable* (*The Inimical Benefactress*, written before 1602) are colorful cloak-and-sword plays that present tragicomic mirrors of life, but are marred by excessive verbal conceits and a lack of imagination.

The most prolific dramatist in the Valencian group, Guillén de Castro (1569-1631), is reputed to have had royal blood and to have been descended from the same family as Spain's national hero, el Cid Campeador. As a young writer, Castro participated, with his poems and prose compositions, in the Academia de los Nocturnos from 1592 until the group went out of existence in 1594; he was also considerably influenced by his personal acquaintance with Lope de Vega, who lived in Valencia from 1595 to 1597 and again in 1599. In addition to his literary interests, Castro pursued political and military careers in 1593 and from 1607 to 1616. He served in the Valencian coast guard, fighting off Moorish pirates, lived in Scigliano, Italy, as its appointed governor, and returned home for interims to join an expedition to transfer the Moriscos expelled from Valencia to Africa, and to recover from an extended illness. In 1616 he came back to Valencia and organized another literary society, which lasted three months. Between 1618 and the time of his death in 1631, he wrote and published many plays and lived alternately in Valencia and Madrid, where he was invited to join the literary society to which Lope de Vega belonged. Five years before he died he married for the second time, this time to a lady from the household of his patron in Madrid, Juan Téllez Girón.[3]

Although the first of Castro's forty-three plays are uneven in merit, each play, when studied chronologically, shows the gradual evolution of his artistic development. His chivalric works include the most faithful and complete adaptation of old Spanish balladry to the stage, and follow the tradition founded by Cueva, who first made use of themes from Spanish history. His fame rests chiefly on two of these that deal with an eleventh-century hero—*Las mocedades del Cid* (*The Youthful Deeds of the Cid*, 1612?-18?) and its less popular sequel, *Las hazañas del Cid* (*The Exploits of the Cid*, 1610?-15?).[4] Since the Spanish medieval epic *El cantar de mío Cid* (*The Song of My Cid*, 1140?) was unknown in seventeenth-century Spain, Castro drew his inspiration and material for his plays from about twenty ballads and some chronicles pertaining to the most famous of all Spanish heroes, Rodrigo Díaz of Vivar (*ca.* 1043-99), whose father and uncle were powerful nobles in the time of Ferdinand I.

In Castro's accurate characterization of the court hero who showed early signs of great military talent, he developed a suspenseful plot that follows the events of the Spanish hero's youth. During an argument at the palace, Count Lozano, the father of Ximena, slaps Diego Laínez, the father of Rodrigo Díaz. After testing his sons' valor and pugnacity, the offended old man asks the youngest, Rodrigo, to avenge his honor. The young man agrees to seek redress without knowing that the offender is the father of his beloved. When Rodrigo learns the true identity of his opponent, he is confronted with a conflict between the duty of honor and love for Ximena. Driven by the chivalric ideal of loyalty, he decides to defend his father's honor, and slays his opponent in a fair contest. Despite the tragic outcome, Ximena still loves Rodrigo, since he did his filial duty; yet she must dutifully implore the king for justice. But the desperate knight departs for the land of the Moors to search for glory, and, after gaining riches, fame, and the agnomen "el Cid" (the lord), he returns and marries Ximena. Centered around the conflict between love and duty, this dramatic play underlines the chivalric ideals of courage, nobility, and courtesy. Its protagonist demonstrates prudence, restraint, and political wisdom—essential traits in the dramatization of a hero.

The varied verse forms and lively dialogue add to the excellence of this drama, but its numerous exaggerated and isolated episodes fragment the action and hinder adequate character delineations. Nonetheless, the play gained much popularity in Spain because of its excellent depiction of colorful medieval customs and its emotional characterizations of eleventh-century historical figures. Although Castro gave his characters the speech and dress of seventeenth-century Spaniards, as was the practice of other Golden Age playwrights, this factor did not detract from their verisimilitude.

Las hazañas del Cid, continuing with the Rodrigo theme, revolves around the siege of Zamora when Sancho II was killed by Bellido Dolfos. The passive portrayal of the otherwise active Cid in the second play served the poet's dramatic intent to present the eleventh-century struggle over the Spanish crown rather than to depict the singular feats of the Spanish hero. Other chivalric plays by Castro that were inspired by ballads are *El conde de Alarcos* (1600?) and *El conde de Irlos* (1605?).

Among Castro's refined works are several comedies of manners that deal with contemporary customs in Valencia and Madrid. The mismatched married couples in several of these plays allude to the playwright's love affair with Helena Fenollar (who eventually sued him) before his unhappy and short marriage to Marquesa Girón de Rebolledo, who died before or shortly after 1600. His satire on marriage, *Los mal casados de Valencia* (*The Ill-Mated Couple of Valencia*, 1595?-1604?), which realistically depicts an adulterous misunderstanding that almost leads to the ruin of two marriages, contains more autobiographical references. In this parody on sexuality, Castro contrived an unexpected turn of events. Don Alvaro lives with his frigid wife, Hipólita, and a mistress, Eugenia. Hipólita ignores her husband's love affair but, after seeing him affectionately embrace Eugenia, who is in the garb of a manservant, she seeks an annulment to their marriage on grounds of sodomy.[5]

Other comedies of manners by Castro in the style of Lope de Vega are *El caballero bobo* (*The Foolish Young Gentleman*, 1595?); *El Narciso en su opinión* (The Self-Styled Narcissus, 1612?), an early *comedia de figurón* (a farcical play in which the protagonist is depicted as a grotesque figure) whose eccentric and presumptuous protagonist represents the antithesis of a *galán;* and *El pretendor con pobreza* (*The Impoverished Seeker of Royal Favor*, 1620?). Castro was the first to dramatize Cervantes' novels in *El curioso impertinente* (*Dangerous Curiosity*, 1606?), *Don Quixote de la Mancha* (1608?), and *La fuerza de la sangre* (*Kinship's Powerful Call*, 1614). He also wrote two mythological plays, *Progne y Filomena* (1608?) and *Dido y Eneas* (1613?).

Another important dramatist in the Valencian group was Gaspar de Aguilar (1561-1623), who excelled in the art of dialogue and plot complication. His *comedias* are of three types: cloak-and-sword, such as *La venganza honrosa* (*Honorable Vengeance*, before 1602); *de ruido* (''noisy pieces,'' so called because they required many properties and mechanical devices), such as *La gitana melancólica* (*The Melancholy Gypsy*, 1590-1607) and *El mercader amante* (*The Loving Merchant*, 1605); and religious, such as *El gran patriarca San Juan de Ribera* (*The Great Patriarch St. John of Ribera*, 1611-15). In Aguilar's plays are found the beginnings of the codification of honor in which death erases dishonor.

Miguel Beneyto (1560?-99) wrote several plays, but only one of any merit was published—*El hijo obediente* (*The Obedient Son*, before 1600), an interesting work that shows the relationship between obedience and honor. Carlos Boyl Vives (1577-1617 or 1621?) was more successful with his only published drama, *El marido asegurado* (*The Reassured Husband*, 1616), in which a man tests his bride to find out if she will be able to safeguard her honor. The last in the Valencian group was a magistrate known by the pseudonym Ricardo de Turia (b. 1578), whose real name is believed to have been Pedro Rejaule y Toledo. His best plays, *La belígera española* (*The Belligerent Lady*) and *La fe pagada* (*Faith Repaid*), show little originality. The first follows Ercilla's epic poem *La Araucana*, and the second, which shows the connection between a man's honor and the fate of his women, reveals Turia's indebtedness to the dramatic plots of Tárrega and Aguilar.

TIRSO DE MOLINA

The immediate follower of Lope de Vega's dramatic precepts and the most apt was a Mercedarian friar, Gabriel Téllez (1581?-1648), known by his literary pseudonym, Tirso de Molina. Why he chose "Tirso" is not known, but it possibly had a festive origin in thyrsus, the wand of the wine god Bacchus. It was also the favored name for a rustic and was used by a number of characters in Tirso's plays. Molina was the name of a city in Aragón, that of an aristocratic family, and also that of a famous Jesuit, Luis de Molina (1535-1600) who espoused the doctrine of free will in a spirited polemic of the time.

Although little is known about Gabriel Téllez's early years, an account of his life as a monk and playwright has been more clearly reconstructed from Mercedarian archives and other records. It is presumed that he was born in Madrid, probably in 1581. Nothing is known of his parentage beyond disputed theories that he may have been either an illegitimate son of a Téllez Girón (the Duke of Osuna) or of Jorge de Alencastre. Certain clues within his life and works indicate that he may have come from the high aristocratic Molina and Mendoza families, since he entered the Mercedarian Order in 1600, he mentions having relatives in Catalonia in *La vida de Santa María de Cervellón* (*The Life of Saint Mary of Cervellón*), he praises the family of Molina in two other plays, and he adopted that name for his pseudonym. On the other hand, he presented himself as a humble shepherd from Manzanares in *Cigarrales de Toledo* (*Country Houses of Toledo*, 1621), a miscellaneous work consisting of narrations, plays, and poetry, so he could also have descended from a humble family.

Gabriel Téllez's lengthy and interrupted schooling included studies in Salamanca (1600-1603), Toledo and Guadalajara (1603-07), and at the University of Alcalá de Henares. When not attending school the young monk resided in Soria (1608), Segovia (1610), and Madrid (1610-11). To preserve anonymity in his discontinuous career as a writer, he probably assumed his pen name first with a hagiographic play, *Los lagos de San Vicente* (*The Miraculous Lakes of Saint Vincent*, 1606-07). While residing in the Convent of Santa Catalina in Toledo after 1612 he wrote and staged *Don Gil de las calzas verdes* (*Don Gil in Green*

Tirso de Molina (1581?-1648)

Breeches) in 1615. The monk was sent to a mission in Santo Domingo in 1616, but he returned to Segovia two years later, and from 1618 to 1620 he traveled in Galicia and Portugal. Finally in 1620 Tirso settled in the Order of Our Lady of Mercy in Madrid, where he was able to write abundantly for the theater, compete in literary contests, and participate in the gatherings of the Poetic Academy in Madrid, which was founded by Sebastián Francisco de Medrano. During this time he associated with leading authors of his day—Quevedo, Góngora, Calderón, Alarcón, and Lope de Vega, the latter of whom dedicated his *Lo fingido verdadero* to him. In return the Mercedarian friar wrote a defense of Lope de Vega's new dramatic art in *Cigarrales de Toledo*.[6]

At the height of his literary career in 1625, charges were brought against Tirso before the Committee for Reform of the Council of Castile. He was accused of writing immoral and scandalous plays. It is probable that his own colleagues—Fray Pedro Franco de Guzmán (a relative of el Conde-Duque de Olivares), Fray Marcos Salmerón, and others— were responsible for the accusation. As a consequence Tirso was forbidden to write, an edict he did not obey, for he continued to write occasionally thereafter until 1632. Additionally, he was transferred in 1626 to a monastery in Trujillo, the birthplace of the Pizarro brothers, where he was isolated for three years from theatrical activities.

Tirso became a zealous worker in his order and was appointed a superior in the monastery at Trujillo, then the chronicler for the Order of Mercy, and finally the superior of the monastery at Soria. Among his later works, *Deleitar aprovechando* (*Pleasure with Profit*, 1631-32), a miscellany of stories, three novels, and many of his *autos sacramentales* stand out. He died at Almazán on February 24, 1648.

In about 1621 Tirso claimed, in his *Cigarrales de Toledo*, to have written three hundred plays, and in 1634 the editor of the third volume of his plays stated that the poet had written over four hundred plays. These figures place Tirso, together with Luis Vélez de Guevara, as the second most prolific playwright after Lope de Vega in the Spanish Golden Age. Of his total output, eighty-five plays are extant, in addition to a number of *autos sacramentales*, *entremeses*, novels, and poems. Most of these were published between 1627 and 1636 and appeared in five collections, four of which contain twelve pieces and one, eleven.

The third and fourth collections were edited by Francisco Lucas de Avila, a supposed nephew of Tirso. Since the publications of Tirso's plays do not reveal when they were written, Blanca de los Ríos, Ruth L. Kennedy, and others have established dates for their composition through their collections of circumstantial evidence and data. The two periods of Tirso's intensive dramatic activity were 1610-16 and 1620-25.

Tirso's life stands in sharp contrast to that of Lope de Vega. Since the monk was confined most of his life to secluded monasteries, except for the time he was given to participate in the theatrical world, he had less opportunity to experience personally the way of life depicted in his plays. But his religious education and experience as a clergyman gave him the ability to penetrate theological questions and to present psychological aspects of his characters. Although less original and spontaneous as a poet than Lope, Tirso displayed a talent for creating strong personalities (Don Juan, Doña María de Molina, and Paulo), for disassociating himself from conventional and chivalrous knightly ideals, and for displaying healthy intellectualism. The poet's dramatic dialogues, unusually comical *graciosos*, wit, vivacity, and frank social criticism make up for his often less carefully constructed plots and trivial dénouements. Occasionally affected with gongoristic mannerisms, Tirso's style, nonetheless, is clear and exemplifies the Spanish dramatic poetry of his age.

The Eschatological Plays. Universally known as the author of *El burlador de Sevilla y convidado de piedra* (*The Trickster of Seville and the Stone Guest*), Tirso created the modern mythological character of Don Juan. This baroque drama, set during a period of sociopolitical and moral upheaval in Spain, presents a character who, repressing religious and moral rules, yields to his own instincts without regard for the consequences. Although various aspects of his character could possibly be traced in legend and earlier literature, the essential figure of Don Juan appeared for the first time in two versions of Tirso's drama: *Tan largo me lo fiáis* (*You Give Me Such a Long Time*, 1612-16) and *El burlador de Sevilla y convidado de piedra* (*The Trickster of Seville and the Stone Guest*, 1616-30).[7]

For his rapidly moving and episodic play, Tirso combined the escapades of an unbridled seducer with a folkloric tale about a ghost of stone who was invited to a banquet. A young nobleman, Don Juan Tenorio of Seville, takes pleasure in pursuing women in all classes of society, from fishermaids to court ladies, despite the continuous warnings of his *gracioso* Catalinón, and others. Nevertheless, the trickster often scoffs at their warnings by expressing a scornful unconcern about divine justice: "Qué largo me lo fiáis!" ("What a long time you [God] give me!"). The philandering youth reveals both his anarchical instincts and his Christian heritage, and he heedlessly continues in his role as a trickster because he expects to have plenty of time left when he gets ready to ask for God's mercy.

The first of his four amorous encounters takes place in the royal palace of Naples, where the dissolute youth impersonates his best friend, the Duke of Octavio, whose fiancée, Duchess Isabel, he seduces. Don Juan eludes arrest with the help of his uncle, who happens to be the Spanish ambassador, and escapes for Spain. When a storm wrecks his ship on a beach near Tarragona, he finds the opportunity to seduce a fishergirl, Tisbea. Upon arriving in Seville the infamous trickster repeats his scheme by attempting to seduce Ana, a daughter of Commander Gonzalo de Ulloa. Discovering the deception in time, Ana cries out, and her father comes to her rescue. In the ensuing scuffle Don Juan kills the Commander and escapes. On the way to Lebrija the fugitive seduces a peasant bride, Aminta, on the eve of her wedding.

When Don Juan returns to Seville he hides in the cemetery, where he chances upon Don Gonzalo's tomb. Youthfully and with much bravura he approaches his victim's statue, tweaks its beard, and invites it to supper the next night. Don Gonzalo not only appears at the appointed time but extends to his host a similar invitation for the following night in the cemetery chapel. When Don Juan shows up, the dead man, repeating the lover's initial command to his victims—"Give me your hand!"—drags his murderer through the flames of Hell without giving him a chance to repent.[8] Seeming to answer the chorus's metaphoric warning, Don Gonzalo's ghost furthermore declares, "Quien tal hace, que tal pague!" ("As a man soweth, so shall he reap!"), a phrase used in Spain by town criers before the execution of a criminal. The play ends conventionally when the trickster's victims seek redress for their grievances and are properly married off by verdict of the monarch.

The swiftly changing scenes, contrasting situations, rapid action, and lively dialogue give this most famous of Tirso's dramas a kaleidoscopic structure. Unity, nonetheless, is achieved through the presentation of a libertine protagonist who approaches each unusual situation with the same stubborn, rebellious nature. Don Juan's comical *gracioso* who warns him, the various reactions of the women in his amorous adventures, and the supernatural elements surrounding his encounter with Don Gonzalo also contribute to the fascination the play has always attracted.

Tirso was not primarily interested in portraying the life of an insatiable lover in his masterpiece, as had been done in several antecedents in classical mythology, medieval legends, and Spanish ballads and drama. Tying an amorous theme to a motif of metaphysical revenge, he exposed, within this eschatological drama, theological issues popular during the baroque period, when the pleasures of terrestrial life were beginning to be regarded more seriously. His invention of the Don Juan character as an iconoclastic sensualist who stands in opposition to all the unwritten laws in Spanish society, was no accident, for Don Juan was a product of the Renaissance. Through the exposure of this libertine, Tirso was not only addressing the problems of a new era, he was also condemning the old conduct associated with the protection of a woman's honor and was directing a message on morality toward the dissolute court of his day. By showing, furthermore, that some women were permissive and others were easy prey, he was exposing the double standard that existed even in the strict society of his day.[9]

Don Juan's attempts to find happiness while moving from conquest to conquest and finally to violence and crime are misguided and doomed to failure. Whereas the sexual offender in Lope de Vega's *Fuenteovejuna* is punished by human justice, Tirso's transgressor is damned by supernatural forces. Warnings of social punishment and divine retribution do nothing to detain him from his illicit activities. He defies the laws of society and also counts on being saved because of his privileged social rank and his youth. Believing there will be enough time for him to confess and be absolved, he cannot be saved by the sole act of contrition because this ritual in its empty form is invalid. Theologically speaking, Don Juan is damned because he has exercised his free will for evil purposes and been overconfident of God's mercy. His rebellious nature gives him heroic grandeur and makes him a tragic hero.

The enigmatic characteristics of Don Juan have attracted much attention.[10] Some suggest that in his search for an ideal woman, he suffered from an Oedipus complex because he was looking for a personified mother in every woman. Others see in him the partly comical figure of an adolescent inexperienced in controlling his natural drives. From biological and psychological points of view, critics have swung from one pole to another when accounting for his behavior as being either overly virile or prematurely impotent; others have found effeminacy in him because of his vice of lying to women. Although Don Juan displays certain sadistic traits and appears to be the victimizer of his paramours, still others consider him in reality to be an unholy martyr, whose death helps cleanse society of certain evils.[11]

In *El burlador de Sevilla*, Tirso dramatically treated one facet within the theme of free will. The casuistic debate whether to trust an ever-forgiving Providence or to seek one's own salvation through good deeds is emphasized further in a complementary drama, *El condenado por desconfiado* (*The Man Condemned for Lack of Faith*, 1615-25).[12] Concerned with theological problems associated with predestination and free will, especially in relation to divine justice and benevolence, this play exposed the heated debate of two theological factions in Tirso's day: one, headed by a Jesuit, Luis Molina, claimed that man through his acts can receive grace for salvation; the other, represented by a Dominican, Domingo Báñez, defended the thesis that God determines who will receive divine grace.

The immediate sources for the play were a legend about St. Pafnucio in *Vitae Patrum* (*The Lives of the Fathers*), Roberto Balarmino's moralistic work *De arte bene moriendi* (*On the Art of Dying Well*), and perhaps the writings of Francisco Zumel.[13] Set in Italy, Tirso's plot involves a pious but cowardly hermit, Paulo, who sinfully asks God about his fate after life. After a demon, disguised as an angel, suggests that his end will be identical with that of Enrico, a hardened criminal, Paulo turns to a life of crime, since he knows he will be damned anyway.

Enrico, however, through his paternal love and sincere faith, repents before his execution and is saved. Paulo never regains his faith because he believes in predestination so strongly that his exercise of free will is inhibited. He is condemned and dies at the hands of an angry mob—an indication of divine retribution.

In this play Tirso succeeds in depicting rural customs, the wily character of peasants, and the lawlessness of criminals. Moreover, the contrasts between the two protagonists are artfully drawn within the framework of this thesis play. Although Paulo exemplifies the perfect hermit, ambition and jealousy finally destroy him. On the other hand, Enrico, a hardened bandit who possesses many flaws, finds salvation because of the finer virtues within his heart. The application of justice in *El condenado* suggests that divine justice cannot be placed in the hands of men, and underlines the importance of faith and repentance. The theme—the lack of faith in God—leads to despair, whereas the theme in *El burlador* (in which the protagonist, although confessing faith in God, procrastinates too long to ask forgiveness) conveys presumptuous overconfidence in him. Both plays stress man's right to choose his actions and thus to direct his own destiny.[14]

The Religious Plays. As a clergyman, Tirso had access to an array of religious writings in which he found natural subjects for the stage. In addition to the characters in Holy Scripture, he made use of numerous accounts of the lives of saints, especially from the *Flos Sanctorum* (*Lives of the Saints*) of Alonso de Villegas and a similar work by Pedro de Rivadeneyra, since they displayed heroic traits suitable for the theater. The playwright enlivened many of his religious plays by interpolating into them romantic episodes and humorous elements.

The earliest and perhaps least perfect of over a dozen of Tirso's hagiographic plays written between 1606 and 1628 is *Los lagos de San Vicente* (*The Miraculous Lakes of St. Vincent*). Its main plot, based on a legend about the conversion of an eleventh-century Moorish woman who became Saint Casilda, follows Lope de Vega's *Santa Casilda*. A trilogy belonging to this group of plays, *Santa Juana* (1613-14), recounts the three periods in the life of a remarkable Franciscan nun, Juana de la Cruz (1481-1534), and is based on Fray Antonio Daza's biography of the saint and the *Memorias* (*Memoirs*) of Sor María Evangelista. The central theme of these plays is that life on earth is a preparation for eternal existence, and each play reflects a different stage of mysticism: the purgative, the illuminative, and the unitive.[15] *Santo y sastre* (*The Saint-Tailor*, 1614-15) dramatizes the life of Saint Homobono, a twelfth-century Italian tailor from Cremona, and sets out to prove that a lowly profession on earth can be combined with spiritual nobility.

Considered a model hagiographic play that also artificially blends secular and religious elements, *La ninfa del cielo* (*The Heavenly Nymph*, 1613) relates the adventures of an Italian lady bandit named Ninfa, Countess of Valdeflor. Although two-thirds of the play are concerned with a simple love triangle between Ninfa, Carlos, and his wife, the ironic dénouement, during which the countess dies at the hand of Carlos's jealous wife, embraces a theological theme, since the dying Ninfa pardons her assassin and goes to Christ, thus uniting with God in mystic union.

The first of four historico-religious plays, *El caballero de Gracia* (*The Gentleman of Grace*, 1620), presents the pious and charitable activity of Jacobo de Gratis (1517-1619), an Italian ascetic who established churches, convents, and hospitals in Madrid. And the good works of the founder of Toledo's Convent of the Conceptionists is the topic for *Doña Beatriz de Silva* (1619-21), whose heroine (1424-1490) eschews her frivolous past and dedicates herself to a religious mission in Toledo.

Tirso's visits in Galicia provided inspiration for *La romera de Santiago* (*The Pilgrim of Santiago*, 1619-20), a play that glorifies the shrine of Saint James within a stereotyped plot of love entanglements in a religious environment. *El mayor desengaño* (*The Greatest Disillusionment*, 1621) is a theological hagiographic drama that was written for university circles. Its first two acts center around the secular existence of the German Saint Bruno (1032-1101), and the third act dramatizes Bruno's monastic conversion and sanctification before founding the Carthusian Order.

Between 1611 and 1622 Tirso produced five plays inspired by the Bible. In the first, *La mujer que manda en casa* (*The Wife Who Rules the Roost*, 1611-12), the dramatist made use of the biblical account of Jezebel's bewitchment of her husband Ahab (King of Samaria and

Israel [*ca.* 875-51 B.C.]), her despotic, lustful powers, and her brutal death at the hands of King Jehu, to caution against the dangers of domineering wives.[16] The first two acts of *La vida y muerte de Herodes* (*The Life and Death of Herod*, 1611-20), a psychological study of Herod Antipas, enact the amorous affairs of that king, while the last act ties his death to the redemptive power of the birth of Christ. The dynamic relationship between this play's plot and action and its ritualistic structure reveals Tirso's perception as a priest and dramatist.[17] *La mejor espigadera* (*The Best Gleaner*, 1614) deals with the stories of Ruth and Boaz, and *Tanto es lo de más como lo de menos* (*Enough Is as Good as a Feast*, 1612-20) incorporates the parables of the prodigal son and the rich miser. The dramatic structure of the latter play, in which Tirso counsels moderation, is like that of an *auto sacramental.*

The title of Tirso's last and most masterfully written biblical play, *La venganza de Tamar* (*The Vengeance of Tamar*, 1621-23), implies its affinity to an honor play. Closely following the account of the immoral behavior of King˙ David's children, as found primarily in II Samuel, chapter 13, the play is almost a classical tragedy. Out of the curse that was put on the House of David after his affair with Bathsheba, the playwright develops an essential theme of incest, a subject rarely staged in Spanish drama;[18] and he makes use of a leitmotiv about the passion of love by frequently inferring that it is like man's appetite for food. In the play Amón, David's oldest son, falls in love with Tamar without knowing she is his half sister. After he realizes who she is, Amón suggests that they act out a love scene in a little drama, and he succeeds in seducing her. Obviously, since Tamar's dishonor cannot be remedied by marriage, her full-blooded brother Absalón—in true Spanish style—avenges the wrong by killing Amón and vowing to annihilate his father.

Tirso provides vivid portrayals of David's household without using the subsequent biblical account of Absalom's rebellion against his father, his tragic death, and his father's continued love for him. Absalón is shown to have a deeper motivation than the avenging of Tamar's dishonor, since he repeatedly expresses his ambition to gain the throne. In Amón's temperamental actions, moreover, his rebellion against his strict yet benevolent father can be discerned; like that of a fatal hero, his death draws little pity. The two domineering brothers stand in contrast to the passive Tamar, who longs for love but not with her brother; she is but a pawn in the hands of others. Although the play's title suggests that Tamar will probably take an active part in her vindication, she only serves as Amón's victim and as an excuse for Absalón's ambitious actions. Finally, Tirso's conception of David's character shows what happens to the loving David of the Old Testament when his sons take advantage of his good qualities. A tragic figure in this play, David possesses an imaginative mind that cannot comprehend the reality of the situation, and when he does, he is resigned to suffer in frustration.

Of the relatively few *autos sacramentales* that Tirso wrote, only five have survived. *El colmenero divino* (*The Divine Beekeeper*, 1609) allegorically depicts man's relation to God and makes use of an extensive metaphor to give meaning to the Eucharist. Supervising a colony of bees in building their hives in an apiary, Jesus, a divine beekeeper, is overwhelmed by sorrow. Under the bees' protection Cuerpo (the Body) builds the hives, but Oso (the Bear) and Mundo (the World) jealously lure the bees away. The weak Cuerpo takes sweet but false honey from Oso, who has disguised himself as a beekeeper, and Abeja (a female Bee) loses her wings because she has taken advantage of Cuerpo, who has worked as a laborer. After confessing her sin, Abeja is offered by the Beekeeper the Honey of Heaven, and her wings grow again, thus giving her a chance to fly to Heaven. The symbolism suggested by the allegorical characters can be easily recognized: the apiary and the hives represent the Church and its branches, the Bee and the Body portray the spiritual and physical sides of man's nature, the Bear represents the Devil, the World symbolizes the sinful elements in life that mitigate spiritual growth, and the Divine Honey is the consecrated bread of the Eucharist.

Tirso's sacramental and morality play *¡No le arriendo la ganancia!* (*Much Good May It Do Him!*, 1612-13?) centers on Spanish honor while making some allusions to the Eucharist. The best of his *autos*, *Los hermanos parecidos* (*The Identical Brothers*, 1615), follows the Pauline notion that Christ was the second Adam, through the use of identical twin actors to represent them. More a morality play than an *auto*, *La Ninfa del Cielo* (*The Nymph of Heaven*, 1619) is an allegorical version of Tirso's full-length play by the same title. In this play Ninfa (the Soul), after falling in love with Sin, repents, is saved, and returns to Christ, thus evoking the mystical union of the soul in Christ. Finally, Christianizing a classical legend in *Laberinto de Creta* (*The Cretan Labyrinth*, 1636?) the playwright converted the pagan labyrinth into a world in which man is tested in the experiences of life. Apparently more interested in the Counter-Reformation than in teaching about the Eucharist in this play, Tirso presents Prester John, king of Ethiopia, as the defender of Catholicism who stands against Tudesco (a German), an advocate of Protestantism.

In addition to these sacramental plays, Tirso's one-act religious play, *Auto de Nuestra Señora del Rosario: la Madrina del Cielo* (*The Play about Our Lady of the Rosary: The Heavenly Sponsor*, 1610-11?), deals with the salvation of a seducer through Grace. This play stands alone because it has the character neither of an *auto sacramental* nor of a morality play.

Although Lope de Vega, José de Valdivieso, Mira de Amescua, and Calderón may have surpassed Tirso as writers of *autos sacramentales*, the Mercedarian achieved certain fame as the baroque moralizer in his *autos* and other religious plays, since he combined in them the medieval mystical view of life with the prevailing religious philosophy of his day. But from the five *autos* of his known today and the other short religious play, it can be seen that, despite his poetic agility and free use of imagination, Tirso showed neither strong interest in nor deep understanding of Eucharistic drama.

The Historical and Legendary Plays. In the historical genre Tirso employed themes from national history. The best among them is *La prudencia en la mujer* (*Prudence in a Woman*, ca. 1622), which portrays in its main plot the political turmoil that existed during María de Molina's regency preceding the reign of Fernando IV (1295-1312). The subplot deals with the legendary rivalry between the Benavides and Carvajales families. Using *La Crónica de Fernando IV* (Valladolid, 1554), among other sources, Tirso situated this play's action in a medieval milieu that recalled the age-old hostility between the Castilians and the Leonese, thereby rekindling an emotional issue still smolder-

ing in Spain at that time.[19] The playwright's secondary purposes in using medieval history were to refer symbolically to Spain's internal situation during the government of the Conde-Duque de Olivares in the
seventeenth century and to call for national unity.

Noted for his characterizations of women, Tirso in this play presented
the regent queen's character in the typical environment of her contemporary world. Setting her against a background of intrigue and in the
presence of ambitious Spanish lords, the dramatist portrays her as a prudent and clement queen who is loyal to the memory of her deceased
husband, circumvents trouble, and protects the throne for her son. The
moral tone, serious dramatic substance, and excellent portrayal of the
queen outweigh the play's stylistic deficiencies, such as its episodic structure and numerous speeches.

Inspired by the old chronicles and Salucio del Poyo's earlier plays,
Tirso wrote two tragedies on the theme of fallen royal favorites: *Próspera fortuna de don Alvaro de Luna y adversa de Ruy López Dávalos*
(*The Prosperous Fortune of Alvaro de Luna and the Adverse Fortune
of Ruy López Dávalos*) and *Adversa fortuna de don Alvaro de Luna*
(*The Adverse Fortune of Alvaro de Luna*, 1615-21). In the latter play,
which was written in the style of a modern romantic tragedy, Alvaro
is victimized by the king's indiscretion and is humiliated when his
beneficiaries, to whom he has been extremely good, fail in expressions
of gratitude.[20]

Episodes from the historical conquest of the New World are recorded
in *Amazonas de las Indias* (*The Amazons of the West Indies*) and the
Trilogía de los Pizarros (*The Trilogy of the Pizarros*). Commissioned
by the descendants of Francisco Pizarro to vindicate their family name,
each play within the trilogy treats the unjust destiny of one of the three
brothers.[21]

Two notable historico-legendary plays are *La joya de las montañas*
(*The Jewel of the Mountains*) and *El cobarde más valiente* (*The Most
Valiant Coward*), which deal with stories from legendary Spain. Tirso's
version of the Romeo and Juliet folkloric legend, *Los amantes de Teruel*
(*The Lovers of Teruel*, 1635), a drama of fate that depends on a succes-
sion of accidents, psychologically develops the self-destructive traits in
Isabel and Marcilla. Another noteworthy play in this group, *Las quinas*

de Portugal (*The Arms of Portugal*, 1638), treats an amorous theme in stock fashion while recounting the heroic deeds of Alfonso Enríquez, the first king of Portugal during the peninsular Reconquest.

The Cloak-and-Sword Plays and Comedies of Manners. Influenced by Lope de Vega, who excelled in the portrayal of women in his *comedias de enredo* (plays of high intrigue), Tirso showed his greatest mastery in this genre. His especially well drawn female protagonists are bold in amorous pursuits and manipulate the rather meek, spiritless men they chase. By making use of the popular dramatic technique of disguising women as men and having them pursue their reluctant lovers, he achieved a peak in plot complication, as can be seen in *Don Gil de las calzas verdes* (*Don Gil in Green Breeches*, 1615).[22]

Considered an early example of escapist theater,[23] this play presents a jilted young lady who cleverly restores her honor by means of a continuous series of entanglements that involve a reversal of sex roles. This play's complicated and hilarious intrigue involves three amorous triangles with just four characters. The cowardly, superstitious Don Martín seduces his fiancée, Juana, then abandons her for a richer and more beautiful girl, Inés. When Juana disguises herself as Don Gil in order to follow her faithless sweetheart, she attracts Inés, who then scorns Martín. The unsuccessful Martín blames his unscrupulous father for his own fiasco. But thanks to her ingenuity in a play-within-the-play, Juana finally wins Martín back. Doña Juana (or Don Gil) has become known as the feminine counterpart of Don Juan Tenorio, since she is more interested in love than in avenging her tarnished honor, and boldly justifies her lies and inventions to achieve her goals. Winning back her lover by means of her superb impersonations in both male and female disguises, she is an excellent example of a "metagonist" who reshapes the expected outcome of the play through her own inventions.

Another side to a young lady's problems in courtship and marriage is farcically treated in *Marta la piadosa* (*Pious Martha*, 1615?). The heroine confronts several difficulties: her lover, Felipe, for whom her younger sister is also competing, kills her brother, and she is being forced to marry a wealthy old man she does not love. To solve her problems, Marta makes a vow of chastity in order to avoid the prearranged marriage and to receive lessons in Latin from her disguised fiancé. She reasons that hypocrisy and dissimulation are justified as long as her purpose of marrying happily is honest. Marta's lifelike delineation superbly portrays a young woman in the dramatic tradition of the *comedia*.[24]

Some plays by Tirso depict as heroines frivolous, susceptible women with picaresque qualities, such as those in *Averígüelo, Vargas (Find It Out, Vargas*, 1619-21), *La villana de Vallecas (The Peasant Girl of Vallecas*, 1620),[25] *Los balcones de Madrid (The Balconies of Madrid*, after 1624), *Mari-Hernández, la gallega (Mari-Hernandez, the Galician*, 1625), and *Desde Toledo a Madrid (From Toledo to Madrid*, 1625-27?). Many other Tirsian lady protagonists, however, as we have already seen, surpass the normal stereotypes and display vivid personalities with psychological traits. The ability of Tirso's heroines to influence the course of action in his plays reveals not only his attitude toward women but also his sociological and cultural concern for them in Spanish society.

Por el sótano y el torno (Through Basement and Hatch, 1623), for example, satirizes cupidity and continence. Two sisters, Bernarda and Jusepa, choose to lead a chaste existence in the house of an old man. Through the help of her servant Santarén, Jusepa finds a cellar cave and a hatch in an adjoining house (sexual symbols) through which she can exchange letters with her lover Duarte. Thus, she eludes her older sister's vigilance, avoids having to marry her old, gray-bearded landlord, and lands the young man of her choice.[26] In *La villana de la Sagra (The Peasant Girl of Sagra*, 1608-14) a young lady follows her exiled brother in order to remain under his protection. Disguised as a peasant girl, she experiences several adventures and finally falls into the arms of a lover who respects her for her honesty. The heroine of *Antona García* (1622) is a rich, pregnant peasant who helps the Spanish army to win in the war against the Portuguese. When a Portuguese officer solicits her in her condition, she tactfully eludes his and his colleagues' advances.

The palace play *El vergonzoso en palacio (The Shy, Young Man at Court*, 1611) presents an excellent example of a Tirsian female portrayal. The main romantic plot, which treats the protagonist's social ascent from shepherd to courtier, is similar to that in Lope de Vega's *El perro del hortelano*. The play's title, derived from an old Spanish proverb, "al hombre vergonzoso el diablo le trajo al palacio" ("the devil brought the bashful man to the palace"), is repeatedly used as a leitmotiv. Magdalena, the impatient daughter of the Duke of Avero, disregards the social rules that divide the classes and woos Mireno, her bashful secretary. She achieves her goal through the use of many clever schemes, including a dream, during which, in a dialogue, she speaks her own part and also that of her lover. The use of this interesting baroque device falls into the category of metatheater.[27] A misalliance that seems likely to result when the two fall in love is averted just in time when the discovery is made that Mireno is in reality Don Dionís, a son of the Duke of Coimbra.

A second pair of lovers in this play's political subplot are entangled in similar problems: Magdalena's sister, Serafina, is being pursued by Antonio, a Portuguese count, who veils his identity. In the carnivalesque play that these characters stage, Serafina's disinterest in marrying and her dreams of pursuing an acting career—not to mention her split personality—are revealed. Disguised as a jealous lover, a madman, and in four other roles, Serafina rejects Antonio when she falls in love with the portrait of herself in masculine dress which is being painted.[28]

Tirso used this play to express his own attitudes about life. Through its theme of a woman's right to choose her mate, he ingeniously challenged the seventeenth-century Spanish custom that prohibited a couple from making their own decision in marriage. Its palace setting, furthermore, indicates his disapproval of life at the Spanish court. Although Mireno's characterization may lack verisimilitude, since he appears to be too timid for the aspiring Magdalena, his ignorance about his true aristocratic rank is thought to mirror the poet's own proud shyness and his life as the supposed illegitimate son of the Duke of Osuna. Moreover, in Antonio's personality a reflection of Tirso's own ingenuity and audacity can be seen.[29]

The twin to *El vergonzoso* is *El melancólico* (*The Melancholiac*, 1611-23?), which contains other autobiographical references to the playwright, since it deals with the mental state of Rogerio, the illegitimate son of the Duke of Bretaña. Disgusted by the bad conduct of his so-called nephew, Enrique brings Rogerio to the court and recognizes him as his heir. But Rogerio, having fallen in love with a shepherdess, Leonisa, before arriving in the city, suffers from melancholy because he is being forced to marry his cousin, Clemencia. His predicament may be parallel to an incident in Tirso's life; furthermore, the play displays the poet's disdain for the injustices that existed in the nobility's strict rules regarding hereditary rights. The metaphoric complexity and contrasting versification in this play contribute to its baroque and vivacious qualities.

Tirso de Molina's dramas became popular with Spanish audiences for several reasons. Their plans of action are usually simple, and his characters echo his interest in social criticism rather than in pastoral, chivalric, and mythological subjects. The poet also departed from a practice of his predecessors by making only occasional references to traditional ballads through a *gracioso*. As a critic of aristocratic society, Tirso directed his dramatic art toward urban corruption. In contrast to Lope de Vega's use of more linear plots and Calderón's dramatic abstractions, Tirso's works rest on tangible reality, as in his characterizations and his transmission of ideas. It has been said that the repertory of his themes encompasses the preoccupations of most early seventeenth-century Spaniards.[30] Known especially for his plays of intrigue and those about theology, and for his portrayals of women, Tirso advanced Lope's theatrical art. He thus stands in the pivotal position between Lope and Calderón.

JUAN RUIZ DE ALARCÓN

The great classicist and the least typical of Spain's Golden Age dramatists, the Mexican-born Juan Ruiz de Alarcón (1581-1639) occupies a special place in the evolution of Spanish theater.[31] Coming from a well-to-do Spanish family, Alarcón studied at the University of Mexico before moving in 1600 to the more prestigious university at Salamanca. Between 1606 and 1608 he practiced law in Seville, but he returned to Mexico in 1608 and received the Licentiate of Laws in 1609. After living in his native country for five years, he returned permanently to Madrid, where he wrote about two dozen plays between 1613 and 1626. He ended his career as a dramatist when he was appointed court reporter for the Council of the Indies in 1626, and he died in Madrid in 1639.

Juan Ruiz de Alarcón (1581-1639)

Called the "Spanish Terence," Alarcón was an urbane dramatist who
strove for perfection. The scale of his dramatic output ranges from the
finest plays to somewhat weak ones. This can be explained by the fact
that, like his contemporaries, Alarcón often wrote in haste in order to
satisfy public demand. He is remembered for his passionless plays that
stand in contrast to the fervent, romantic pieces his colleagues wrote,
and also for his lively comedies of manners. Having adopted neoclassical
tendencies that anticipated those of Moratín nearly two centuries later,
he acquired a number of enemies, who ridiculed his physical defor-
mities, Creole origin, claims of nobility, and literary aspirations. The
embittered hunchback with red hair and bowlegs responded to the cruel
witticisms of his critics—Góngora, Suárez de Figueroa, and the Count
of Villamediana—by praising in his plays such virtues as faithfulness
in friendship, chivalric loyalty, abnegation in love, and innocence. At
the same time he attacked such vices as slander, lying, ingratitude, injustice, and greed.

Since Alarcón was concerned with social problems within his own experience, his theater is moral and intellectual rather than aesthetic. His
social criticism is conveyed through the ethico-psychological depiction
of characters and the study of customs. Rather than elaborating complex plots, the playwright introduced into Spanish drama the depiction of morals and character, especially in the characterization of Spanish
gentry. In order to achieve realism he sacrificed the use of plots of intrigue and concentrated on character analysis.

Alarcón's most mature and polished of plays of character and social
observation are *La verdad sospechosa* (*Suspect Truth*, 1619), *Las paredes
oyen* (*Walls Have Ears*, 1621), and *El examen de maridos* (*The Test
of Suitors*, 1623-25?). The first and last of these plays are drawn from
the same sources that Shakespeare used in *The Merchant of Venice*.
In *La verdad sospechosa*, a moralizing play that chastises the vice of
mendacity, Don García makes a sport out of lying.[32] Interrupting his
studies at the University of Salamanca, he returns with his tutor to his
home in Madrid to receive the primogeniture that falls to him after
the death of his brother. After the tutor reveals to García's father that
his son has a great defect—lying—the father, Don Beltrán, makes plans
to marry him as soon as possible to Jacinta.

Stage scene from Act 1, scene 5, of Ruiz de Alarcón's *La verdad sospechosa* (*Suspect Truth*), at the Palacio de Bellas Artes (Mexico) under the direction of Antonio Castro Leal, 1934.

Don García has already fallen in love with Jacinta, having met her on the street and pretended to be a rich Peruvian recently arrived in Spain. Unfortunately, however, since the young man mistook Jacinta for her companion, Lucrecia, he thinks he is in love with Lucrecia. The intrigue of the *comedia* rests on the confusion of names. When García speaks to Jacinta, he swears he loves Lucrecia, and when his father proposes that he marry Jacinta, García untruthfully declares that he has already secretly married in Salamanca. As a result of his confusion and lies, García not only loses the woman he loves but also is forced by his father to marry the woman he dislikes.

The ironic ending of this play teaches that mendacity harms not only the lier but all others who are involved. The play's theme—the greatest deceiver is the one who deceives himself—shows indebtedness to Aesop's fable about the boy who cried "Wolf, wolf!"[33]

A play that is considered to be a jewel in Spanish *comedia*, *Las paredes oyen*, provides a moral through the character portrayals of two antithetical rivals who compete for the love of a beautiful widow, Doña

Ana. Finally the rich and handsome but gossipy Don Mendo loses out to the less endowed but more generous and amiable Don Juan. With his fine presentation of Don Mendo as the perfect gossip, Alarcón was actually mimicking his critics, whereas the qualities of Don Juan were meant to reflect the playwright's philosophy that nobility exists in nature and not because of heredity. For Alarcón the doctrine of social equality was manifested in good actions and dignity rather than in noble birth.

In *El examen de maridos*, regarded as Alarcón's last play, Marquise Inés accepts her deceased father's advice to examine the qualifications of her numerous suitors. After narrowing her choice down to the more handsome Carlos, whom she does not really like, and the less dashing but more lovable Fadrique, she lets the two men debate her predicament with the understanding that the winner will gain her hand in marriage. Although Carlos unwittingly argues in his own disfavor (thanks to false rumors spread by Fadrique's jealous former girlfriend, Blanca, about Fadrique's physical defects and Inés's long-time passion for Carlos) and wins the debate, he yields Inés to Fadrique when he finds out the truth. Then, feeling sorry for Blanca, he marries her.

In this play's suspenseful plot, which leads to an unexpected resolution, the characters display different traits related to friendship, loyalty, and marriage. Blanca capriciously changes her mind as fortune shifts; and since Fadrique's main interest is his friendship with Carlos, he expresses little concern for the lady he will win. Carlos's aggressiveness works in his disfavor, but his generosity is revealed when he marries Blanca. Finally, the incredibly objective posture that Inés maintains throughout the play eventually wins for her the mate she originally favored.

Alarcón is particularly known for his plays about the occult and the Devil.[34] His *Quien mal anda mal acaba* (*He Who Follows an Evil Way Ends Evilly*, 1601-11?) is the first dramatic treatment of a man's pact with the Devil to appear in Spain. In this play Román Ramírez fails to attract the attention of Doña Aldonza until he signs a pact with the Devil, who agrees to help him become a doctor. Before their marriage, however, two representatives from the Inquisition arrest the doctor as a heretic and wizard. The playwright's interest in black magic can be found in another early play, *La manganilla de Melilla* (*The Stratagem at Melilla*, 1602-8), whose plot is based on a trick of military strategy that Captain Pedro Vanegas used to defeat Moorish forces at Melilla.

La cueva de Salamanca (*The Cave of Salamanca*, 1617-20), somewhat autobiographical and episodic, makes references to two historical figures linked to the practice of the occult against the background of student life. The dramatist based the main plot on the legend that the Devil was tricked by one of his students, who left his shadow behind and repented before the Devil was able to drag him off to Hell. It is thought that the learned magician, Enrico, who teaches his art in a windowless house that resembles a cave, is a reflection of Enrico Martínez, a well-known Dutch magician in Spain who died in 1632. His student, Villena, is presented as a fictional son of the childless Enrique de Villena, a fifteenth-century Spanish marquis whose zealous contribution to the learned arts wrongfully gained for him a reputation as a practitioner of necromancy. Alarcón attempted to squash these false accusations about the marquis with an invented descendant's explanation that he did not go to Hell, and with Enrico's final acknowledgment of error. Although the lengthy discussions about the practice of black magic detract from this play, interest is maintained in the slapstick scenes dealing with student life.

Alarcón's skillfully drawn plot for another play about sorcery, *La prueba de las promesas* (*The Test of Promises*, 1618), is derived from Juan Manuel's thirteenth exemplary tale in *El conde Lucanor*. A necromancer, Illán of Toledo, plans to marry his daughter Blanca to Enrique, since he is eager to terminate a feud between the two families. Blanca, however, is in love with Juan, who asks Illán to teach him the art of black magic so that he can be close to her. Unwilling to force his daughter into an unhappy marriage, Illán tests Juan's character. Turning on his magical power, he makes the young man rise above the social status of Blanca. In this state Juan loses interest in Blanca, but as the spell is broken he changes his mind. The disillusioned Blanca comprehends the untrustworthiness of her humiliated lover and happily consents to marry Enrique. The playwright's double purpose in this play of intrigue was to focus on the theme of ingratitude and to show that, although knowledge of the occult is permissible, its practice is inadvisable.

In Alarcón's only attempt at religious drama, *El anticristo* (*The Antichrist*, 1623), he invented a heretical plot around passages from Malachi, Daniel, the gospels, and the Book of Revelation, as well as a book about the Last Judgment that appeared in Salamanca in 1588 that antithetically contrasts the Devil with Christ. The indecent inversions in this play were much too unorthodox for the public in seventeenth-century Spain, and it is no small wonder that Lope de Vega and some other playwrights are reputed to have hired spectators to disrupt its staging by throwing cucumbers during its premiere.

Themes on social consciousness can be perceived in other plays by Alarcón. The futility of worldly success and honor is presented in *Los favores del mundo* (*The Favors of This World*, 1616-17). Fickleness is the subject in *Mudarse por mejorarse* (*Changing for the Better*, 1618). Unswerving allegiance to a sovereign and true friendship are found in *Los pechos privilegiados* (*The Hearts of the Elite*, 1619-21) and *La amistad castigada* (*The Chastized Friendship*, 1620-21). And the heroic restitution of the lost honor of a nobleman is treated in *El tejedor de Segovia* (*The Weaver of Segovia*, 1619-22).

Although the women in his dramas lack the vivacity of those in the plays of Lope de Vega and Tirso de Molina and contribute less to the development of the intrigue, they are known for their independence. The marriageable young ladies have the ability to calculate their matrimonial possibilities coldly, and those of noble birth usually act in accordance with their social station. Some of the women possess superior character, and those who conduct themselves improperly lose their lovers.[35] On the other hand, many of Alarcón's *graciosos*, whom he made more intelligent and less comical than their counterparts in other Golden Age dramas, contribute significantly to the development in his plays. Their frequent expressions of dissatisfaction and grief are considered to be reflections of Alarcón's own beliefs.

The structural arrangements of Alarcón's plots rely on the defects or virtues of his characters, and the human situations he depicts proceed out of the conceptual development of his theses. While adopting a realistic style devoid of euphuistic embellishments, he clearly expresses through his lively dialogues, short monologues, and lengthy narrations a baroque vision of life. A moralist with high regard for man's dignity, the poet capably polarizes truth and falsehood, friendship and enmity, loyalty and faithlessness, generosity and avarice. Although his better plays may lack imagination and spontaneity, the well contrived characterizations, dignified versification, and sedate diction reflect the workmanship of a conscientious dramatist.

Despite his contribution of twenty-five urbane plays, Alarcón is regarded as the least prolific among the giants of the Golden Age. Since his plays were less frequently staged than those of the more renowned playwrights of his time, Alarcón's reputation as a serious dramatist was not established until reworkings of his plays appeared in France, England, and Italy after his death.

ANTONIO MIRA DE AMESCUA

Antonio Mira de Amescua (1574-1644) was a southern dramatist in the Lopean cycle who wrote while serving in several ecclesiastical positions. Born in Guadix as an illegitimate son of Melchor de Amescua and Beatriz de Torres, he studied canon law in Granada and received a doctorate in theology in 1598. When Mira returned to Guadix in 1600 he was appointed the town's mayor, but six years later he moved to the court in Madrid to develop a literary career. Soon the young lawyer, priest, and writer became a censor, and in 1609 he was named the royal chaplain in Granada. He resided in Naples from 1610 to 1616 while in the service of the viceroy, the Count of Lemos. In 1622 Mira became the royal chaplain to Infante don Fernando of Austria in Madrid. His production as a playwright continued until 1632, when he decided to devote his entire time to his ecclesiastical duties in Guadix. During his later years Mira de Amescua's reputation suffered because of his neurasthenic temperament and arrogance. He died on September 8, 1644.

Mira's dramatic production includes fifty-three plays and fifteen one-act pieces. Mainly known for his religious plays with familiar subjects, he is also remembered for historical dramas about fallen royal favorites and for some secular plays. In his religious works the Andalusian poet dramatized theological problems, as did Tirso de Molina, whereas his plays of intrigue adhere in style to the typical *comedia de capa y espada* because of their amorous dialogues, comic passages, narrations, and polymetric versification.

Mira's masterpiece, *El esclavo del demonio* (*The Devil's Slave*, 1612), treats the topic of a man's pact with the Devil, which had already been used in Juan Manuel's *El conde Lucanor* (45th *ejemplo*) and Alarcón's *Quien mal anda mal acaba*; it was to be used later by Calderón in his *El mágico prodigioso* (*The Prodigious Magician*). Like his predecessors, Mira based his play on a Portuguese hagiographic legend about Frei Gil de Santarem, who was born in 1190. Mira's Don Gil signs a pact with the Devil for the possession of beautiful Leonor, but after he embraces her she turns into a skeleton. Sorry for his mistake, Don Gil calls on his guardian angel, who snatches the evil pact away from the Devil. Don Gil then imposes on himself the severe penance of living as a recluse the rest of his life.

The dramatic irony in this play arises from conflicting interpretations of reality in a conversation between the saintly Don Gil and his servant, whose ambiguous replies misinform his master and cause him to become a sinner. Other baroque aspects can be seen in the play's affected metaphors and strained conceits that elaborate on the problematic relationship between predestination and free will. Rebelliously choosing to offend God, the protagonist loses the intercessory power of the Virgin Mary; however, he remains willing to appeal to his guardian angel, who leads him to salvation. The playwright's own character is thought to have been reflected in the dynamic, egocentric, and contrary Don Gil. Although the play possesses vigorous, imaginative actions and sonorous versification, it is often episodic, and the secondary plot is sometimes unrelated to the main plot.

Mira's second best hagiographic play, *La mesonera del cielo* (*The Innkeeper of Heaven*, 1620-32), deals with the redemption of a fallen woman. The poet also wrote a biblically inspired play, *El arpa de David* (*The Harp of David*, 1611?), and a devotional play, *El amparo de los hombres* (*The Protector of Men*, 1616?). His *teatro menor* (one-act plays) consists of three *autos de nacimiento* (nativity plays), ten *autos sacramentales*, one *auto mariano* (Marian play), and an *entremés* (interlude).

Outstanding among Mira's *autos sacramentales* are *Pedro Telonario*, *Las pruebas de Cristo* (*The Examination of Christ*), *El sol de me-*

dianoche, y estrellas a mediodía (*The Sun at Midnight and the Stars at Noon*), *La fe de Hungría* (*The Faith of Hungary*), and *El erario y el monte de la piedad* (*The State Treasury and the Mount of Piety*). The protagonist in the first *auto* truthfully reflects the impetuous personality that the Apostle Peter was thought to have had, the play about the sun and stars deals with man's slavery to life, while the last two works issue a caution about the dangers of heresy. The play about Hungary, which uses as its subject the split between Roman Catholicism and Protestantism in that country, underscores the value of the Bread of the Eucharist and praises the Habsburgs' resistance to heretics. In *El monte de la piedad*, the *vellón*, a devaluated coin, is allegorically equated with the tokens of faith. Although Mira's politico-religious message is strong in these *autos*, their lyrical expression and humane background outweigh their allegorical and symbolic content.

Mira drew from national history, classical mythology, and the histories of the Roman Empire, Italy, France, the Netherlands, and Hungary for his historico-legendary plays. Some of those that deal with fallen court favorites are *El ejemplo mayor de la desdicha* (*The Greatest Example of Misfortune*, 1625), a dramatized history of General Belisario, which was modeled on Rotrou's *Belisaire*; *La rueda de la Fortuna* (*The Wheel of Fortune*, 1604), which relates the misfortunes of Prince Teodosio; and *El conde Alarcos* (1620?), whose action in France is derived from Spanish folklore. The most renowned among these, however, is one of many dramatizations of the legendary love affair between Alfonso VIII and the Jewess of Toledo—*La desgraciada Raquel* (*The Unfortunate Rachel*, 1625?). Somewhat inferior to Lope de Vega's *Las paces de los reyes*, Mira's play nonetheless reveals no evidence that he borrowed from or was indebted to Lope.

Two of Mira's three novelesque plays of intrigue—*La tercera de sí misma* (*The Go-Between for Herself*, 1616?) and *La fénix de Salamanca* (*The Phoenix of Salamanca*, 1610?)—contain stock presentations of women who successfully pursue their lovers in masculine attire. The third play, *No hay burlas con las mujeres, o casarse y vengarse* (*Women Cannot Be Tricked, or Revenge Through Marriage*, 1621?), consists of a love intrigue involving two women and four men. The play's veiled heroine, Laura, avenges her honor, makes peace with her perturbator, and finally happily marries him.

Mira's popular palace plays anticipate certain stylistic traits of Calderón. *El palacio confuso* (*The Confused Palace*, 1624?) stages a classical story from Plautus's *Menaechmi* about the twin sons of a Sicilian king. One boy was raised secretly by the queen as a peasant, and the other was left at sea to perish because of predictions that he would grow up to be a cruel king. The jumble of confusion that follows is untangled finally when Carlos regains his rightful crown and Enrico happily accepts his lot. *Gálan, valiente y discreto* (*Gallant, Valiant, and Discreet*, 1632) retells the Duchess of Mantua's careful selection of an appropriate mate. The subject for this palace play follows Ruiz de Alarcón's *El examen de maridos*, and it in turn served as a model for Moreto's *El desdén con el desdén* (*Disdain for Disdain*).

Mira is considered to be a transitional dramatist in the Spanish Golden Age, standing between Lope de Vega and Calderón. The southern dramatist, whose strength lay in the imaginative use of lyricism and baroque techniques, was venerated by his contemporaries. After his death, however, his work was neglected and left in oblivion until the twentieth century, when a revival of interest has been sparked by recent scholarly editions of his dramatic works.[36]

LUIS VÉLEZ DE GUEVARA

One of Lope de Vega's immediate followers and imitators was Luis Vélez de Guevara (1579-1644). Born in Ecija of a poor nobleman, Diego Vélez de Dueñas, and Francisca Negrete de Santander, he graduated from the University of Osuna in 1596. After participating in a military expedition in Italy, the young man returned to Spain in 1600 and settled permanently in Madrid as a poet. In 1608 following the publication of an opuscule in praise of Prince Domingo, he abandoned the name Vélez de Santander for the name by which he is known today. Married four times, Vélez de Guevara experienced financial difficulties throughout his life, despite the several court positions he held. In 1642 his son, Juan, replaced him in his post as palace poet, and on November 10, 1644, Vélez died in Madrid.

After Lope de Vega, Tirso de Molina and Vélez de Guevara share rights as the most productive playwrights in the Spanish Golden Age. While presiding at a poetic-burlesque contest in the palace at the Buen

Retiro in 1637, Vélez de Guevara claimed authorship of four hundred plays, and in 1641 he published a novel, *El diablo cojuelo* (*The Lame Devil*). From his vast output, about eighty plays have been preserved, some of which were written in collaboration with other authors.

Having assimilated the best in Lopean technique, Vélez de Guevara produced artificial and complicated works. Despite the superficiality of his style, which is often characterized by superfluous verbal ornaments, his diction is concise, natural, and flexible. On occasion his language is witty and sharp. His best plays, which are founded on peninsular heroic themes, nobly interpret history and combine it with fantasy.[37] Certain qualities of Golden Age Spaniards, furthermore, can be observed in his strong-willed characters.

The most perfect of Vélez's dramatic works, *Reinar después de morir* (*Queen after Death*), was written in his later years. This poetic drama, which resembles a classical tragedy of fate, was reconstructed from medieval historico-legendary accounts of Crown Prince Pedro and Inés de Castro, common to both Portuguese and Spanish literatures. The story of her tragic death in 1355 appeared often in chronicles, ballads, and *cancioneros* (collections of poems), and also in Luis Camoens's *Os Lusiadas* (*The Lusitanians*, 1572). It was dramatized in Antonio Ferreira's *Dona Ignez de Castro* (1553-67) and was subsequently adapted by Jerónimo Bermúdez in *Nise lastimosa* and its sequel, *Nise laureada*, in 1577. Other playwrights used the same story: Lope de Vega in *Doña Inés de Castro*, Tirso de Molina in *Siempre ayuda la verdad* (*Truth Always Helps*), and Mexía de la Cerda in *Tragedia famosa de Doña Inés de Castro*.

In Vélez de Guevara's version, Pedro, the unfortunate Portuguese prince, disobeys his father's order to marry Blanca de Navarra and secretly marries Inés, thereby giving up his right to the throne. The king is consequently forced by his noblemen to order Pedro's arrest and the death of Inés, since she refuses to renounce her claim as the future queen. After the king's sudden death, however, Pedro ascends the throne and condemns the accomplices in Inés's death. Then he places the disinterred cadaver of his wife on the throne, crowns it, and bestows on it all the honor due to a queen.

The clash between romantic love and political duty in this play is centered not so much on the action of the protagonists as on that of the noblemen and the king. The young couple's submissiveness in facing the unfavorable events contributes to the tragic end. Moreover, the error that leads to Inés's fate originates in her insistence on remaining Pedro's wife rather than his concubine.[38]

Vélez de Guevara achieved great poetic effects in several of his plays while dramatizing legends and themes from national history. *La niña de Gómez Arias* (*The Girl of Gómez Arias*), which was later adapted by Calderón, depicts the figure of a seducer. After abusing a young lady and selling her as a slave, Gómez Arias is condemned to death by order of the Catholic kings. *La luna de la sierra* (*The Moon-Maiden of the Mountains*) dramatizes the energetic resistance of a beautiful village woman, who opposes the immoral advances of two noblemen. A free adaptation of Lope's *Peribáñez*, this play was later used as a model by Rojas Zorrilla in his masterpiece, *El rey abajo, ninguno* (*Below the King All Men Are Peers*). The action in Vélez's play is more intricate than in Lope's work, and the female protagonist, Antona García, speaks the language of the upper class.

Together with Lope de Vega and other playwrights of the *Siglo de Oro*, Vélez de Guevara revealed certain changes in attitudes toward Spanish women in the seventeenth century. The stage was used as a medium to present a new type of woman who could defend herself in society. Heroines possessing manly traits of bravery and arrogance were given roles in which they freed themselves from the watchful protection of the masculine members of their families. Even more, they challenged the men who tried to deceive them. From this new concept arose the term *mujer varonil* (manly woman), a product of the baroque mentality. The aggressive actions of these characters provided an outlet for Spanish women's longings for freedom and adventure. The *mujeres varoniles* expressed hatred of masculine liberty, resentment toward society's belief in the superiority of man, and jealousy of man's access to pleasures that were denied women.[39]

Excellent examples of *mujeres varoniles* can be found in Vélez de Guevara's *La serrana de la Vera* (*The Mountain Girl from Vera*), which is based on a ballad of the same name, and *El amor en vizcaíno, los celos en francés* (*Love in Biscayan, Jealousy in French*). The latter play, with an abundance of pastoral scenes from Navarra, is about a Biscayan woman, Dominga, who avenges her dishonor by killing the Dauphin of France. The dramatist artistically created a woman with masculine characteristics to play a double role—the avenger of an affront and the leader of her people. Dominga's rustic, ungrammatical Biscayan speech creates confusion and serves as comic relief. Vélez de Guevara's dramatic experiment of creating women with masculine characteristics can be traced to the heroines of earlier plays, such as Cristóbal de Virués's Semíramis and Tirso de Molina's María de Molina and Doña Juana.

A popular historical play by Vélez de Guevara is *Si el caballo vos han muerto* (*If They Killed Your Horse*). The plot is based on a generous deed in the Battle of Aljubarrota: Pedro Hurtado de Mendoza saves the life of Juan I at the price of his own when he gives the king his horse by which to escape. The incident about the horse is fictitious, but it was based on the first part of a ballad by Alfonso Hurtado de Velarde.[40] In this play the customs of medieval nobility are masterfully presented.

The legend of Guzmán el Bueno, the second most venerated Spanish hero, is dramatized in *Más pesa el rey que la sangre, y Blasón de los Guzmanes* (*Duty to King above Family, and the Glory of the Guzmán Family*). In this drama, facts from Spanish traditional history and the poet's own inventions are successfully blended. The play is a presentation of the turbulent politics in the second half of the thirteenth century, when the cruel but patriotic defense of Tarifa won immortality for its defenders. Guzmán's barbarous but sublime sacrifice of his son for the defense of the fort from the Moors has been compared in Spanish tradition to Abraham's offering of Isaac.

Another of Vélez de Guevara's popular historico-legendary plays is *El diablo está en Cantillana* (*The Devil Is in Cantillana*), which recounts one of the adventures of Pedro I.

Three other plays pertaining to military life written by Vélez de Guevara are worthy of mention. The bravery and generosity of Spanish soldiers are vividly depicted in *Los amotinados en Flandes* (*The Insurgents in Flanders*).[41] The novelesque play *El asombro de Turquía y valiente toledano* (*The Fear of Turkey and the Valiant Toledan*) is an account of the exploits of a famous sailor, Francisco de Ribera, in the victorious naval battle with the Turks in 1616. The unity of the play's action would have been improved if some of the sea deeds had been omitted. In *El marqués de Bastos*, a servant-soldier of a marquis is the protagonist. After leading a life of many excesses, he enters military service under his master and dies in battle.

Novelistic qualities are present in *La desdichada Estefanía* (*The Unfortunate Stephanie*). This play is based on a true story that came from the court of Alfonso VIII of Castile, but it also has certain similarities to Ariosto's tale about Ariodante and Ginebra. Estefanía, the sister of the king, marries Fernán Ruiz. When the new husband is absent, the princess's lady-in-waiting, impersonating her lady, invites and receives an ex-suitor of the princess, Count Vela. When false rumors of his wife's infidelity reach the jealous husband, he returns and, without finding out the truth, kills the count and mortally wounds his wife. Realizing the catastrophe she has created, the lady-in-waiting throws herself from the balcony, and the unfortunate widower implores the king to condemn him to death. This tragic drama excellently portrays human affections and violent passions.[42]

Vélez de Guevara's best-known play having a setting outside of Spain is *Cumplir dos obligaciones y Duquesa de Sajonia* (*Fulfillment of Two Obligations and the Duchess of Saxony*). During an official visit in Germany, a Spanish ambassador, Rodrigo de Mendoza, is saved from an assassin by a German count, Ricardo. Taking refuge in a castle, Mendoza meets the lord and his wife, Estefanía, who is a victim of her husband's jealousy. After returning to the imperial court, the Spaniard discovers that the lord of the castle had been influenced in his jealousy by the slander of Ricardo; consequently, he challenges Ricardo to a duel and makes him confess his knavery. When the jealous duke wants to punish Ricardo, Mendoza defends him, thus repaying his debt to him for having saved his life.

Vélez de Guevara dealt with foreign history in other plays, such as *Hazañas de Escandemberg* (*The Exploits of Skander Bey*), *Atila, azote de Dios* (*Atila, the Scourge of God*), *Tamerlán de Persia* (*Tamerlane of Persia*), and *El príncipe esclavo* (*The Prince-Slave*). Some of these works and others on Spanish national history fall into the category of *comedias de ruido*, which can be described as turbulent plays that require huge backdrops and large casts.

During his lifetime the dramatist became known for his religious dramas, such as *La hermosura de Raquel* (*The Beauty of Rachel*) and *Santa Susana*. *La creación del mundo* (*The Creation of the World*) is an adaptation of a similar play by Lope de Vega and is also a *comedia de repente*—an improvised play written in a short period of time. Vélez's sacramental play most true to that genre, *Auto famoso de la Mesa Redonda* (*The Famous Play of the Round Table*), presents the capture of Jerusalem by Charlemagne, who symbolically represents Christ. His *Auto sacramental de la Abadesa del Cielo* (*The Sacramental Play on the Abbess of Heaven*), which is based on the popular legend about a nun who repents after eloping with a lover, has no allegorical reference to the Eucharist and belongs to the cycle of *autos* on the miracles of the Virgin Mary. His other *auto*, *Auto del Nacimiento*, is a stereotyped Nativity play.

Attractive for their dramatic motifs and interesting situations, Vélez de Guevara's plays display his talent for presenting lively descriptions and his lyric intensity with Andalusian overtones. Their swift action, liveliness, and variety in dramatic exposition merit special attention.[43] Believing that his purpose was to please his audience, the playwright avoided deep psychological analyses and placed more emphasis on the development of action.

JUAN PÉREZ DE MONTALBÁN

Lope de Vega's immense influence on Juan Pérez de Montalbán (1602-38) began when the great master encouraged the seventeen-year-old youth to write for the stage with a play, *Morir y disimular* (*To Die and to Conceal*, 1619). Montalbán inherited a love for letters from his father, who was a bookseller and the editor of Lope de Vega's plays. Upon receiving a doctorate in theology in 1625, Montalbán was ordained as a priest. The young man suffered some personal losses, however. His father's pirated edition of Quevedo's *Buscón* (*The Searcher*) caused a long, heated controversy, and after the death of Lope de Vega shortly afterward, mental illness progressively overtook Montalbán. He died in 1638 in Madrid.

Montalbán's theater, which consists of fifty-eight known pieces, is not perfect. The plot development is defective because of weak passages;

nonetheless, the plays are full of passion, delicate images, and especially skillfully delineated female characters. The dramatist had a special talent for presenting dramatic situations and popular stories. His best work is a legendary play, *Los amantes de Teruel* (*The Lovers of Teruel*), which had previously been treated on the stage by Rey de Artieda, Yagüe de Salas, and Tirso de Molina.

The frequent references to Pedro el Cruel in early Spanish poetry and drama are echoed in Montalbán's two-part *comedia*, *La puerta macarena* (*The Macarena Gate*). The dramatist, however, omitted the incidents pertaining to Alburquerque's revolt and the king's alliance with the Black Prince. The play concentrates on the life of the impetuous young monarch, and the delineations of the main characters are excellent. Pedro's strong disposition, tricky character, and cruelty are fascinating. Queen Doña Blanca is viewed sympathetically, and Don Fadrique is well delineated; but the appearance of Doña Leonor de Guzmán is anachronistic, since she was put to death in 1351, two years before the king's marriage to Blanca.

The three plays in a series of historical dramas that extol Philip II in different periods of his reign represent Montalbán's most ambitious work. The first of the two-part *El segundo Séneca de España* (*The Second Seneca of Spain*, 1625-28) shows how Philip stoically approached his personal and public problems in 1569-70, a decisive period in his life following the deaths of his son, Carlos, and his third wife, Isabella, and before his marriage to Anne of Austria. The more inferior Part II, covering the last decade of his reign (1588-98), just after defeat of the Spanish Armada, places much emphasis on pageantry and court life. In a third separate drama, *El señor Don Juan de Austria* (1628), the playwright presents a five-year period (1571-76) not covered in *El segundo Séneca de España*, beginning with the victorious Battle of Lepanto and ending with the death of Don Juan of Austria. In this play, particularly, Montalbán displays his talent for character delineation by contrasting the proud, chivalrous, and devout disposition of Don Juan with the extreme jealousy of his half brother, Philip II.

Montalbán's cloak-and-sword plays are *Como amante y como honrada* (*Like a Lover and Like an Honorable Woman*), which has a complicated intrigue, and *La monja alférez* (*The Nun Ensign*), which was inspired

Juan Pérez de Montalbán (1602-1638)

from the roving life of Catalina de Erauso. His religious plays, however, met with much less success. The best-known of them is a *comedia de santos*, *San Antonio de Padua*, which recreates the life of this Portuguese saint.

Virtues are exalted, vices are debased, and historical events are realistically dramatized in Montalbán's plays. Although the playwright was an adapter rather than a creator, his plays contain ingenious and unexpected situations and skillfully developed plots that sustain continued interest. His style is usually free from elaborate rhetoric, though in some scenes that were designed to impress, artificial and bombastic language can be found. Basically, Montalbán wrote to please his audience.

DIEGO JIMÉNEZ DE ENCISO

One of the less prolific dramatists in the Lopean cycle was a Sevillian poet, Diego Jiménez de Enciso (1585-1634), whose livelihood did not depend entirely on earnings from writing for the stage. As a descendant of a noble family, he held responsible governmental positions. He died in his late forties, having been afflicted with a crippling disease.[44]

Among his eleven well versified plays, the most prominent are two *comedias a cuerpo* (true historical plays), *La mayor hazaña del emperador Carlos V* (*The Greatest Deed of Emperor Charles V*) and *El príncipe Don Carlos* (*Prince Don Carlos*). In the former, dealing with the emperor's abdication and retirement to the monastery of Yuste, the characters of Charles V and Don Juan of Austria are masterfully drawn.

Enciso's masterpiece, *El príncipe Don Carlos*, is the most genuine dramatic presentation of the sickly, lonely, first-born son of Philip II, who is believed to have suffered greatly from quartan or malaria and who died at the age of twenty-three in 1568. Traditionally considered to be the first play to use as its theme the life of the unfortunate Spanish heir, it reveals the stubborn, ambitious, conceited, ill-tempered, and hostile character of Don Carlos, and his relationship with his haughty, pedantic father. Other early seventeenth-century playwrights, such as Vélez de Guevara and Montalbán, who included Don Carlos in their works, also realistically presented the effects of his illness on his personality.

Enciso's religious piece, *Santa Margarita*, abounds in lyricism.‘ Although it is dramatically inferior, the play has a highly spiritual character.

The quality in Enciso's works is uneven. The scenes are seldom well linked, and his feminine characters, who are insufficiently developed, have more masculine traits than charm. One of his dramatic strengths is to present opposite traits within a single character, thus underlining individuality and personality. The playwright manages his dialogue with sobriety, and the rapidity of action in his plays prevents an unnecessary flow of words; therefore, his poetic language possesses a simplicity that is not characteristic of the baroque style. Although Enciso was from Andalusia, where witticism was an important feature in life and literature, his plays lack this sprightly quality.

LUIS BELMONTE BERMUDEZ

A Sevillian poet and playwright, Luis Belmonte Bermúdez (1587?-1650?) wrote about twenty-five plays, some of which were composed in collaboration with others. His best known works are *El diablo, predicador* (*The Preacher Devil*, 1623), *El gran Jorge de Castrioto* (*Great George of Castrioto*, which deals with the defense of Epirus against the Moslems), and *El sastre del Campillo* (*The Tailor from Campillo*, 1624, which treats different topics of loyalty).

In the first of these plays, based on Lope de Vega's *Fray Diablo* (*Brother Devil*), Belmonte ironically blends the serious with the comical to portray the strife between good and evil. In the play's inventive and daring action, Lucifer estranges the inhabitants of Lucca from some Franciscan monks, who, in turn, have to make plans to abandon their abbey because they are not collecting enough alms. God punishes the Devil by transforming him into a friar and making him serve as an enthusiastic preacher in order to reconcile the people with the Franciscans. The two character portrayals in this play give the audience an opportunity to applaud the Devil's originality and to sympathize with the grotesque figure of Friar Antolín.

ANDRÉS DE CLARAMONTE

The little that is known of the theatrical activity of Andrés de Claramonte (d. 1626) has been gleaned from various early sources, including Agustín de Rojas Villandrando's *Viaje entretenido* (*The Entertaining Journey*, 1600), which cites Claramonte as an actor who played in farces.[45] This Murcian actor, playwright, theatrical director, and writer composed a number of plays, eighteen of which are known. One of his first, *La ciudad sin Dios o El inobediente* (*The Godless City or the Disobedient One*, 1603), is based on the biblical King of Nineveh and his pagan worship and orgies. In 1607 Claramonte, with Alonso de Olmedo, formed a theatrical company which was active for a while in southern Spain before moving to Castile for a number of years. Claramonte's book *Letanía Moral* (*Moral Litany*) appeared in 1610; its approval was signed by Vargas Machuca. On June 12, 1613, Juan de Salazar presented Claramonte's *La católica princesa* (*The Catholic Princess*).

Claramonte's most interesting play, *De esta agua no beberé* (*I Shall Not Drink This Water*), is probably an adaptation of *El rey don Pedro en Madrid*[46] and Calderón's *El médico de su honra*, since it presents similar amorous incidents in the life of Pedro I. His *El valiente negro en Flandes* (*The Brave Black in Flanders*) narrates the heroic life of a black soldier, Juan de Mérida, whose valor wins for him the rank of a general in the war in Flanders. Another black appears as one of the Magi in his *El mayor rey de los reyes* (*The Greatest King of Kings*). According to a heated debate in the last fifty years, it was Claramonte, not Lope de Vega, who wrote *La Estrella de Sevilla* (*The Star of Seville*);[47] Marcelino Menéndez y Pelayo attributed the play to Lope de Vega but its later emendations to Claramonte. A recent critic has also ascribed the authorship of *El burlador de Sevilla* to Claramonte because its style is closer to that of the Murcian than to that of Tirso de Molina.[48]

ALONSO DE COSTILLO SOLÓRZANO

As a dramatist, Alonso de Castillo Solórzano (1584-1648) wrote some nine plays, outstanding among which are *El marqués del Cigarral* (before 1634), *El mayorazgo figura* (*The Conceited Heir*, 1640), and *La vic-*

toria de Norlingen. The first play, a *comedia de figurón*, presents a character much like Don Quixote who has lost his common sense because he has read too many books about nobility.

ALONSO JERÓNIMO DE SALAS BARBADILLO

Less gifted as a dramatist than as a novelist, Alonso Jerónimo de Salas Barbadillo (1581-1635) left six plays, of which the best known are *El galán tramposo y pobre* (*The Tricky and Poor Lover*), *El gallardo Escarramán* (*The Gallant Escarramán*), and *La escuela de Celestina* (*The School of Celestina*, 1620). He also wrote over a dozen witty *entremeses*, including *El caballero bailarín* (*The Gentlemanly Dancer*) and *El buscaoficios* (*The Job-Finder*).

FELIPE GODÍNEZ

Much like Mira de Amescua, Filipe Godínez (1585-1659) preferred religious subjects, as can be observed in three of his biblical plays that were written between 1603 and 1613—*Los trabajos de Job* (*The Toils of Job*), *Las lágrimas de David* (*The Tears of David*), and *La reina Esther* (*Queen Esther*). Because the Inquisition declared the last two plays heretical in 1624, the Sevillian dramatist, who was also a priest, was sent to prison for one year for allegedly practicing the Jewish faith in secret. Among several devout plays written during his residence in Seville were *Ludovico el piadoso* (*Pious Ludovico*), *El soldado del cielo, San Sebastián* (*The Soldier of Heaven, St. Sebastian*, 1613), and *El príncipe ignorante y discreto* (*The Ignorant But Discreet Prince*, 1622).

The first secular play Godínez wrote after moving to Madrid was *La traición contra su dueño* (*The Betrayal of His Master*, 1626). It illustrates the complexity of reality through the complicated interaction between the characters, who act out of misunderstandings and confusion. The resolution upholds the thesis that God's justice does work in the world. The conflict in another cloak-and-sword play attributed to Godínez, *Aun de noche alumbra el sol* (*Even at Night the Sun Shines*), arises from a love triangle between Don Juan de Zúñiga and Crown Prince Don Carlos, who compete for the love of Doña Sol; the play ends happily with two weddings. Although the playwright's heroic drama *Cauteles son amistades (Caution Goes with Friendship)* is skillfully conceived, it is marred by too many shifts in the plot and an excess of ambiguities, disguises, schemes, and traps.

LUIS QUIÑONES DE BENAVENTE

Writing *entremeses* almost exclusively, Luis Quiñones de Benavente (1593-1651), a priest from Toledo, penned about 900 such interludes, of which 150 are extant.[49] These works are known to have been performed between the acts of *comedias* that were staged between 1620 and 1650. An excellent comic poet, Benavente brought this farcical genre to its highest excellence by providing it with flexibility and sincere joy. He replaced the sarcastic bitterness of earlier *entremeses* with gentle irony, practical jokes, and witty puns that amuse and provoke laughter. In these one-act plays, which seldom exceed 300 verses, Benavente displays a clear, elegant style and the ability to handle different verse forms. His colloquial and select language produces lively dialogue. The dramatic minimizes the distinguishing characteristics that had previously separated this genre from early short humorous plays. Several categories of these short pieces can be found among his works—the *entremés*, the *mojiganga* (a short burlesque piece presented with caricatures and masks), the *jácara* (a merry ballad), and the *loa* (a monologue or dialogue seeking the audience's good will), each of which retains some of its original characteristics. Benavente also replaced the term *baile* (a short dancing and singing piece) with *entremés cantado* (sung interlude).[50]

In one of his best known interludes, *El talego niño (The Swaddled Moneybag)*, he combines the elements of a traditional folkloric farce with those of a moralizing satire. In it, a miser, Taracea, who has fired his maids for swallowing whole eggs, is moving to a new house. He disguises his servant Garrote as a nurse so that he can transport his valuable moneybag swaddled like a baby. Upon spotting Garrote, the dismissed maids, with their new mistresses, divert his attention by telling him about a place where doughnuts grow on trees and fall into honey. In the disarray that follows, they steal the moneybag, and the play ends in an all-around drubbing.

In another interlude, *El miserable* (*The Miser*), another excellent portrayal of a penny-pincher appears. Peralvillo marries a small woman, Tilde, in order to save money in buying her dresses. To conserve her clothing further, he instructs her to walk in long strides, to sleep in the nude, and not to cry. In his madness, Peralvillo convinces his neighbor to make an opening in the wall that separates their houses so they can share the light they will get from a lamp filled with the oil that is left over from their salad dressing. He even parcels out portions of food and other kitchen items—one dozen lentils, one grain of salt, one piece of charcoal.

Other representative interludes by Benavente have intriguing titles: *Los gallos* (*The Rooster Chase*), which depicts a picturesque carnival custom; *El negrito hablador* (*The Talkative Negro*); *El guardainfante* (*The Farthingale*), which is a protest against contemporary fashions; *El borracho* (*The Tippler*), about a young lover and a soldier who deceive a barber; *La capeadora* (*Gusarapa's Fishhook*), showing a battle between the sexes; and *Las civilidades* (*Clichés*), containing an attack on the pedantry of language. The panoramic backgrounds in Benavente's farcical pieces display a variety of customs and social situations that he chose to censure. The follies and weaknesses of his eccentric people produce such hilarity that his purpose of teaching common sense is fulfilled.

FRANCISCO DE QUEVEDO

As the greatest satirist of Spain, Francisco de Quevedo (1580-1645) also displayed some talent in playwriting, especially with interludes. A wealthy courtier and literary genius, Quevedo lived an exciting life in several dangerous political positions. When the Duke of Ossuna was the viceroy of Naples, the satirist served as his minister of finance, but when Ossuna lost his power in 1619, Quevedo was also put out of office and thrown into prison. After returning to Madrid in 1623, he regained favor in the court of Philip IV and held an honorary position as a secretary to the king. Among the intellectuals in Madrid he soon became known for his excellence in satirical and lyric poetry. While his picaresque novel, *Buscón* (*The Searcher*) and his moral essays *Sueños* (*Visions*) stand out as his best moral-satirical works in prose, his most important didactic work is *Política de Dios* (*The Politics of God*, 1626).

Quevedo continued with an attack on the favorites who ran the government in *El discurso de todos los diablos o infierno enmendado* (*The Discourse of All the Devils or Hell Reformed*, 1627). His sharp exposures of court corruption finally sealed his fate. On the occasion of a banquet in 1639, Olivares found under the king's napkin a memorial that Quevedo had written denouncing the prime minister's dictatorial power. This angered the royal favorite so much that he had Quevedo put into a dungeon in León, where he remained until the prime minister's fall in 1643. After Quevedo left the prison, his health was broken and he died in poverty.

Realizing that his satirical propensity and caustic humor were unsuitable for the stage, Quevedo composed his theatrical works with more vivacity and in more haste. Of his three extant three-act plays, *Cómo ha de ser el privado* (*The Qualities a Prime Minister Should Have*, 1628?) is the most important. Giving no hint of the rift that developed between the satirist and the prime minister, this political work pays tribute to the Conde-Duque de Olivares and reflects bright hopes for the Spanish nation at the beginning of Philip IV's reign. Set in Naples but clearly alluding to Madrid, the play presents characters who are reflections of the notable figures in the Spanish court, but in the guise of Neapolitans. The rather slow action is filled with historical episodes, long speeches, and an insipid romance between the king and Serafina. After the king decides to select his prime minister in the midst of a royal festivity, a lengthy discussion takes place about the qualities he should possess. Although this play appears to have been hurriedly improvised, it has some ingenious traits and interesting situations. Within its polymetric versification the long verse forms show excellent craftsmanship.

Quevedo showed more dramatic talent in his *teatro menor* (one-act plays), where he displayed more fantasy and invention. He deserves an honorable place among the innovators of the *entremés* for giving the form a new focus on human psychology. Using multiple types of people in his satirical works, he gave new life to the interlude, which he wrote in prose and verse. Their themes are the problems of reality and illusion, the struggle between the sexes, love, and money.

Most of Quevedo's interludes are lost because of prohibition during the Inquisition, his imprisonment, and the unfulfilled promise of his nephew to publish them. Outstanding among the nine extant ones is *El hospital de los mal casados* (*The Hospital of Mismatched Marriages*). In it, two crooks, disguised as a quack and his assistant, examine a variety of patients who show symptoms of being mismatched in marriage. Among them are a woman whose husband is an unfaithful, idle gambler; a housewife whose irritable mate is bandaged up after having been run over by a wagon; and an old man whose young wife is barren.

Quevedo showed the influence of other works in several of his interludes. In *Los refranes del viejo celoso* (*The Proverbs of an Old Jealous Man*) he revealed his fascination with Cervantes' interlude *El viejo celoso* (*The Jealous Old Husband*). He brought material from his own *Visions* to the stage in *El sueño de la Muerte* (*The Dream of Death*); furthermore, *La endemoniada fingida* (*The Deceptive Woman Possessed by the Devil*) and *El marido fantasma* (*The Phantom Husband*) display the agility and witticism that are characteristic of Benavente's interludes.

Among other extant short pieces by Quevedo are seven *loas* (laudatory prologues), ten *bailes* (short skits with dancing and singing), five *diálogos*, several *autos sacramentales*, and sixteen *jácaras* (musical playlets for the dance). Enjoying as much fame as his picaresque novel, these short works are interesting for their literary, philosophical, and sociological content. They are saturated with witticism and gallantry, and depict many characteristics of the Spanish people. Their vivid style is based on contrasts, linguistic puns, and neologism.[51]

His *loas*, intended to be performed before the performance of a three-act play, expound on various subjects, such as a town, a particular day, colors, certain countries, love, thieves, or even a fly. His first *loa* was written for Tirso's *Amor y celos hacen discretos* (*Love and Jealousy Make People Discreet*). The best among his *bailes*, which were presented between the first and second acts of a play, is *Los galeotes* (*The Galley Slaves*). Many of Quevedo's *autos sacramentales* convey the satirist's message through the mouth of a shouting devil, while Christ appears in a passive role.

Quevedo's brilliant *jácaras* contain the *romance* verse form—octosyllabic lines with imperfect rhyme. The theme of vagrancy becomes an accepted category in his most famous *jácaras: Carta de Escarramán a la Méndez (Escarramán's Letter to Mrs. Méndez), Respuesta de la Méndez a Escarramán (Méndez's Answer to Escarramán)*, and *Romance del testamento que hizo Escarramán (The Ballad of Escarramán's Testament*, 1611). The satirical element in these short pieces is humorously presented through the *jerga germanesca* (slang of thieves) of Escarramán and Méndez. The speech they use during their love affair parodies that of a courtier and the lady he is wooing.

Athough Quevedo was much more famous for his satirical works, he holds an important place in seventeenth-century Spanish drama, as has been shown, as author of various kinds of short pieces.

CRISTÓBAL DE MONROY Y SILVA

An Andalusian, Cristóbal de Monroy y Silva (1612-49), who wrote about thirty-eight plays that were published in 1646, excelled in depicting historical and mythological figures in various facets of society. He portrayed Francis I of France as a great warrior in *La batalla de Pavía (The Battle of Pavía)*, Pedro Girón as an exemplary vassal in *Embidias vencen fortunas (Envies Destroy Fortunes)*, the brave and passionate Neoptolemus in *La destrucción de Troya*, and the intelligent and brave Hector in *Héctor y Aquiles*. Popular for his effervescent dialogue, wit, and excellent versification, Monroy also attracted attention for his depictions of intelligent, beautiful, and passionate women. Among his plays employing themes from Andalusian society are *Las grandezas de Sevilla (The Grandeur of Seville)*, which gives a magnificent vision of that city, and *Los celos de San José (The Jealousy of Saint Joseph)*, which paints the customs of Andalusian shepherds.

OTHER PLAYWRIGHTS

The four historical plays written by Damián Salucio del Poyo (1550-1614) toward the end of the sixteenth century appear to have influenced the composition of other dramatic works. Having been inspired by the *Golden Legend* of Jacobo de Varaggio (1230?-98) to write *Vida y muerte de Judás (The Life and Death of Judas)*, Salucio depicted Judas as a totally evil figure who destroys the lineage of his family. The morally blind traitor faces the three criminals, who are presented in a subplot, at Calvary. Beneath the Cross the unyielding robbers, Dimás and Barrabás, finally repent and are saved, while Grimás, the hardened thief who asks for no mercy, is condemned along with Judas, who hangs himself. Resembling Tirso de Molina's later play, *El condenado por desconfiado* (1615-25), this pseudo-biblical piece was also imitated by Zamora and Hoz y Mota.[52]

Salucio's *La próspera y adversa fortuna del condestable don Ruy López de Avalos el Bueno* in two parts (*The Prosperous and Adverse Fortune of the Constable Ruy López de Avalos the Good*) and *La privanza y caída de don Alvaro de Luna* (*The Favorite at Court and the Fall of Don Alvaro de Luna*), both reflecting the inestimable property of Fortune, were later imitated by Tirso. Salucio's plays, nonetheless, are overladen with characters and episodes, lack love intrigues, and have weak characterizations of women.

The three extant plays written by Miguel Sánchez (1545?-after 1615), a clergyman and secretary to the Bishop of Cuenca, were probably composed between 1590 and 1610. They are *Cerco y toma de Túnez y la Goleta por el Emperador Carlos Quinto* (*The Siege and Seizure of Tunis and La Goleta by Emperor Charles V*), *La guarda cuidadosa* (*The Careful Guard*), and *La isla bárbara* (*The Barbaric Isle*).[53] The linear plot in the historical play develops out of a succession of episodes that underline Charles V's qualities as a ruler. The novelesque *The Careful Guard*, having a more sustained plot, is concerned with a love triangle in which the Prince is rebuffed by Nisea, who is enamored of Florencio. There is an ironic turn of events when the jealous, vengeful Prince hires a forest guard, who is a disguised Florencio, to seduce Nicea. Following the scheme, Florencio deceives the Prince with his double deception. The didactic message in *The Barbaric Isle*, another novelistic play, shows that a king should be moderate in his use of authority.

A friend of Lope de Vega and Cervantes, José de Valdivieso (1560-1638) wrote almost exclusively on religious subjects. Having published his *Doce autos sacramentales y dos comedias divinas* in 1622 in order to prevent others from plagiarizing him, he exhibited an originality with the *auto sacramental* that was not surpassed until

Calderón. Seventeen of his numerous *autos* remain extant. Valdivieso achieved dramatic balance in his works by combining poetic language with prevailing artistic trends. His merit lies in his elaborately developed dramatic action, his choice of allegories to illustrate theological concepts,[54] and his use of popular songs. His lyricism can be observed especially in *El villano en su rincón* (*The Peasant's House Is His Castle*), *La serrana de Plasencia* (*The Shepherdess from Plasencia*), *La casa de los locos* (*The Madmen's Hospital*), and *El árbol de la vida* (*The Tree of Life*). The last play, considered his best, taken from Genesis 2:9, covers man's history from his Fall to the Redemption through Christ, and allegorically presents a theological debate between Divine Justice and Divine Mercy. Man's moral decisions are elaborated in *El hijo pródigo* (*The Prodigal Son*, 1605), which also makes references to the parable of the banquet, and *El fénix de amor* (*The Phoenix of Love*), whose structure is closer to a cloak-and-sword play than to an *auto*.

Numerous other less active dramatists who belong to the Lopean cycle produced original works as well as *refundiciones* (recast versions of plays by other dramatists). Gaspar de Avila, who presented Philip II's life in *El gran Séneca de España*, is also known for two plays of intrigue, *El Iris de las pendencias* (*The Disputes of Iris*) and *Las fullerías de amor* (*The Trickery of Love*). Luis Mexía de la Cerda (1580?-1635) is known for adapting the story of Doña Inés de Castro in another play. Alonso Hurtado de Velarde (1580?-1638) produced a *refundición* on the Princes of Lara (1612-15), *El conde de las manos blancas* (*The Count with White Hands*), and *El Cid, doña Sol y doña Elvira* (1630?). Other lesser dramatists in this group and their works are as follows:

Alfonso Velásquez de Velasco (1560?-1620): *El celoso* (*The Jealous Man*, 1602).

Julián Armendáriz (1585?-1614): *San Juan Facundo* (*Eloquent St. John*, 1603) and *Burlas veras* (*Earnest Jokes*).

Matías de los Reyes (1588-1642): *Dar al tiempo lo que es suyo* (*Give in Proper Time What Is Yours*, 1629) and *Di mentira y sacarás verdad* (*Tell a Lie and Get the Truth*), and four less successful plays.

Rodrigo de Herrera y Ribera (1585?-1657): *El voto de Santiago* y batalla de Clavijo (*St. James's Vow and the Battle of Clavijo*) and *Del cielo viene el buen rey* (*A Good King Comes from Heaven*).

Jerónimo Villaizán (1604-33): *Ofender con las finezas* (*To Offend with Favors*) and *A gran daño, gran remedio* (*For Great Harm, a Great Remedy*).

Cristóbal Lozano (1618?-62?): *Las persecuciones de Lucinda* (*The Persecution of Lucinda*) and *El rey penitente David* (*Penitent King David*).

Francisco Castro (1618-79?), a satirical poet and *entremesista*: *El novio miserable* (*The Miserable Suitor*) and *El inglés hablador* (*The Talkative Englishman*).

CONCLUSION

During the fifty years in which the Lopean cycle flourished, Spanish theater was firmly established and the new *comedia* acquired the traits that distinguished it as Spanish national drama. Various factors contributed to its success. Theatrical activity in Spain at the turn of the sixteenth century provided the fertile ground out of which the nation's greatest dramatic poet could arise. Lope de Vega, profiting from his countrymen's theatrical interest, broke away from the classical past, provided the theater with new aesthetic principles, and adjusted his playwriting to public likings. Although the spectacular reputation of Lope de Vega eclipsed that of his contemporaries, many of his followers made worthwhile contributions to the advancement of the *comedia*. They gradually replaced the episodic, linear dramatic action of their predecessors with closely intertwined plots.

The leader of the Valencian group, Guillén de Castro, enriched the *comedia* by adapting old Spanish balladry to the stage. As the staunchest defender of Lope de Vega's dramatic precepts, Tirso de Molina showed a gift for penetrating theological questions, expressing ideas, and depicting women and *graciosos*. The Mexican-born Juan Ruiz de Alarcón introduced into the *comedia* well-polished dramas of character, which were later effectively developed by the seventeenth-century French playwrights. Antonio Mira de Amescua, treating well-known themes with originality and using a Gongoristic style, displayed unusual dramatic vigor, especially in his religious dramas. Vélez de Guevara's heroic plays, despite the presence of certain stylistic superficialities, interpreted history with poetic fantasy and portrayed strong-willed characters. Among the works of the minor playwrights in the Lopean cycle are occasionally well drawn historical and character plays, while other authors distinguished themselves with one-act pieces which added special glamor to the Spanish stage.

The political, social, and economic situation in Spain changed drastically during the third decade of the sixteenth century, and the tastes of theatergoers became more sophisticated. As they became more selective about the repertory, the productivity of the aging Lope de Vega diminished while the works of his contemporaries won more acceptance because of their more refined rhetorical style, their satirical exposure of political and social issues, and their more calculated plot structures. Thus Calderón de la Barca and his followers, emerging out of the Lopean cycle, brought the *comedia* to its full growth in the following years.

Chapter IV

Calderón: The Apogee of the *Comedia*

After Philip III became king in 1598, Spain entered an era of theatrical brilliance in which the prolific and original output of the great Spanish playwrights attained its greatest height. Lasting for thirty-seven years, this period of Spanish drama made a permanent impression on the literature of the world. Its end coincided with the death of Lope de Vega in 1635, when another giant of Spanish drama was attaining recognition. Pedro Calderón de la Barca inherited a legacy established by Lope and his followers and brought it to maturity. Carrying the inventive genius of the previous generation to the level of perfection, Calderón, as the leader of the new school of dramatists, stylized and refined Spanish dramaturgy. With their new approach to plot structure and rhetorical style, the Calderonians not only composed original works but also chose to rewrite older plays, to which they applied their more sophisticated dramatic techniques.[1]

Considered the most polished Spanish dramatist by many Spanish and foreign critics, Calderón actually should not be exclusively singled out, since he was a link in a long chain of poets. Calderón escaped the chaotic formulative period through which Lope de Vega and his followers went, since the state of dramatic art was firmly established in many respects and Spanish theater was full-grown by the time Calderón began to write. He also benefited from the vast improvements in staging that had evolved since the rudimentary beginnings during Lope's career. Elaborate decorations, lighting effects, advanced stage machinery, and the use of background music had come to be accepted by the time Calderón began to write his plays.

Because he was writing for a more sophisticated audience, Calderón was obliged to develop a refined style. Whereas Lope de Vega wrote commercially attractive romantic plays mostly for presentation in the *corrales*, Calderón, the court favorite of Philip IV, composed urbane, delicate, and discreetly satirical commissioned dramas that were usually staged as ornate shows in the royal theaters. Perhaps realizing his limited imaginative talents, and pressured by the court and theatrical managers to produce attractive plays, Calderón relied on the inventiveness of his predecessors and dedicated himself to the perfection of dramatic art. Borrowing from earlier major works, he remade the *comedia* by tightening previous loosely connected plot structures, eliminating irrelevant material within a dramatic story, and introducing psychological problems more suitable to logical analysis. His dramaturgy, therefore, represents the most systematic development of Spanish drama during the Golden Age.

The craftmanship of Calderón is displayed in his majestic stories, clear concepts, and lofty diction. His well structured plots begin with favorable situations, develop steadily with intensely passionate conflicts, and progress into decisive dénouements with shocking outcomes. He achieved superior characterizations by a calculated juxtaposition of individuals in opposing situations. His versification meets the standards of fine dramatic composition, and the imagery in his well disciplined diction is appropriate to the movement of his poetic illusions. These factors contribute to the lyrical beauty of his dramas, which are unequalled in the history of Spanish dramaturgy.

Pedro Calderón de la Barca (1600-1681), who was born and died in Madrid, came from a noble family from northern Castile. His mother, who was of Flemish descent, died when Pedro was ten years old, and his father, an employee of the royal treasury, died five years later. As the third child in an orphaned family of seven, Calderón was subjected to great stress from an early age. Perhaps because of the adverse conditions during his childhood, he developed much astuteness and perspicacity.

After studying for nine years at the Jesuit Imperial College in Madrid and graduating in 1614, Calderón took up theology at the University of Alcalá de Henares. But after his father's death he abandoned his

Pedro Calderón de la Barca (1600-1681)

ecclesiastical studies and moved to the University of Salamanca (1616-19), where he studied canon law and developed a liking for logic. Although he attained academic distinction and had a desire to become a priest, it appears that worldly interests claimed his attention.

Calderón made his debut as a poet in the contests at San Isidro from 1620 to 1624, and won some important prizes there. He also wrote his earliest plays during this period. The detailed geographical description in several of his plays, especially in *El sitio de Bredá* (*The Siege of Bredá*, 1625),[2] indicate that he must have served in the military forces in Italy and Flanders sometime between 1625 and 1635. During this decade, when he also resided in Madrid and composed at least fifteen plays, he was involved in amorous escapades and disputes that ended with duels and brushes with the law.

Two recorded incidents document his unruly behavior. While Calderón served in the household of the Duke of Frías, his three brothers killed Nicolás de Velasco, the son of a servant of the duke; their sentence for the crime was a fine of 600 ducats. Then in 1629, while avenging the injury his half brother suffered in a duel at the hands of an actor, Pedro de Villegas, Calderón, in company with friends and police, pursued the offender into a nunnery and, in the fracas that resulted, tore off the veils of the nuns. Since one of the nuns was Marcela, the daughter of Lope de Vega, who filed a complaint with the Duke of Sessa, Calderón and his friends were detained for a few days. After Fray Hortensio Paravicino rebuked them, the dramatist retaliated by sneering at him sarcastically in a passage in *El príncipe constante*. Rather than damaging his career, this incident enhanced Calderón's popularity at the court.

After the success of *La vida es sueño* (*Life Is a Dream*) in 1635 (the year of Lope de Vega's death) and the magnificent presentation of a mythological play, *El mayor encanto, amor* (*The Greatest Enchantment Is Love*, 1635), which celebrated the opening of the new palace at the Buen Retiro, Calderón was named a court dramatist by Philip IV. In 1636 his younger brother, José, edited a volume of the dramatist's plays. The following year the poet was knighted in the Order of Santiago and began his military service. After his second volume of works was published in 1637, his fame as the author of forty secular plays was established. As Calderón approached the zenith of his career, however, his creative power suffered somewhat because of commissions to write spectacular productions for the royal theater.

After taking part in a campaign to suppress a Catalan uprising (1640-42), Calderón retired from military service on account of failing health and immediately wrote his most popular play, *El alcalde de Zalamea* (*The Mayor of Zalamea*, 1640-44), which presents a sympathetic view of Spanish peasants who have been abused by Spanish soldiers. His dramatic activity suffered in the following years when the theaters in Madrid were temporarily closed to observe mourning for deceased members of the royal family. During this time the poet's two brothers were killed and his sweetheart also died after giving birth to his child. These national and personal misfortunes forced the saddened poet, out of economic necessity, to serve for four years (1645-50) in the household of the Duke of Alba. After joining an ecclesiastical order in 1651, he restricted his production to the writing of *autos sacramentales* for the municipality of Madrid and musical comedies for the court. As a priest he spent some of this time as a chaplain in Toledo. Finally, in 1663, his former post at the court was returned to him. Calderón died on May 25, 1681.

CALDERÓN'S DRAMATIC WORKS

Calderón's works include about one hundred and twenty plays, about eighty *autos*, and twenty *entremeses*, *loas*, *mojigangas*, and *jácaras*.[3] His theatrical works fall into three periods: his apprenticeship, when the poet wrote under the artistic influence of Lope de Vega, Tirso de Molina, Vélez de Guevara, and Mira de Amescua; a middle stage when, as a mature dramatist, he emancipated himself by developing his own style; and a final period devoted mostly to *autos sacramentales* and some zarzuelas. Since he wrote various types of plays during his first two periods, it is feasible to discuss them according to categories.

The Cloak-and-Sword Plays. Although Calderón followed at first the established dramatic art of his predecessors, he found ways to improve on it by consolidating plots and correlating subplots more advantageously. In 1623 he wrote what is considered his first major play of intrigue, *Amor, honor y poder (Love, Honor, and Power)*, which was based on a short novel by Bandello.

He incorporated an old anonymous farce in one of his most renowned cloak-and-sword comedies, *La dama duende (The Phantom Lady*, 1629), in order to create a fanciful vision of live and to defy common superstitions of his time. In this play Doña Angela, an adventurous young widow who hides her face behind a mantle, is caring in her home for a young gentleman, Don Manuel, who has been hurt while defending her. A secret passage between their adjacent rooms facilitates the confusion they both create to such a degree that neither can distinguish dream from reality. Don Manuel believes he is being visited by a phantom when the widow repeatedly enters his room, when she thinks he is asleep, for the purpose of discovering his true identity. After her chimeric appearances are uncovered and explained, the play ends happily with their marriage.

Although not as ludicrous or spontaneous as Tirso's Don Gil or Lope's Finea, Doña Angela also entertainingly transgresses the accepted code of behavior in Spain by breaking through walls and using fantasy and imagination. In his reworking of the *comedia de capa y espada*, Calderón achieved greater clarity by better organizing the incidents in his plot structure, and playfully criticized the Spanish code of honor.[4]

In another famous cloak-and-sword play, *Casa con dos puertas mala es de guardar (The House with Two Doors Is Hard to Watch*, 1629), Calderón employed dramatic techniques similar to those found in Roman comedy.[5] The complicated love intrigue, furthermore, mirrors social life in the Spanish court in Calderón's time. The play's main plot is centered around the love affair of Lisardo and Marcela, who is dominated by her vigilant brother, Félix. The subplot deals with Félix's jealous courting of Laura, who he suspects is stepping out on him. The play's rapid action takes place in an occasionally darkened house with two doors from which the characters, often in disguises, enter and leave, causing continuous confusion, mistaken identities, trickery, and suspense. Finally, the two young couples marry in a double wedding.

Other representative Calderonian plays of intrigue are *El maestro de danzar (The Dancing Teacher*, 1651-52), *El astrólogo fingido (The False*

Astrologer, 1631), *El escondido y la tapada* (*The Hidden Man and the Veiled Lady*, 1636), and *Dicha y desdicha del nombre* (*The Advantages and Disadvantages of a Name*, 1660-61). The last is also a palace play, since its characters represent personages of high nobility. These plays involve questions of honor and contain an abundance of disguised ladies, guardian fathers and brothers, and shrewd *graciosos*. With their stories about love escapades in upper-class society and their clever dénouements, they fulfill Calderón's main purpose to entertain.

The Philosophical Dramas. After becoming a theologian, dramatist, soldier, and courtier, Calderón produced two philosophical plays: *En esta vida todo es verdad y todo mentira* (*In This Life Everything Can Be True and False*, 1659), and his masterpiece, *La vida es sueño* (*Life Is a Dream*, 1631-35). The themes of both plays stress the monarchical right of succession through inheritance rather than through use of force or astrological prophecies. In the Byzantine story of the first drama, a bandit, Focas, kills Emperor Mauricio and sets himself up as a tyrannical ruler. Realizing that he must secure his succession, Focas returns to his native island of Trinacria in search of his long-lost son and finds Euraclio and Leonido, one of whom is identified by their tutor, Astolfo, as the son of Mauricio. When Focas threatens to kill both young men, Astolfo reveals that one of them is Focas's son. Although everyone refuses to answer the tyrant's inquiries, Euraclio, out of loyalty to his friend, finally identifies himself as Mauricio's son. Before Focas can complete his plans to crown Leonido as the prince and to kill Euraclio, the Prince of Calabria unexpectedly arrives in pursuit of battle and saves the true heir's life. When the truth of Focas's crimes is revealed, Euraclio is rightfully proclaimed as the new emperor. Although the play ends with the marriage of Leonido and Euraclio's sister, the principal motif is loyalty between two young men rather than the usual motif of courtship.[6]

La vida es sueño merits the fame it has attained as the greatest Spanish play of all time. It is about a Polish crown prince, Segismundo, who, according to the stars and other predictions, was to become a monster of impropriety and cruelty. More concerned for his Polish subjects than for his son, King Basilio spreads a rumor that his new son was born dead, and confines him to a solitary tower in a forest. The heir to the throne is raised like an animal, having no contact with people except for an old tutor, Clotaldo.

Both remorseful for his cruel action and fearful that the horoscope prophesying his own downfall and disgrace will be occasioned by his only son, Basilio makes plans to test Segismundo. He orders the young prince to be drugged and brought to the royal palace. Upon awakening and finding himself surrounded by courtiers, Segismundo believes he is dreaming. After learning his true identity, he rebels against established social rules by treating his father disrespectfully, making advances to Rosaura (a court lady who happens to be the daughter of Clotaldo), and throwing a servant through a window. Frightened by his son's beastly behavior, the king has him drugged again and returned to his lonely tower. After this experience, the confused prince is troubled to decide which of his two existences is reality.

Meanwhile the Poles, angered by Basilio's announced plan to leave the Polish throne to his nephew, Astolfo of Moscow, attack the prison tower, free the unhappy Segismundo, and reinstate his rights to the crown. Now the young sovereign quickly adjusts to his new situation and becomes a prudent ruler. In contradiction to the prophecy, he forgives Basilio for his unwise policy and pardons Clotaldo for obeying the deposed king; furthermore, Segismundo overcomes his passion for Rosaura and restores her honor by approving her marriage to her former suitor, Astolfo. Then he marries Estrella in order to maintain peaceful relations with the powerful neighboring nation of Moscow, thus restoring peace to Poland.

One of the reasons Calderón based his imaginative play on Polish history was the fact that seventeenth-century Spaniards were becoming interested in that exotic country on the other side of Europe, which had grown in fame as a vast empire of wealth and power. Poland and Spain held analogous positions on opposite sides of the continent— one of the culturally rich and Catholic countries was the defender of Christendom against the Turks from the east, and the other was a stronghold against the Moors and Turks in the south and west and the Protestants in the north.

It appears that Calderón had a continuing interest in basing works on historical events from Eastern Europe. His first personal contact with Poland may have been when he was a soldier in Flanders, since he included a Polish prince, who must have been present there, in the plot of *El sitio de Bredá*. A year before writing *La vida es sueño*, he wrote, in collaboration with Antonio Coello, another play dealing with recent Eastern European history, *Yerros de naturaleza y aciertos de la fortuna* (*The Errors of Nature and Prudence of Fortune*, 1634). And many years later he wrote *Afectos de odio y de amor* (*The Affects of Hatred and Love*, 1658?), in which he alluded to Poland and Sigismund.

In writing *La vida es sueño*, Calderón may have been influenced by Lope de Vega's *El reino sin rey* (1599-1612) and even more by *El gran duque de Moscovia* (1606), since the latter play is apparently concerned with a similar dynastic dispute.[7] The paradoxical metaphor in Calderón's title, furthermore, suggests his fascination with the popular baroque mode of contrasting contradictory values to find truth.[8] His choice of the theme of reality and illusion may also have been inspired by lines spoken by characters in the plays of Lope: Fabio in *El galán de la Membrilla* (1615), who says, "Dejadle desvanecer,/que los sueños, sueños son" ("Put it aside, since dreams are only dreams"); and Federico in *El castigo sin venganza* (1631), who speaks to his *gracioso* about man's imagination and daydreams: "nuestra vida/es sueño, y que todo es sueño;/pues que no sólo dormimos,/pero aun estando despiertos,/cosas imagina un hombre/ . . . con frenesí" ("Our life is a dream, and everything is a dream; since not only do we dream, but, even being asleep, man imagines things . . . with frenzy").[9] The impracticability of believing in dreams is even discussed by Magdalena in act 3 of Tirso's *El vergonzoso en palacio*, who states: "no creáis en sueños,/ que los sueños, sueños son" ("don't believe in dreams for dreams are only dreams").

The idea that life is a dream, nonetheless, existed much earlier. In Buddhist tradition it can be found in a folk tale, "Sleeper Awaken," from the *Arabian Nights*. The Hindus, Hebrews, and Greeks also taught that the instability of life can be modified through mystical experiences. Christian mystics, likewise, believe that throught the use of illusory dreams, one loses his selfish thoughts of superiority and obtains prudence and temperance.[10]

The complex thematic design and elaborate structure of *La vida es sueño* has generated various interpretations, pointing to the innovative talent of its author. This exceptional drama, whose essential theme is the understanding of human life, treats several universal problems that were being examined during the baroque period: greed for worldly power, the triumph of human liberty due to the victory of free will over destiny, and the struggle of reason over natural impulses. The main plot, dealing with the conversion of Segismundo and his relationship with his father, Basilio, is closely linked to the subplot that is concerned with Rosaura and her grievance with Astolfo.[11] These two closely intertwined plots expose the central theme: the realization that only death awakens man from his illusory existence in this life. Like other baroque dramatists, Calderón did not clearly separate his plot and subplot but densely combined them and their motifs to give unity to the dramatic action.

The characters in this play who act unjustly are compelled to convert, for they learn to act well, since life is only a dream. After having been brought to a humbling position for being overly proud, their conversions lack progressive development except for Segismundo's regeneration, which evolves in stages. At first his appeals and appearances are like those of a primitive man; possessing neither practical intelligence nor fortitude, the prince is empowered by his innate impulses and responds only to Rosaura, who acts as the main agent in his dramatic conversion. While enduring the trials forced upon him, however, he gradually comes to self-realization, regains his freedom, and becomes a prudent ruler.[12]

The theme of individuals as the prisoners of their own situation, whether by other men's making or by unforeseen events, is expressed in *Life Is a Dream*, as well as in other Calderonian dramas of serious import. The poet's intention in presenting a character who frees himself from the bondage of fate was to inspire an ethical awakening within the monarchy of his own country. By transferring his sociopolitical viewpoints to a distant Polish setting, he was more easily enabled to present his ideas on how the Spanish absolute monarchy could be improved. He drew attention to the salient features in Polish internal affairs, and with penetrating psychological realism he demonstrated the specific situation in that powerful country. By presenting the causes for the decline of the autocratic Polish monarchy and emphasizing the regenerative power of a new king whose experience was gained from human failure and from contact with the people, Calderón advocated changes that could be made to humanize future Spanish monarchs.

Remarkable for its lyricism, this play displays brilliant imagery, representative symbols, and ingenious metaphors. The hyperboles, strained phrases, and chiaroscuros, which are characteristic of the baroque poetic style, were directed toward a courtly audience, as were also the complex versification and sophisticated diction of the royal characters, who are involved in philosophical arguments. Furthermore, the concept of metatheater is much in evidence with the use of the play-within-a-play technique and the characters' awareness of their own role-playing.[13]

The Honor and Jealousy Plays. As we have already observed, the honor motif in the plays belonging to the Lopean cycle developed into a stereotype that became a popular convention. Whereas Lope de Vega's honor plays disclose his fascination with the diverse possibilities for adventure, Calderón, in his dramas of honor, set forth certain ethical principles about the laws of honor for the purpose of discrediting them. Calderón's themes became a living force through which he exposed his view of the world and his art. In his hands the treatment of this theme reached its highest point.

During Calderón's time the feudal notion of honor continued to thrive, with modifications, and even intensified in strength during the absolute monarchy and the baroque period. Rooted in the patrilineal laws of inheritance of medieval Christian Spain, which had also inherited some laws from the polygamous Hebraic and Moorish society, the unwritten laws governing seventeenth-century honor continued to presuppose the moral obligation of a nobleman to defend his family's name and heritage at all costs. In view of the public eye, the gentleman brought fame to himself by his virtue or heroic action; likewise, the women in his household brought him good repute by their modesty and prudence. Any sullying of a family's honor and any transgression of the prescribed rules required swift and silent revenge.

The elaborate social laws that grew out of a gentleman's obsession to check the conduct of his female relatives imposed severe restrictions on women. Always having to be veiled, living in the seclusion of their homes, and never allowed outside without proper escorts, women could bring dishonor to their household for anything from a flirtation to being victimized by rape. Men, on the other hand, enjoyed great self-esteem for their authoritative responsibilities and were free to conduct themselves in whatever way they pleased without losing their honor. With his legalistic mind, Calderón capitalized on the incongruities that could arise within these unwritten rules. He not only dramatized passionate conflict between a married couple but also showed the corruption that existed because of the customs dealing with honor. In three of his earliest plays of honor, and in another on jealousy, social values are unreflective and brutal. In them the code of honor is carried to such sanguinary extremes that the innocent heroines die tragically at the hands of their cruel husbands, who have merely suspected them of unfaithfulness. Calderón's exaggerated presentation of problems of honor does not so much mirror seventeenth-century Spanish life as distort reality. Thus, his dramaturgy actually represents a step away from the *comedia de capa y espada* and toward classical tragedy.

Recently interest has emerged in Calderón's artistic interpretation of the moral justification of honor. According to newer explications, the Calderonian honor plays, which dramatize conflicting solutions to the problem of honor, are actually theses arguing against the enforcement of the old code of social conduct. Having in mind his spectators—mostly seventeenth-century gentlemen, who were sensitive to their social class and their obligation to maintain their honor, especially in regard to their women—Calderón led them to become morally aware and critical of the unspoken laws that demanded violence and murder. He accomplished this by means of shock and exaggeration; nonetheless, he gave no hint of his intent. In his plays of honor the heroes' sanguinary actions are admired by the characters left alive, and after the final, bloody scene, the audience is left with the impression that the protagonist's stained honor has been cleansed by the spilled blood.

The unchristian actions, which were accepted for the sake of the play, actually follow a somewhat perverted pattern of Christian discipline.

Instead of expressing the quality of mercy, his protagonists are reconciled to their code through bloodshed. They usurp the vengeance that belongs to God alone. To them, honor becomes a religion of perfection; they avenge themselves with what they love most—their women. The dramatist effectively carries his point by structuring the ideals (e.g., love, honor, obedience, and death), ritual, and symbolism in these plays after those of the Christian religion.[14]

The main source for Calderón's most discussed honor drama, *El médico de su honra* (*The Physician of His Honor*, 1635),[15] was probably a play by the same title attributed to Lope de Vega. A nobleman from Seville, Gutierre, who broke his first engagement to Leonor because of an apparent deception, marries Mencía. At first he attempts to dismiss his feelings of jealousy toward her when she meets her former fiancé, Prince Enrique. Later, however, Gutierre's uneasiness about his honor is rekindled when Mencía expresses the opinion that he is becoming mean and may kill her. Finding a parallel to his situation in a rumor that King Pedro's life is threatened by his half brother Enrique, Gutierre concludes that an honorable man can imagine his dishonor without being sure of it. Deciding that he has been dishonored, Gutierre uses another figment of his imagination and hires a surgeon, Ludovico, to drain Mencía's blood and to announce that she has died accidentally when a bandage slipped. Although the king condones the nobleman's cruel action at the conclusion of the play, he orders him to marry Leonor in order to restore the honor he had caused her to lose. This play's title metaphorically refers to a treacherous avenger who, while satisfying an alleged dishonor, amputates the presumably diseased part of his marriage. Like a "metagonist," he symbolically assumes the role of the surgeon, whom he uses like an instrument to guide the play to its tragic end.[16]

Although the presentation of the Sevillian's brutality is of primary importance to the play's action, the playwright is also commenting on the cruel—and not necessarily just—character of Pedro I when the king in the play threatens Coquín, the *gracioso*, with the punishment of having his teeth pulled if he cannot force the king to laugh within a month. This early incident prepares the audience to expect, although not necessarily accept, the humorless king's severe condoning of the innocent young wife's murder.[17]

Calderón selected a Portuguese scenario for *A secreto agravio, secreta venganza* (*Secret Vengeance for Secret Insult*, 1635), probably having been influenced by the practice prevalent among Spanish writers in his time of depicting Portuguese noblemen as jealous and vengeful. A riddle on love and jealousy, this play deals with adultery. A suspicious Portuguese gentleman, Don Lope de Alameida, having an intuition that his honor has been secretly damaged, avenges the supposed offense by stabbing Don Luis to death in a sinking boat, and then causes the death of his wife, Leonor, by setting his house on fire. After committing these acts, he makes plans to end his own life by going to battle. The immediate model for this play was Tirso's *El celoso prudente* (*The Prudent But Jealous*), and its title alludes to the Old Testament philosophy of justice, which advocates "an eye for an eye."

A later honor tragedy, *El pintor de su deshonra* (*The Painter of His Dishonor*, 1648-50), displays an especially elaborate dramatic technique. Constantly searching to provide different milieus and unusual sets of circumstances, Calderón placed this play's dramatic action in Barcelona and Italy, where he related the themes of honor and jealousy to the practice of painting. The self-centered imagination of a painter, Roca, leads him to misunderstand his wife's abduction. In a jealous rage he kills his wife and Don Alvaro before taking his own life. In his last "bloody picture," he passionately depicts his wife's infidelity and her punishment, forcefully making his audience believe that her castigation was deserved. According to Calderón's baroque interpretation, both the guilty and the innocent participate in this chaotic world while compounding offenses against each other.[18]

These Calderonian plays, with their ritualistic proceedings upholding the sanctity of honor, appear to have satisfied public expectations. The plays' popularity can be attributed to the psychological tones present in both the women's and the men's portrayals. In their attempts to purify themselves, the idolized courtly women display few human qualities but sacrifice themselves on the altar of love. In contrast, the men's pseudo-virtuous actions toward their helpless victims arouse the public reaction these plays had and continue to have.

While the motif of jealousy is used to intensify the conflict in the three dramas of honor which have just been discussed, jealousy itself is the passion that leads to the crime in *El mayor monstruo, los celos*

(*Jealousy, the Greatest Monster*, 1634). When the Jewish king Herodes believes his wife, Mariene, has had an affair with Octaviano, he mistakenly stabs the innocent woman while attempting to kill the Roman emperor. After the king discovers his error, he jumps into the sea to his death. Lacking character and prudence, Herodes suffers from excessive pride and jealousy. His deteriorated mental state leads him to his outrageous actions and final self-destruction. The historical theme of this play, whose action is condensed into several days, its catastrophic ending, and its elevated linguistic style contribute to give it the character of a true classical tragedy.

The Portuguese war in 1640, which regained for that country its independence from Spain, probably inspired Calderón to write *El alcalde de Zalamea* (*The Mayor of Zalamea*, 1640-44). Recast from Lope de Vega's earlier improvised piece by the same title, and set in Estremadura in 1580, when Philip II waged a military campaign to claim and hold the Portuguese crown for Spain, Calderón's social drama depicts a conflict of honor between a well-to-do peasant mayor and aristocratic army officers. The village mayor, Pedro Crespo, puts a haughty captain to death for dishonoring his daughter and refusing to marry her. Although the military general desires to punish the mayor for going beyond the limits of his jurisdiction, the king exonerates Pedro. The girl's virtue is restored by Pedro's announcement that she has entered a convent. While presenting life in a society that is governed by an established system, the playwright shows how human passions and the free will of an individual can upset the order.[19] If Captain de Ataide had agreed to marry Isabel, the clash between the military and civil classes would not have been created, and the play would have ended happily but also pointlessly. The tragic outcome inspires discussion on whether or not civilian officials have jurisdiction over the military.

In most of his dramas Calderón presents upper-class society, portraying his protagonists as aristocrats and ridiculing peasants. Thus his depiction of a hero who is a common man who defies the social abuses of a higher class is unusual.[20] Considered Calderón's masterpiece by some critics, *El alcalde de Zalamea* displays his talent for closely integrating main and secondary plots. The main plot deals with the villainous actions of the captain, and the secondary concerns the jurisdictional argument between the mayor and the general. The succinct presentation of the dramatic conflicts, the realistic depiction of the characters and milieu, the sublime versification, and the direct style helped to make this play one of the most frequently performed in Spanish and European theaters in the nineteenth century, and have contributed to its popularity even today.

The Historical Plays. Calderón selected widely in his choice of subjects, characters, and nationalities, and in accordance with already established practice he transformed his characters from other epochs and countries into contemporary Spanish citizens, to whom the Spanish audience could more easily relate. While he drew from peninsular history and the Bible for his tragedies of honor and jealousy, he was inspired by the characters in antiquity, the Old Testament, legends, and Spanish imperial accounts for other dramas. His historical heroes, moreover, were the great figures already dramatized by his predecessors.

His noteworthy historico-legendary play *La hija del aire* (*The Daughter of the Air*, ca. 1637) dramatizes the life of the ambitious, egocentric queen of Assyria, Semiramis (*ca.* 800 B.C.), who was famous for her beauty, wisdom, and seductive charm. Although the playwright had access to ancient histories, he probably modeled his two-part drama after Virués' *La gran Semíramis* and Lope de Vega's play on the same subject.[21]

Calderón's play takes the form of an open, circular structure. Raised in seclusion in a cave, much as Segismundo was, Semiramis rapidly ascends to become the queen and founder of Babylon, only to fall suddenly because of her intemperate ambition. Having been possessed by the passion to govern, she turns into a tyrant. As a blind instrument of ambition, she loses because she is unable to turn over the reins of government to her son when he becomes of age. The proud queen dies on the battlefield and her spirit vanishes in the air.

This drama closely approaches a classical tragedy, since the tragic destiny imposed by the stars on the feminine protagonist is fulfilled. Its rich Oriental theme underlines the inscrutability of fortune. The extravagant heroine, the bizarre turn of events, the shocking narrations, and the sanguinary scenes turn the play into a spectacular baroque production which is permeated with moral symbolism.

In the last three decades of his life, when Spanish national power was declining, Calderón attempted to remind his fellow countrymen of their glorious past by dramatizing imperial myths and decisive episodes from ancient Greek and Roman history. Especially fond of Alexander the Great (356-23 B.C.), he portrayed the king of Macedonia, who conquered the Eastern World, in *Darle todo y no dar nada* (*To Give Everything and Not to Give at All*, 1651). Modeling his play on Lope's mediocre, episodic play *Las grandezas de Alejandro* (*The Great Deeds of Alexander*), the baroque dramatist improved the form by making the plot more coherent and bringing out a legendary episode in the life of the great general. Enamored of his slave, Campaspe, Alexander controls his emotions and gives her up to his painter, Apeles, who is also in love with her. Through a stoic disposition, the Calderonian protagonist achieves moral victory in his internal struggle. This incident serves to demonstrate Alexander's high moral principles, for if he has control in matters of passion, he also possesses the qualities to be an exemplary statesman. Shortly before his death the poet wrote another play about the remarkable deeds of Alexander the Great in *Duelos de amor y lealtad* (*The Duel between Love and Loyalty*, 1678).

One of Calderón's plays on Roman history *Las armas de la hermosura* (*The Weapons of Beauty*, 1652) centers on an early historical event when the Sabine women were enslaved after having been accused by the Roman senate of making the Roman soldiers effeminate. Besieging Rome with his army, Coriolano threatens to annihilate the entire city, including his loving lady friend, Veturia, so that the dishonorable injustice will be corrected. In an unexpected dénouement, a peaceful solution dissolves the warlike situation between the Sabines and the Romans, and Coriolano and Veturia declare their love. Epitomizing the distorted values in the Roman senators' code of honor, this play was recast from an earlier play on the same subject, *El privilegio de las mujeres* (*The Privilege of Women*, 1636), which Calderón wrote in collaboration with Coello and Pérez de Montalbán.[22]

El segundo Escipión (*Scipio, the Elder*, 1677), which glorifies the imperialistic expansion of Rome, is concerned with a story from the early life of Publius Cornelius Africanus (237-183 B.C.) and the capture of Nova Carthago in 210 B.C. Another play based on a later period of Roman history, *La gran Cenobia* (*The Great Zenobia*, 1634), relates the conquest of Palmyra and the defeat of Zenobia by Lucius Domitius Aurelius (212?-75 A.D.). After uniting the Oriental part of the Roman Empire, a beautiful Assyrian queen, Zenobia, became a dominant political figure in the East. In 272 her aggressiveness pushed the Roman emperor to the east before he defeated her in two battles at Palmyra. After razing the city in 273, he took her as a prisoner to Rome, where she spent the rest of her life. Later, however, Aurelius was assassinated by his own officers during an expedition against the Persians.

In Calderón's interpretation, Cenobia exemplifies intelligence, justice, and valor, while Aureliano represents the opposite qualities. Decio, a fictitious character who completes the amorous triangle in this play, kills the tyrannical emperor and is elected by his officers to fill his position. Calderón's occasional deviations from historical facts are made to sustain the plot structure of his drama, whose theme underlines the mutability of Fortune.[23]

Several Calderonian plays on ancient history are based on the Apocrypha and the Bible. *Judas Macabeo* (1623) stages several episodes from the glorious rebellion of the Maccabees against the persecution of Antiochus Epiphanes of Syria. *La sibila de Oriente (The Sibyl of the East*, 1634-36), belonging to a cycle on biblical subjects, is based on the Queen of Sheba's visit to King Solomon. A prophetess of highest wisdom, the black queen foresees that the sacred wood of Lebanon will be used for the Cross of the Crucifixion. Having basically the same subject, Calderón's *auto El árbol del mejor fruto (Three of the Best Fruits*, 1661) merges an Old Testament story with the redemption of Christ.

Another biblical story exposing Calderón's tragic theory of life is found in a drama about incest, excessive ambition, and hatred, *Los cabellos de Absalón (Absalom's Hair*, 1634). Act 2 is for the most part a transcription of the third act of Tirso's *Venganza de Tamar*, but Calderón finishes his play with a continuation of the biblical account of this family. Seeking to avenge his sister's dishonor and to win the throne at all costs, the rebellious Absalón murders Amón. Then, after returning from exile, he conspires to organize a rebellion against his loving father, King David. But his vindictive force leads him to destruction. As recorded in II Samuel, chapter 18, Absalón, after returning on horseback through the woods from battle, is caught by his hair on the branch of an oak tree and is fatally stabbed by the enemy.[24]

Among the interesting features of this play are Amón's role as a "metagonist" and a play-within-the-play that he invents when he needles Tamar into playfully taking the role of his lover; their play-acting, however, turns into an incestuous affair in reality.[25]

Calderón showed his interest in sixteenth-century Spanish history in several plays. The historical setting for *Amar después de la muerte (Love after Death*, 1633) recounts the uprising of the Moors (1568-71) in the Alpujarra region during the reign of Philip II. Displaying Calderón's mastery in transforming historical material on the stage with poetic imagination, this play includes a pre-Romantic theme about the unfortunate love between Alvaro Tuzaní and Clara Malec during the Moorish rebellion. Making use of adverse fate in the development of his plot, Calderón presents a conflict caused by the code of honor that is reminiscent of Diego Laínez's offense in Castro's *Las mocedades del Cid.*

An incident from another Moorish uprising in Albaicín in 1501 serves as the basis for Calderón's *refundición, La niña de Gómez Arias (The Girl of Gómez Arias, ca.* 1637-39). Modeled on Vélez de Guevara's play by the same title and containing a folkloric motif taken from a stanza of a ballad, Calderón's artistically superior play retells the story of Dorotea, whom Gómez Arias seduced and sold as a slave. At the play's end, Queen Isabel avenges the wrong by ordering him to marry her and then having him decapitated. His villainous exploitation of an innocent girl and the resulting catastrophe are parallel to the experiences of Fernán Gómez in Lope's *Fuenteovejuna.* Both seduce women, rebel against society, and die for their treachery.[26]

Among Calderón's works dealing with contemporary Spanish events are *El sitio de Bredá (The Siege of Bredá,* 1626) and an *auto, El segundo blasón del Austria (The Second Glory of Austria,* 1679), which eulogizes the Spanish Habsburgs. Realizing his countrymen's political and religious interest in the war in Flanders, the playwright vividly dramatized in the first play the valor of the Spanish army in the ten-month-long siege of Bredá, which in 1625 was surrendered to the Spaniards under the command of General Spínola. (Two years later the Dutch recaptured the city, but this had not taken place when Calderón wrote his play.) The main plot basically follows the siege of the fortified city, while an historico-fictional subplot involves a sentimental intrigue revolving around a feminine character, Flora. Calderón's cinematographic treatment of the events and his presentation of numerous characters masterfully convey both the dangerous environment and the personal agony that was suffered. Understandably, the protagonists undergo no character changes. Spínola is given all the qualities of an epic hero, while his opponent, Justino de Nassau, is portrayed negatively. In composing his epic-like drama, Calderón must have been influenced by Lope de Vega's historical plays, such as *La nueua victoria de D. Gonzalo de Cordoua* (1622) and *El asalto de Mastrique por el Príncipe de Parma* (1600-1606).

The Religious Plays. In a number of Calderón's religious plays the motif of patriotism predominates. In *Afectos de odio y amor* (*Affections of Hatred and Love*, 1654) and the *auto sacramental, La protestación de la fe* (*The Profession of Faith*, 1656) Calderón treats the religious wars in Northern Europe and, in particular, the conversion to Catholicism of Queen Christine of Sweden in 1654. But her conversion failed, as history proved, to bring about the conversion of her country, as both the Pope and Calderón expected.

Calderón's *El príncipe constante* (*The Steadfast Prince*, 1629), regarded as the finest Spanish play on religion and chivalry, deals with the expedition of Prince Fernando of Portugal to Tangiers in the fifteenth century, which ended with his capture and death. Its immediate sources are considered to be *La fortuna adversa del Infante don Fernando de Portugal* (which has been attributed to Lope de Vega), Góngora's ballad entitled "Entre los sueltos caballos" (1585?), and Luis Vélez de Guevara's *Comedia famosa del Rey don Sebastián* (1607?).

Confronted with the choice between worldly existence and eternal life, the heroic Prince Fernando refuses to save his own life and surrender the colonial Christian city of Ceuta to the Moslems. Eventually overpowered, he suffers degradation and torture before dying as a prisoner of the enemy. The unusual dénouement, however, presents the resurrected Fernando, who leads the Portuguese army in a victorious battle. His martyrdom, reminiscent of the passion, death, and resurrection of Christ, is not interpreted as a defeat but as a victory for himself, Spain, and the Church. Moreover, Ceuta symbolically becomes the lady with whom he mystically unites in holy matrimony.

Fulfilling the requirements of Christian constancy and renunciation, Fernando plays the role of a saint rather than that of a tragic hero. Acting on his own will rather than being a victim of Fate, the flawless knight forces upon himself the roles he must play. While some critics may consider that he is going through a process of self-discovery over which he has no control, others argue that the religious view of his ethical conduct gives him the traits of a "metagonist."[27]

The dramatic action of the play arises from the clash of two conflicting attitudes and ideas. The forbearance in suffering of the Portuguese prince is contrasted with the cruelty of the King of Fez. Christian life, which transcends human experience, stands in opposition to Moslem belief, based on the material universe. By exposing the human dimensions of the principal characters, Calderón projects even more clearly the discordant attitudes of the two worlds. All the characters share the common trait of constancy, as the title suggests for the prince: Prince Fernando in religion, the King of Fez in politics, Muley in love, and Fénix in melancholy. The playwright, furthermore, implies in this play that moral conflicts are often entangled with political interests, thus justifying the need for Christians to seek eternal values over transitory worldly goals.

Calderón presents England's separation from the Roman Church in *La cisma de Ingalaterra* (*The Schism of England*, ca. 1634) according to the interpretation of the Counter-Reformation. He divides the key figures in the historical conflict into three overlapping triangles, with Henry VIII at the center of each: the religious group (the Catholics, the king, and the heretics), the matrimonial characters (Queen Catalina-Catherine, Henry VIII, and Anne Boleyn), and the lovers (Anne Boleyn, Henry VIII, and Charles, the ambassador of France). All of the characters stand in the shadow of Cardinal Wolsey, whose ambition to become the new English religious leader appears to unite the three plots. Holding the key to the intricate situation, the cardinal, who is depicted as a tragic hero, falls because of an excess of pride and arrogance.[28] In his double role as tempter and deceiver, he represents the psychological rather than the theological side of the Devil. Henry VIII is not deceived by the cardinal, however, but accepts his deception as a means to rid himself of Catherine in order to marry Anne. When the king's goal is obtained, nonetheless, he assumes the tragic veil of destiny, for he knows he is guilty but also has been victimized.

Calderón's philosophical-religious play, *El mágico prodigioso* (*The Wonder-Working Magician*, 1637), is based on the Faustian theme and deals with the fourth-century legend about St. Cyprian of Antioch's pact with the Devil; it also shows similarity to Mira de Amescua's *Esclavo del demonio*. In the Calderonian play Cipriano, symbolizing Everyman, finds God after encountering several cunning deceptions by Demonio. After realizing that his guise as a professor of theology is hollow, Demonio attempts another approach. Pretending to be Floro and visiting the house of Justina, he precipitates a jealous fight between Lelio and Floro, who are both in love with Justina. Cipriano, acting as the friend of the two men, makes peace between them only to fall deeply in love with the girl. Demonio seizes the opportunity and appears before Cipriano during a violent storm as a shipwrecked man. They become friends, and upon learning that the man is a magician, Cipriano accepts his offer to teach him necromancy for a year for the purpose of winning the love of Justina. After the pact is signed in blood, Demonio incites another fight between Lelio and Floro, who end up in jail. Soon afterward, the sorcerous attempts of both Demonio and Cipriano fail to influence the strong-willed Justina to love Cipriano. The false figure of the girl, which Demonio has desperately devised, turns into a skeleton when Cipriano tries to kiss it, and the duped man finally nullifies his pact with the Devil and invokes God's mercy. This scholastic play is best understood through the irony of Demonio and his "metatheatrical" schemes.[29] It teaches the uselessness of necromancy, the importance of free will in a man's life, and the infinite mercy of God.

Among Calderón's plays based on religious chronicles are *Las cadenas del demonio* (*The Chains of the Devil*, 1635-36), which enacts the evangelization of Armenia by Saint Bartholomew, and a hagiographic play, *El gran duque de Gandía* (1671),[30] which dramatizes the life and sanctification of Francisco Borja. In the latter play an amorous secondary plot involving Carlos and Magdalena serves as a contrast to the duke's betrothal to religion.

Calderón's vision of the Andean world appears in his politico-doctrinal play *La aurora en Copacabana* (*Dayspring in Copacabana*, 1661), which is concerned with the appearance of an image of the Virgin in Peru. This play eulogizes the evangelization of the Incas with the implementation of the Marian cult. Within it, two topics converge. As a theologian, Calderón employs the ancient debate between the heathen and the Christians to explain the nature of the conflict between the Incas' paganism and Spanish Catholicism. But as a jurist, the dramatist uses the views of St. Thomas Aquinas to support the Incas' natural right to a legitimate government. The playwright, concludes however, that, since the Indians lack Divine Grace, their Christianization through Marian miracles and their conquest by the Spaniards are justified.

Among Calderón's devotional plays are *La devoción de la Cruz* (*The Devotion of the Cross*, 1633), *El purgatorio de San Patricio* (*The Purgatory of St. Patrick*, 1634), and *El gran príncipe de Fez* (*The Great Prince of Fez*, 1668).[31] The first two deal with the question of predestination and the last with a Moroccan convert, Baltasar de Loyola, who propagated the Christian faith after his baptism in 1656.

Calderón probably wrote *La devoción de la Cruz* while in military service in Italy, since its setting and characters are Italian. Using a pious legend as the source for this poetic play, he blended novelesque and mystic-romantic elements to expound the Antinomian doctrine that faith alone is necessary for salvation. While the principal theme suggests the redemptive power the Cross has for those who believe, its structure is built on two opposing motifs: the barbarous, unwritten law of honor, and the Cross, representing repentance and forgiveness. The syllogistic expositions of the characters reveal abstract ideas about man's fall and redemption, much as was done in some earlier *autos sacramentales*.[32]

The theological debate in *El purgatorio de San Patricio* could easily have been devised by Tirso, and its historical source was in fact Pérez de Montalbán's *Vida y purgatorio de San Patricio* (1628). The Apostle of Ireland, San Patricio, disguised as a supernatural spirit, leads Ludovico, an inborn criminal, on a tour of purgatory. After witnessing the scene of death there, Ludovico calls on God's mercy, repents, changes his ways, and is saved.

Two other devotional pieces are about the Virgin Mary. *Origen, pér-*

dida y restauración de la Virgen del Sagrario (*The Origin, Loss, and Restoration of the Virgin of the Sanctuary*, 1629) dramatizes a legend from Toledo about the Virgin's image. The pictorial presentation of the subject evokes the history of the Black Virgin, which appears on the front and side panels of the altarpiece in the Cathedral of Toledo.

Other Types of Dramatic Works. Equal to Tirso as a writer of *comedias palaciegas* (palace plays), Calderón showed great ingenuity and subtlety in this genre. Good examples among many of his in this genre are *La banda y la flor* (*The Band and the Flower*, 1632), *Dicha y desdicha del nombre* (*The Advantages and Disadvantages of a Name*, ca. 1660-61), and *El galán fantasma* (*The Fantastic Lover*, 1634-36). Resembling the cloak-and-sword plays, many of these melodramatic pieces are set in distant, idealized Italian or imaginary courts. They were also staged entirely by courtiers before courtly audiences in the royal palaces.

Like Lope de Vega, Calderón found subjects for novelesque plays in famous works of fiction. His *Celestina* and *Don Quijote*, which are now lost, and *La fingida Arcadia* (*The False Arcadia*, 1663) were taken from well-known works. Several other dramatic works follow stories found in Old French epics or romances of chivalry; these include *La Puente de Mantible* (*The Bridge of Mantible*, 1632),[33] *El castillo de Lindrabridis* (*The Castle of Lindrabridis*, ca. 1661-63), and *Los hijos de la fortuna, Teágenes y Cariclea* (*The Children of Fortune, Teágenes and Cariclea*, 1651-64). The latter play dramatizes the extensive text of Heliodorus's *Aethiopica*, a third-century Greek romance that influenced the works of Cervantes and Pérez de Montalbán. Condensing the plot and transforming the characters, Calderón employed the techniques of counterpoint to depict Persina and Admeta, and parallelism to portray Teágenes and Cariclea. The coherent and entertaining actions of the two sets of protagonists present life's adventures through its many obstacles and misfortunes.

As a playwright for the court, Calderón experienced success early in his career with *El mayor encanto, amor* (*The Greatest Enchantment Is Love*, 1635). Written for the inauguration of the palace in the Buen Retiro, this play dramatizes the encounter of Ulysses and Circe on the

"Love, Wind, and Nymphs' choir," a stage scene presumed to have been made for Calderón's *El mayor encanto, amor* (Biblioteca Nacional, Madrid).

Interior stage decor for a play by Calderón (Biblioteca Nacional, Madrid).

Island of Ea in the Tyrrhenian Sea. Calderón's romantic hero, involved in love and adventure, including a shipwreck, the drinking of a magic potion, and being the victim of mistaken identity, conquers his sensuality and abandons Circe. When the play was first presented, the spectacular scenery designed by Cosme Lotti reproduced the scene of the shipwreck on the large pond in the park and used a magnificent water car drawn by dolphins. The performance was accompanied by music and fireworks, and members of the court watched from gondolas.

Following the example of the great poets, Calderón continued to use Greek mythology as a rich source of symbolism in his other mythological and quasi-operatic plays. As the greatest baroque dramatist among the Spanish playwrights, he achieved excellence in this genre. These three-act plays, written between 1652 and 1670, and devoid of sociological and religious content, present refined and exotic scenarios, fabulous characters, trivial themes, unusual dramatic effects, mistaken identities, anagnorises, and happy dénouements. Commissioned by the king to celebrate royal weddings, birthdays, and state visits, they were staged in the palace or royal garden. In *La estatua de Prometeo* (*The Statue of Prometheus*, 1669) the light-hearted tones of a baroque romance stand in contrast to the cold classical setting. Among other plays in this category are *El hijo del Sol, Faetón* (*The Son of the Sun, Phaeton*, 1661), *El monstruo de los jardines* (*The Monster of the Gardens*, 1650-53), *Apolo y Climene* (1661), *Fortunas de Andrómeda y Perseo* (1653), and *Eco y Narciso* (1661).[34]

Calderón is credited with creation of the zarzuela, a two-act musicodramatic production having a mythological-pastoral theme. The ancestry of this indigenous Spanish genre can be traced to the early plays of Juan del Encina, Lucas Fernández, and Gil Vicente, and other scenic productions dating from the fifteenth to the seventeenth century in which musical compositions from the wealth of folk music in Spain were interpolated in the dialogue. As masters of lyric drama, Lope de Vega and his contemporaries also realized the contribution that vocal and instrumental music could make to drama, and provided for its inclusion in their works.

The new term that Calderón used is derived from the palace of La Zarzuela, which was originally built as a hunting lodge by Prince Fernando in the royal estate of the Pardo near Madrid. After the prince left for Flanders in 1634, Philip IV enlarged and beautified the gardens, turning the estate into a country retreat. At first the king was entertained there by comedians, who acted and presented short musical pieces, but their spontaneous performances soon developed into musical plays, which became known as *fiestas de Zarzuela*. Later they were simply called zarzuelas.

Although Lope de Vega's eclogue, which was set to music in 1629, is considered to be the first operatic work in Spain, Calderón's "Piscatory Eclogue" *El golfo de las sirenas* (*The Gulf of the Sirens*), which was performed at La Zarzuela for the first time in 1657, is considered to be the first text of a *fiesta de Zarzuela*. Having an Italian seaside setting near the famous strait of Messina, this one-act piece contains a *loa* (prologue) and a *mojiganga* (a sung conclusion to a dramatic performance). The story deals with the dangers that Ulysses and his companions encounter when the beautiful Scylla and the sweet-singing Charybdis attempt to seduce them.

An earlier zarzuela by Calderón, *El jardín de Falerina* (*The Garden of Falerina*, 1648), was first performed not at the king's country estate but at the Royal Palace in Madrid. Considered to be the second play set to music in Spain (after Lope's), this work dramatizes the episodes in Boiardo's *Orlando innamorato* (*Orlando in Love*) that tell of Falerina's enchantment of Rugero at the palace of Charlemagne.

Although Calderón's two-act *El laurel de Apolo* (*The Laurel of Apollo*) was commissioned for performance at La Zarzuela, it was first staged at the Coliseo del Buen Retiro in 1658, where also his last two zarzuelas were performed. Juan Hidalgo, a court musician of superior skill, is the supposed composer of the master's *La púrpura de la rosa* (*The Blush of the Rose*, 1659), and he is the known composer of *Celos aun del aire matan* (*Jealousy, Even When It Comes from the Air, Can Kill*, 1660), the longest extant specimen of Spanish operatic music from the seventeenth century. The subject of the one-act *La púrpura de la rosa* is the mythological fable about the love of Venus and Adonis and the jealous vengeance of Mars. The three-act *Celos aun del aire matan*, which was based on the fable in Ovid's *Metamorphoses* about Cephalus and Procris, begins with the goddess Diana's condemnation of Aurora for neglecting her vows of chastity when she falls in love with a shepherd. Another nymph, Procris, who was critical of Aurora, is unable to learn from the mistake of her compeer and heedlessly falls in love with Cephalus. As a result, she is punished and transformed into a star, while her lover is turned into a zephyr.

The zarzuela was forced into retreat when the Italian opera troupes invaded Madrid in the early eighteenth century, and such poets as José de Cañizares, whose *Angélica y Medoro* (1722) was the first Spanish opera written in the Italian style, gained control. Nonetheless, Calderón's mythico-legendary zarzuelas were again recalled by a faction in Spain that reversed public opinion toward the earlier popular Spanish art form during the second half of the eighteenth century.[35]

The few *entremeses* (interludes) that Calderón wrote are *El dragoncillo* (*The Little Dragon*), a reworking of the theme of Cervantes' *La cueva de Salamanca* (*The Cave of Salamanca*); *El sacristán mujer* (*The Sacristan Women*); and *La casa de los linajes* (*The House of People of High Lineage*).

The "autos sacramentales." Sacramental plays began to flourish in seventeenth-century Spain during the reign of Philip III. During the Counter-Reformation the presentation of these one-act theological pieces became a public institution. Didactic in purpose and exalting Catholic theology and Scholasticism, they stimulated the laity to become more knowledgeable about the Bible and man's relationship to God.[36]

Calderón, refusing to accept blindly the lyrical structure of the *auto sacramental* as it had been formulated during previous generations, creatively experimented to produce in his *autos* a harmonious balance between lyrical and dramatic elements. In his artistic hands, the Eucharistic play grew in refinement to achieve its greatest perfection. With his sacramental pieces he not only surpassed Tirso de Molina and Lope de Vega but also José de Valdivieso, whose only medium was religious plays.

Continuing in the tradition of dramatizing the Eucharist and presenting subjects from Holy Scripture, legends, history, and mythology, the poet personalized abstract theological concepts relating to the mystery of redemption. Calderón employed various plots to show acceptable

"The Sacred Form of an *auto sacramental*," a painting by Claudio Coello.

attitudes in Christian life, and by reinforcing them with symbolism and allegory, he reconciled the spiritual life of man with his physical existence. In all of his *autos* he demonstrated two worldly concepts: the spiritual, based on man's service to God, and the material, based on a vassal's loyalty to his lord.

Containing farcical characters who resemble *graciosos* and other characters who express themselves in comic puns and word plays, Calderón's *autos* became colorful spectacles. His inclusion of both singing and dancing attests to his ability to bring to life the incomprehensible mysteries of faith through his appeal to the senses. These works are considered to be forms of sacred opera, since his poetry, which includes paraphrases of biblical texts, provides for occasions of music ranging from simple, prosodic chants to instrumentally accompanied melodies and expressive recitatives.[37]

The eighty *autos sacramentales* of Calderón have been divided into the following groups: philosophical-theological, mythological, biblical (Old and New Testaments), those written for special occasions, historical-legendary, and Marian.[38] In the first of these categories, *El gran teatro del mundo* (*The Great Theater of the World*, 1648-50) has exerted much influence on some modern critics, who have found a basis for their metatheatrical theory in this *auto* and in *Life Is a Dream*. The *auto*'s theme emphasizes man's need for charity as a condition for salvation. Making use of an ingeniously designed "metaplay" and utilizing metaphors freely, the playwright presents both divine and human characters onstage.[39] After creating the world, Autor (God) presents a *comedia* on a stage—Mundo (World). His actors must act well in accordance with La Ley de Gracia (Prompter, who enforces the law of grace), and their actions are guided by *libre albedrío* (free will) to do good or evil. With the introduction of the theme of the Dance of Death, the symbolic characters, such as the King, Beauty, and Laborer, repent of their sins. Discretion goes to Heaven for acting well, and Wealth, incapable of repenting because of lack of charity, is damned. Calderón's figurative characterization of Poverty, who is obedient to God but takes advantage of free will in his refusal to work, reveals his attitude to the moral problem concerning him; his only alternative, according to the dramatist, is to stop existing. Nonetheless, Poverty goes to Heaven.[40]

The most celebrated of the master's Eucharistic plays, *La cena del rey Baltasar* (*King Belshazzar's Supper*, 1632), interprets the biblical account of Belshazzar and Daniel, according to Daniel, chapter 5, to illustrate the sanctity of Holy Communion. With the addition of allegorical characters and emphasis on certain details, Calderón's work acquires the characteristics of a Golden Age drama. The play opens on the eve of the wedding banquet of King Baltasar, who, although already married to Vanidad (Vanity), is taking a new bride, Idolatría (Idolatry). Having been called before the king, Daniel (a Hebrew prophet living in captivity in Babylon) and his *gracioso*, Pensamiento (Thought), have the unpleasant task of predicting that the king's happiness could be broken by the hand of God. After Vanidad and Idolatría prevent the king from angrily killing Daniel, the prophet saves the king's life from the sword of Muerte (Death), who wanted to assist Daniel in avenging himself.

Possessed with Fear since he thinks he is being followed by Sombra (Shadow), Baltasar promises to respect the Jewish laws, and Muerte returns to him his lost book of memory, in which it is stated that the king will die. Nonetheless, Daniel again prevents Muerte from stabbing the king when he falls asleep. Upon awakening when his wedding feast has already begun, Baltasar immediately drinks wine from the consecrated vessels (the Law of Grace) that had been taken from the temple in Jerusalem. Seeing that Baltasar has broken his agreement, Muerte poisons the wine. Immediately a violent storm arises and a paper on which a strange inscription is written appears in a cloud. Called again to interpret, Daniel reads that the days of Baltasar have ended because of his sacrilegious deed. Thereupon Muerte finally kills the dying king with a sword.

Although Calderón retains the facts as recorded in the Bible, his suggestion that the poison from the sacred cup is the major cause of Baltasar's death symbolizes the sacrilege and resulting punishment of partaking unworthily of the Eucharist. The Bible records only that the king was slain in the night after the great feast at which he desecrated the holy vessels. Calderón's unification of teachings from the Old and New Testaments, together with his personification of the biblical events, contributes to the uniqueness of this *auto*.

Among the sacramental plays inspired by the New Testament,[41] *La viña del Señor* (*The Vineyard of the Lord*, 1674) is taken directly from the parable of the vineyard, as recorded in Mark, chapter 12, and shows resemblance to Lope de Vega's *El heredero del cielo*. In Calderón's interpretation, Padre de Familias (Father of Families, or God) rents out his land in the country to Hebraísmo (the Hebrews). Padre sends Isaías (Isaiah), Jeremías (Jeremiah), and Lucero del Día (the Light of the Day—John the Baptist) to collect the rent. Since they all die in vain, God finally sends his own son, Jesus, who sacrifices himself for man's redemption. The land is then taken from Hebraísmo and given to Gentilidad (the Gentiles).

The setting for an *auto* written for one of many famous hunting parties during Philip IV's reign is *El valle de la Zarzuela* (*The Valley of the Zarzuela*, 1655). This play contains a debate between three powers of the soul in which Voluntad (Will) wins.

Among Calderón's historical-legendary *autos* are *El santo rey Don Fernando* (*King Ferdinand, the Saint*, in two parts, 1671) and *La devoción de la misa* (*The Devotion for the Mass*, 1637). The first play, pertaining to the time of Ferdinand III of Castile, combines the history of the construction of the Cathedral of Toledo by the captive Moors, the siege of Seville, a related story about the image of the Virgin, and the death of the king. The play's theme, which emphasizes charity and faith, promulgates the triumph of Christianity over Mohammedanism, the Albigensian religious sect, and Hebraism. The second historical *auto* is about a legendary warrior who, through his devotion in attending Mass, frees himself from the dangers he encounters while fighting the Mohammedans during the Reconquest. The continuous war in Castile symbolizes the primitive medieval Church and the protagonist represents man, who submitted to sim but was helped by Divine Grace to achieve victory.

La hidalga del valle (*The Noblewoman of the Valley*, 1634), is categorized as a Marian *auto* that makes no allusion to the Eucharist. Written to be presented at the festivals commemorating the Virgin Mary, it was never staged during the Feast of Corpus Christi. In this play, which is preceded by a *loa* under the same title, Culpa (Guilt) and Placer (Pleasure) argue about the nature of the Virgin. If she was born without sin, they say, she could not have been redeemed by Christ's blood; however, if she was redeemed, she must then have been born in sin. Finally, Placer satisfactorily concludes that the Virgin's protection from sin and her participation in Redemption are not contradictory; therefore, she can be considered to have been redeemed by Christ, even though she may have been conceived without sin.

A Marian *auto* to which the Eucharist is tied, *La piel de Gedeón* (*The Fleece of Gideon,* 1650), makes use of incidents in Gideon's victory over the Midianites and Amalekites, as recorded in Judges, chapters 6 and 7. At the end of the play, Aurora, personifying the Virgin Mary, appears to explain that the dry fleece that proved to Gideon that God was speaking to him, symbolically represents the concept of the Immaculate Conception, and ties it to Christ's death and the Eucharist.

The incorporation of mythological subjects, which was a popular practice in all the arts during the Golden Age, influenced Calderón to write other *autos*. A medieval interpretation of the myth about Orpheus is adapted in his *El divino Orfeo* (*The Divine Orpheus, ca.* 1634), which supports the theological argument that God is always victorious over the power of the Devil. While Orfeo represents the figure of Christ in this play, the main protagonist is Aristeo, who portrays the Devil. The dramatist's unorthodox presentation of Satan's views was derived from St. Thomas Aquinas's paradoxical interpretation of St. Paul's teaching that, although God and divine things may appear weak, they are in reality strong. In another mythological *auto*, *Los encantos de la culpa* (*The Enchantment of Guilt,* 1649), the dramatist uses the myth of Ulysses and Circe, in which the concept of guilt is absent, to illustrate the sacrament of penitence.

During Calderón's career the sumptuous staging of *autos sacramentales* became an immensely popular tradition for the Feast of Corpus Christi. The celebration began at daybreak with an artillery salute and the ringing of bells. After Mass was said, religious and charitable organizations, guilds of tradesmen, the armed forces, high governmental dignitaries, and the king participated in a procession in which the Host was displayed to the public. Several bands and numerous floats joined the religious parade.

After a midday *siesta*, the public gathered before five o'clock in the places where the Eucharistic exhibitions were to be presented. It was necessary for the two different *autos* which were to be staged to be performed at least four times, if not more, in order to accommodate the king, then the Councilors of Castile, next the Councilors of Madrid, and finally the populace. The two-storied wagons, with their elaborately painted scenery, moved in procession along the streets until their final performances were held at the Plaza Mayor and the Puerta de Guadalajara. A second wagon, which served as a stage for the first with its scenic background, was usually a part of the procession. Eventually a third *carro*, and even more, made it possible to convert the sites into permanent acting places at various locations in the city.[42]

Toward the end of Calderón's life, the celebrations on Corpus Christi Day ran into trouble because the actors supplemented their repertoires with *jácaras* and *bailes*. The lack of novelty and verisimilitude in the *autos* of other dramatists, the stereotyped content and carnivalesque aspect of later productions, and the rise of Neoclassicism contributed to the decline of this popular Spanish genre. In 1765 a decree signed by Charles III prohibited its performance, and eventually intellectual and theatrical critics regarded the *auto* as a ridiculous art form.

CONCLUSION

Together with Lope de Vega, Calderón offered the highest expression in peninsular drama. As a poet and thinker, Calderón elucidated the truths and mysteries of life and turned the puzzles and confusion in man's world into sense and order. Filling his works with startling metaphoric imagery, exaggerated conceits, contrasts, and neologisms, he systematically employed metrical passages, pompous figures of speech, distortions, and exuberance. In his quest to improve Spanish drama, Calderón synthesized seventeenth-century theatrical art, methodically transforming many earlier Golden Age plays into pieces of art. Rather than depicting the traits of individuals, his dramatic characters embody ideas and abstractions. His productions, enriched with innovative concepts, modern techniques, and the inclusion of the plastic arts and music, reflect the imperial Spain which was beginning to crumble. If comparisons must be made with his predecessors,

Calderón was less spontaneous and original in subject matter than Lope de Vega; and compared to Tirso de Molina he was less perceptive in his character portrayals of women; but he was superior to both in profundity and baroque expression.

Calderón was, however, the last star in the Spanish Golden Age. In fact, during the last forty-five years of his life, Spanish drama underwent a period of gradual decay as Spain experienced politico-economic decline and resulting moral deterioration. Already in the works of Calderón, and more so in those of his successors, uncertainty about the future of Spain is expressed. In their choice and treatment of themes, they preferred to escape from reality by turning to fantasy and by weaving adventurous love stories. Likewise, they questioned Spanish life more often by exposing the moral implications in the code of honor and by finding fault with old customs, such as the degrading treatment of women.

After Calderón's death, a sharp drop in dramatic production created a vacuum in Spanish literature. His much less talented successors were unable to make further improvements, and a period of decline quickly followed. Toward the end of the seventeenth century, Calderón's popularity also waned and his works came to be regarded as dogmatic, absolute, and fanatical. They remained in disrepute until nineteenth-century German scholars began to reverse the stigma that had been attached to them in Spain. Dissociating themselves from the negative attitude of the Spaniards in the last century, German, British, and American scholars have been able to reevaluate Calderón as one of the greatest of baroque dramatists.[43]

Chapter V

The Decline:
Calderón's Contemporaries
and Imitators

THE NEW generation of playwrights who were contemporaries of Calderón de la Barca continued in the tradition of court drama with even more refined forms and styles. In the midst of this intensely productive and heterogeneous period, the young dramatists, like their master, profited from the inventiveness and diffusion that was characteristic of the Lopean school while writing for court audiences. The works of the Calderonians show more adequate character delineations, refined and affected styles, and pathetic sensibility.

During Calderón's long career a large number of playwrights associated themselves with him, competing with him in a friendly way and also imitating him. Among several dramatists in his cycle who deserve to be mentioned are Rojas Zorrilla and Agustín Moreto.

FRANCISCO DE ROJAS ZORRILLA

The foremost Spanish dramatist among Calderón's followers was Francisco de Rojas Zorrilla (1607-48). Born and raised in Toledo, this poet studied at the University of Salamanca and lived in Madrid, where he participated in several literary competitions. By the age of twenty-five he had already acquired fame as a dramatist. In his early career Rojas Zorrilla collaborated with Luis Vélez de Guevara, Montalbán, and Calderón. After Lope de Vega died in 1635, Rojas became one of the favorite court playwrights in Spain.

With his unusual talent for wit, Rojas offended several persons during a literary contest in 1638, and subsequently was stabbed. During his youth he fathered an illegitimate daughter, who, after his death, became the famous actress called "la Bezona." Married in 1640 to Catalina Yáñez Trillo de Mendoza, he had one son, Antonio Juan, born in 1642. Three years after obtaining membership in the Order of Santiago, he died suddenly in 1648.

Of the total dramatic output of over seventy plays attributed to Rojas, only thirty-five full-length plays are extant. He also wrote nine *autos sacramentales*, two interludes, and more than fifteen plays in collaboration with Vélez de Guevara, Montalbán, Coello, Cáncer, Rosete Niño, Belmonte, Mira de Amescua, and Calderón. During Rojas's lifetime two collections of his plays appeared, in 1640 and 1645. They can be divided into six groups: tragic plays, honor dramas, religious plays and *autos sacramentales*, cloak-and-sword plays, novelistic plays, and comedies of manners and customs.[1] Known for Senecan dramatic traits, the poet exposed violence, sensationalism, and stoic virtues in his dramas. Although the tragic plots of some of his plays contain comic elements, their total effect is tragic.

Among his ten tragic plays several are outstanding. Those based on classical subjects are *Los áspides de Cleopatra* (*Cleopatra's Serpents*, 1640-45) and *Los encantos de Medea* (*Medea's Sorcery*). *Numancia cercada* (*The Siege of Numancia*, ca. 1630) and *Numancia destruída* (*The Destruction of Numancia*, ca. 1630) constitute a two-part series based on episodes from early Spanish history that had been treated earlier by Cervantes. *No hay ser padre siendo rey* (*A King Cannot Act as a Father*, 1635) and *El Caín de Cataluña* (*Cain of Catalonia*) deal with father-son conflicts. A drama on the theme of vengeance is *Morir pensando matar* (*To Die with the Intent to Kill*), and one of his honor dramas, *Casarse por vengarse* (*To Marry for Revenge*), treats a conventional theme of honor in which a husband kills his wife for being courteous to another man.

The action for Rojas's most celebrated honor play, *Del rey abajo, ninguno* (*Below the King All Men Are Peers*, 1651), is set in the fourteenth century when Alfonso XI had trouble curbing the power of his rebellious feudal lords. Although the play has a baroque and pastoral setting, it deals with exaggerated loyalty to a king and makes allusions to the doctrine of the divine right of kings that was adhered to during the reign of the Spanish Habsburgs. The protagonist, García del Castañar, a Spanish nobleman, lives in disguise in the country. His honor is stained when a courtier, Mendo, attempts to seduce his wife. Believing the villain to be the king, García refrains from avenging the wrong, since he regards his king more highly than his own honor. But when he learns that the offender was not the king, García kills the real intruder. Thus the nobleman shows that although he would make an exception for the king, he will not suffer dishonor from anyone else. Blanca, his virtuous wife, also highly values her husband's reputation and plays an active role in seeking to restore her own lost honor.

The gripping action, intense tone, emotional conflict, and sonorous versification make this drama remarkable, despite its partly euphuistic style. The play's theme develops from its title—the monarch, considered God's representative on earth, can do no wrong and therefore is unapproachable. All those beneath the king are peers among themselves and each is obliged to avenge his own personal honor. Several minor themes can also be found: the enjoyment of idyllic life, a courtier's dependence on his king, and the interaction between reality and illusion.[2]

The presentation in this play of country life, as opposed to courtly life, is similar to that in Antonio de Guevara's prose essay *Del menosprecio de corte y alabanza de aldea* (*On the Scorning of the Court and in Praise of the Village*). In both can be seen the Horatian theme of *beatus ille quid procul negotii*, which eulogizes country life. Several earlier plays may have served Rojas as sources, such as Lope de Vega's *El villano en su rincón* and *Peribáñez y el comendador de Ocaña* and Tirso's *El celoso prudente*.

Rojas's religious plays lack emotional inspiration and fall short in doctrinal content. Generally each play portrays a sinner who is converted by means of Divine Grace; some of the protagonists become martyrs. Two of his noteworthy plays on saints are *La vida en el ataúd* (*Life Is Found in the Coffin*, in the 1640s), an account of Saint Boniface's martyrdom, and *El mejor amigo el muerto* (*The Dead Man as the Best Friend*, in the 1640s), dealing with the conversion of a young Scot, Jorge Lesleo, from Calvinism to Catholicism. Two of Rojas's three extant sacramental plays, *El gran patio de palacio* (*The Palace's Great Courtyard*, 1647) and *La viña de Nabot* (*Naboth's Vineyard*, 1647?) have meritorious qualities but interpret theological doctrine inadequately.

The melodramatic adventures in Rojas's novelistic plays are better suited for reading than for the stage. His *Persiles y Segismunda* (1633), a dramatized version of Cervantes' Byzantine novel of the same title, suffers because the plot appears to be poorly planned and because of an endless number of characters who speak in monologues. For *Los celos de Rodamonte* (*Rodamonte's Jealousy*, before 1640) the playwright borrowed from Ariosto's *Orlando furioso*. *Los bandos de Verona* (*The Rival Houses of Verona*, 1640) is based on the Romeo and Juliet story, except that Rojas brings the lovers to a happy ending.

Conforming to the typical characteristics of the cloak-and-sword plays, Rojas's works in this genre are better than average. *Donde hay agravio no hay celos* (*Dishonor Leaves No Room for Jealousy*, 1637) and *No hay amigo para amigo* (*Honor-Bound Friendship Means More Than Friendship Alone*, before 1640) excel in characterizations, well-ordered plots, and humorous situations that arise out of the cowardice of *graciosos*.

In comparison to Rojas's cloak-and-sword plays, his comedies of manners and customs are less important for their plot development than for their portrayal of social life. Comically viewing Madrid's society, Rojas depicted such problems as the double dealings between the sexes. Another play, *Lo que son mujeres* (*The Ways of Women*, before 1645), revolves around two sisters and their attitudes toward the opposite sex.[3]

Of great merit is Rojas's *Entre bobos anda el juego* (*Merry Sport with Fools*, 1638), one of the earliest *comedias de figurón* (farcical plays in which the protagonist is depicted as a grotesque caricature) that gained popularity during the second half of the seventeenth century.[4] This play singles out an anti-lover in the character of Lucas, a wealthy Toledan and ridiculous maniac who loses his much younger fiancée to his cousin, Pedro. Criticizing a father's dominance in the selection of his daughter's husband, this play speaks out for true romantic love. Also through the new humorous character of a *figurón*, who is more skillfully drawn than most *graciosos*, Rojas satirizes contemporary Spanish life.

Since Rojas Zorrilla cultivated sensationalism within the Spanish style of his tragic dramas, he aroused renewed interest in the Spanish tragedies of the Renaissance. In his honor plays emotional intensity reaches a high point, whereas in his lighter dramatic pieces he contributed to the evolution of the *gracioso* by giving him a more prominent role in the comical secondary plots.

AGUSTÍN MORETO Y CABAÑA

The second most important author of the Calderonian school was Agustín Moreto y Cabaña (1618-69),[5] who, together with Calderón and Rojas Zorrilla, benefited from the popularity of theater in the seventeenth century. Born in Madrid of Italian parents, Moreto studied at the University of Alcalá and became a courtier and court dramatist. Before entering a sacred order in 1657 he wrote about fifty plays, mostly imitating and adapting the better-known plays of his predecessors. They were published in three volumes, in 1654, 1657, and 1681. Moreto compensated for his lack of imagination and inventive power by gaining distinction in dramatic refinement and in the arranging and perfecting of previously traced plots. Although he wrote all types of *comedias*, his style approaches that of seventeenth-century French comedy.

The work that has won for Moreto immortal fame is a drawing room comedy, *El desdén con el desdén* (*Disdain for Disdain*, 1654), which is based primarily on Lope de Vega's *Milagros del desprecio* (*Miracles of Scorn*) and *La vengadora de las mujeres* (*The Avenger of Women*). The love game or test in Moreto's play revolves around the psychology of rejection. Count Carlos falls in love with Countess Diana, whose beauty and reluctance to marry are widely known. Through the ingenious arrangements and advice of his intelligent *gracioso*, Polilla, Carlos jolts the indifferent Diana, who had previously been pampered by her suitors. First Polilla acts as Carlos's spy when he assumes the role of servant-councellor in Diana's house under the name Caniquí. He advises Carlos to return her disdain with even more indifference and then teases Diana about Carlos's lack of interest in her. In his role as a "metagonist," he succeeds in curing the countess of her fault and makes it possible for the play to come to a happy resolution.

Although the theme of a maiden's free will is deliberated from a man's point of view, Moreto raises sensitive questions about women's right to make important decisions in their own lives. He questions whether they should blindly accept the courtship of every suitor without being in love, and marry just to fulfill unwritten social laws. The ending of this play points out that a woman should be free to decide her own destiny and to marry the suitor with whom she truly falls in love. This play deserves the extraordinary fame it has attained because of its tightly constructed plot, its operatic quality, and the psychological delineation of its characters.

Moreto's *El lindo don Diego* (*The Conceited Mr. Wonderful*, 1662) shares with *El desdén* almost equal fame. This lively comedy of manners, inspired by Guillén de Castro's *El Narciso en su opinión* (*The Self-Styled Narcissus*, 1625), is one of the best *comedias de figurón*. It entertains with its witty dialogue, comic situations, and the portrayal of a conceited protagonist who is castigated in a cleverly planned dénouement. The elegant but provincial Don Diego intends to marry a rich heiress, Doña Inés, in Madrid. His eccentricity, however, not only irritates his beautiful fiancée, who is in love with another suitor, but also offends his future father-in-law. Don Diego's plans fail when his vanity leads him into an ingenious trap that is planned by the servant of his rival, the *gracioso* Mosquito. The clever lackey introduces the dandy to an important lady, who in reality is a harlot. The fop realizes the truth about his new conquest too late. Offended by Don Diego's bad conduct, Doña Inés's father gives her in marriage to Don Diego's competitor. The defeated, vain pretender returns home full of shame without having achieved his goal.

Although Moreto borrowed his plots from earlier plays, he abandoned the established genres, such as the honor plays and *comedias de capa y espada*, for *comedias de figurón*. He also neutralized the traditional sharp contrast between the servant-figure, the *gracioso*, and the *galán*, often placing the *gracioso* in the position of a "metagonist." The playwright's new satires on the urban manners of flirtation and courtship focus on the behavior of people of marriageable age in seventeenth-century society. In his plays no one is hurt by the loss of honor and no transcendental ideas are debated. Only certain social faults are exposed, such as vanity and eccentricity, which become the butts of ridicule. Three of his adaptations are especially well known. *El valiente justiciero* (*The Valiant Judge*, 1657), a recasting of Lope de Vega's *El infanzón de Illescas*, depicts Pedro I as he changes from an unruly youth into a trustworthy, politically influential king. *Como se vengan los nobles* (*The Vengeance of the Nobles*, 1668), an imitation of Lope's *El testimonio vengado* (*The Avenged Testimony*), is about the first-born but illegitimate son of the king of Navarre, who vindicates false accusations about his stepmother by defeating his three half brothers. And in *Licenciado Vidriera* (*The Glass Licentiate*), an adaptation of Cervantes' exemplary novel by the same title, the protagonist feigns insanity in order to criticize the social illness of ingratitude, but after proving his point he becomes sane again.

Although Moreto's fame rests with his plays of intrigue, eight of his hagiographic plays are outstanding. Composed to commemorate the cult of St. Francis of the Seine that was established in 1651 in Madrid, *San Franco de Sena* (1652) shows a resemblance to Tirso's *El condenado por desconfiado* (*The Condemned Man for Lack of Faith*), since it depicts the conversion of a sinner because of his love for his crippled father, and illustrates the paradox that the worst sinner makes the best saint.[6] This play displays Moreto's successful use of conceits to achieve dramatic irony—his instrument for social criticism.[7] His forceful intent in his only extant *auto*, *La gran casa de Austria y Divina Margarita* (*The Great House of Austria and Divine Margaret*), diminishes the work's artistic qualities.

Moreto ranks next to Cervantes and Quiñones de Benavente as one of the best *entremisistas* (writers of one-act plays). Most of his thirty-eight *entremeses* satirize social climbers, roguish characters, and women of ill repute. An example of each is *Entremés del aguador* (*Interlude of the Water Vendor*), *Entremés de los gatillos* (*Interlude of the Little Pickpockets*), and *Entremés de doña Esquina* (*Interlude of Miss Street Corner*).

ALVARO CUBILLO DE ARAGÓN

Aside from the works of Rojas Zorrilla and Moreto, the dramatic production of Calderón's numerous successors declined in quantity and quality. Although many of the lesser-known playwrights in the period of decline possessed less theatrical talent and enjoyed shorter-lived fame than the great masters, some of their plays are exceptionally good. In this group are the works of Alvaro Cubillo de Aragón (1596-1661), who claims in the dedication of *El enano de las Musas* (*The Dwarf of the Muses*, 1654) to have written over one hundred dramatic pieces. Twenty-four of these are extant.

Although Cubillo's plays display little creativity, they show that he possessed the skill to dramatize stories. The baroque influence of Góngora can be noticed in Cubillo's ability with word games, and Calderón's influence can be seen in his plot structures. Cubillo's fondness for minute details, furthermore, is reminiscent of Moreto's art. The sensitive poet was a good judge of feminine passion, as can be seen in *Las muñecas de Marcela* (*The Dolls of Marcela*, 1636) and *La perfecta casada* (*The Perfect Wife*, 1636). *Las muñecas de Marcela*, classified as a marionette play, psychologically portrays Marcela, who awakens to life after falling in love and changes from a tender maiden to a woman. The characters resemble marionettes engaged in love games, quarrels, and activities related to the avenging of honor. The heroine in *La perfecta casada* not only follows the model-wife ideal that was exposed in Fray Luis de León's book of the same title, but also defends her unfaithful husband. The psychological traits in both plays give them a modern air.[8]

In Cubillo's other play of customs, *El señor de noches buenas* (*The Gentleman of Happy Nights*, 1635), two brothers who are identical twins—one being rich but stupid, the other poor but intelligent—fall in love with the same lady. She is confused because in the night her lover speaks beautiful words and during the day her admirer is completely stupid. The baroque technique of polarizing good sense and stupidity within the comic treatment of deception makes this play ludicrously comical.

Other plays by Cubillo are worthy of mention. *El invisible príncipe del baúl* (*The Invisible Prince with the Trunk*, 1637?) is a caricatural *comedia de figurón*. A heroic-legendary theme appears in the two-part *El rayo de Andalucía* (*The Lightning of Andalusia*, before 1632), which deals with the deeds of Mudarra, who avenged his brothers' treacherous deaths. The legend of Bernardo del Carpio is dramatized in the two-part *El conde de Saldaña* (1641). *Los triunfos de San Miguel* (*The Triumphs of Saint Michael*, before 1654) and *El bandolero de Flandes* (*The Brigand of Flanders*) are religious in content.

JUAN BAUTISTA DIAMONTE

Of Greek and Sicilian origin, Juan Bautista Diamante (1625-87) emphasizes scenographic and musical aspects in his fifty plays and dozen short pieces, some of which were published in two volumes in 1670 and 1674.[9] Possessing exuberant baroque style, his plays lack inventiveness. Diamante excelled in incorporating national tradition within his works. *El honrador de su padre* (*The Son Who Honors His Father*, 1657) and its sequel, *El cerco de Zamora* (*The Siege of Zamora*) were inspired by Guillén de Castro's *Las Mocedades del Cid* and Pierre Corneille's *Le Cid*. Diamante's *El valor no tiene edad* (*Valor Has No Age*, 1636?) exalts the brave feats of the famous knight García de Paredes. *El Hércules de Ocaña* (1647) glorifies the celebrated swordsman Céspedes. And *La judía de Toledo* (*The Jewess of Toledo*, before 1667) is an adaptation of Mira de Amescua's *La desgraciada Raquel* and Lope's *Las paces de los reyes y judía de Toledo*.

Diamante also wrote a number of zarzuelas and other types of dramas. *La reina María Estuarda* (1660) deals with British history. In his dramas of intrigue, *Juanilla la de Jérez* and *Pedro de Urdemalas*, the heroines disguise themselves as men to win their lovers. *La devoción del rosario* (1651) is his best religious piece; it was inspired by the legend about the salvation of a bandit who prayed the rosary every day.

ANTONIO HURTADO DE MENDOZA

Belonging to the transitional period between Lope de Vega and Calderón, Antonio Hurtado de Mendoza (1586-1644) was known as a poet and a dramatist. As a courtier he was active in literary circles in the court and in Madrid. Mendoza composed a dozen plays, which were presented before royal audiences in the theaters at the Buen Retiro and Aranjuez.[10] *Querer por sólo querer* (*To Love for the Sake of Love*) premiered in 1622 in Aranjuez and won for him royal recognition. As can be expected of court productions, this drama and other works of his are filled with euphuisms and mythological allegories. Staged as a summer festive court spectacle in which the queen's maids of honor played, this long play, with some 6,400 lines, consists of chivalric and pastoral episodes against a background of music and supernatural effects.

Cada loco con su tema (*Everyone Is Crazy in Some Way* 1630), a cloak-and-sword play, exposes in witty dialogue the weaknesses and foibles of human nature. Resembling the eccentric protagonist in a *comedia de figurón*, Hernán Pérez, an *indiano* who has just returned to Spain from Peru, seeks to establish his family in Spanish society by marrying off his two daughters to men of his own choice. As the title suggests, each of the characters displays his own maniac philosophy.

A comedy of manners by Mendoza, *Los empeños del mentir* (*Perseverance in Lying*), was commissioned for presentation in the Coliseo Theater in the Buen Retiro around 1634. This satirical drama, which ridicules Madrid's social climbers, shows the influence of the picaresque novel, since all the characters gullibly attempt to advance themselves at all costs. The play's depiction of the life of courtesans is reminiscent also of Cervantes' *La entretenida* (*The Entertaining Comedy*). A fine psychological drama, Mendoza's *El marido hace mujer* (*The Husband Rears the Wife*, 1631-32), is the antecedent of Molière's *L'École des maris* (*The School for Husbands*). Dealing with marriage as a social relationship between husband and wife rather than as a sacred union, the play shows how a marriage can fall apart when put under great stress. Another lofty play with lively dialogue, *Más merece quien más ama* (*He Who Loves Best Deserves More*, 1622?) deals with love within court life.

Other plays by Mendoza that deserve mention are *El premio de la virtud* (*The Reward of Virtue*, before 1621), *Celos sin saber de quién* (*To Be Jealous of an Unknown*, 1630-32), *Los riesgos que tiene un coche* (*The Risks of a Carriage*, 1630-44), and *El galán sin dama* (*The Gentleman without a Lady*, 1635). The best among his *entremeses* are *Examinador miser Palomo* (*Examiner, Mister Palomo*, 1617) and its sequel *El licenciado Dieta* (*The Licentiate Diet*, 1618), which are discreet satires on courtly life and the pastimes of courtiers.

ANTONIO COELLO Y OCHOA

A skillful adapter of other playwrights' works, Antonio Coello y Ochoa (1611-82) often collaborated with colleagues in writing plays.[11] His greatest piece, *El conde de Sex, o dar la vida por su dama* (*The Earl of Essex, or To Die for His Lady*, 1633), which has also been attributed to Philip IV, treats for the first time the infatuation of Elizabeth of England for the Earl of Essex. Several years of history are consolidated into an invented plot in which Essex sacrifices his life in order to save his sweetheart, Blanca, whose family had conspired against Elizabeth.

Two noteworthy dramas that Coello wrote in collaboration with Rojas and Vélez de Guevara are *El catalán Serrallonga* (1635), containing a lively description of medieval game disputes in Barcelona, and *La Baltasara* (before 1637), which gives an account of the frivolous life of the famous actress Baltasara de los Reyes and her conversion and entrance into a convent. Coello joined with Calderón in writing *Yerros de naturaleza y aciertos de la fortuna* (*The Errors of Nature and the Prudence of Fortune*, 1634), which was probably the source of Calderón's *La vida es sueño*.

FRANCISCO DE LEIVA RAMÍREZ

A playwright of Calderonian orientation, Francisco de Leiva Ramírez (1630-76) came from Málaga. His most famous play of intrigue, *La dama presidente* (*The Lady President*), is about a woman who conducts herself as if she were a man. Although the intelligent Angela scorns men, she is seduced by an adventurous lover, César. In the disguise of a man, she departs for Florence in pursuit of him. The talented woman succeeds in obtaining a court appointment as magistrate of justice, and while presiding at the trial of her seducer, she orders him to marry his victim, who is, of course, herself.

Leiva's *Cuando no se aguarda y príncipe tonto* (*When One Does Not Wait and the Foolish Prince*) is one of the best *comedias de figurón*. His *Marco Antonio y Cleopatra* and *La mayor constancia de Mucio Scévola* (*The Great Loyalty of Mucius Scaevola*) are based on Roman history.

ANTONIO DE SOLÍS Y RIVADENEYRA

An imitator of Calderón who displayed little creative talent was Antonio de Solís y Rivadeneyra (1610-86), who wrote a dozen plays of intrigue that display the fictional ambience of love within caricatural satire. Endowed with gifts of discretion and comic power, Solís approached the art of Moreto. *El amor al uso* (*Stylish Love*) ridicules love. In it an engaged couple, who in reality are in love with each other, are involved with other partners.

El doctor Carlino, an improved adaptation of Góngora's play by the same title, deals with a procuring doctor whose loquacious and foolish wife spoils his pandering. Three couples involved in love affairs with different partners are the focus of *Un bobo hace ciento* (*A Dunce Makes One Hundred More*). *La gitanilla de Madrid* (*The Little Gypsy Girl from Madrid*), inspired by Cervantes' *Gitanilla*, shows Solís's ingenuity with plot development and his agility in style. Among his heroic dramas, the most Calderonian in style is *El alcázar del secreto* (*The Castle of the Secret*).

JERÓNIMO DE CÁNCER Y VELASCO

As a gifted poet of quips and caricature, Jerónimo de Cáncer y Velasco (1594-1654) was a forerunner of the grotesque in Spanish theater. Francisco de Quevedo's satirical jokes can be traced to Cáncer's comic plays *Mocedades del Cid*, *La muerte de Baldovinos* (*The Death of Bowdoin*, 1651), and *Los siete infantes de Lara*. These plays are parodies of earlier serious works, whose protagonists belong to the medieval chivalric tradition. In them Cáncer introduces an entirely different atmosphere, in which the deeds of the heroes and kings and their speech habits are ridiculed. He succeeds in transforming the grandeur of the medieval heroes into mediocrity. The grotesque occurrences, low comic expressions, common dialect used by the high nobility, and scenic effects suggested by the characters' hands provoke continuous laughter. Cáncer created this new kind of caricatural theater by changing the style and tone of the conventional *comedia* and by degrading epic history, historical characters, and highly dramatic situations.[12] Cáncer's farces, such as *La visita de la Cárcel* (*The Visit in the Jail*), *Los gitanos* (*The*

Gypsies), and *La mula* (*The Mule*), display ingenious humor within violent situations. Cáncer also wrote plays in collaboration with six other dramatists.

JUAN DE LA HOZ Y MOTA

Best known for a highly comical character in *El castigo de la miseria* (*The Punishment of Poverty*, 1650-60), Juan de la Hoz y Mota (1622-1714)[13] found inspiration in María de Zayas's novel of the same title, in Cervantes' exemplary novel *El casamiento engañoso* (*The Deceitful Marriage*), and in Plautus's *Aulularia* (*The Miser's Money Pot*). For this character study dealing with morality, La Hoz was not influenced by Molière's *L'Avare*, however, since Don Marcos is more repugnant than the French playwright's Harpagon. In *El castigo de la miseria* a cunning young woman tricks a cynical student into marrying her by pretending she has inherited a fortune from her first husband, who she claims was the governor of Havana.

The best among La Hoz's twelve extant plays is *El montañés Juan Pascual, primer asistente de Sevilla* (*The Mountaineer John Pascual, the King's High Assistant in Seville*), considered to be an adaptation of a play by Lope de Vega. Its plot revolves around Peter the Cruel's amorous adventures and ends with a noble application of justice. This play was the antecedent of several Spanish Romantic works, such as Fernández y González's *La cabeza del rey don Pedro* (*The Head of King Don Pedro*), the Duke of Rivas's "Una antigualla en Sevilla" ("An Old Tale of Seville"), and José Zorrilla's *El zapatero y el rey* (*The Shoemaker and the King*). The most important among his religious plays is *Morir en la cruz con Cristo* (*To Die on the Cross with Christ*).

JUAN DE MATOS FRAGOSO

A Portuguese playwright writing in Spanish, a skillful adapter of many well known *comedias*, and a collaborator with Moreto, Cáncer, and Diamante, Juan de Matos Fragoso (1608-89) reworked many old plays to suit the public's taste.[14] While he was deficient in dramatic invention and lyric power, he showed special ability in constructing plots, especially those having themes on honor. Nonetheless, the old models of the theater were becoming exhausted and the decline of Golden Age drama was beginning to be evident in his time.

Among the half-dozen plays that show Matos Fragoso's lively talent is *La corsaria catalana* (*The Catalan Privateer*). *El traidor contra su sangre* (*The Traitor against His Blood*), which deals with the legend of the Princes of Lara, left a profound mark on Romantic literature. Matos Fragoso wrote a second part to Vélez de Guevara's *Reinar después de morir*, entitled *Ver y creer* (*Seeing Is Believing*), and the poet also was a productive writer of *entremeses*.

OTHER DRAMATISTS

During the Spanish *comedia*'s period of decline, nearly fifty other less gifted authors produced plays, some of which are worthy of mention. The following abbreviated list provides their names, dates, and more important works:

Antonio Enríquez Gómez (1600-1663): *Celos no ofenden al sol* (*Jealousy Does Not Offend the Sun*) and *A lo que obliga el honor* (*To What Does Honor Oblige Itself?*).[15]

Pedro Rosete Niño (1608-59): *Madrid por dentro* (*Inside Madrid*) and *Errar principios de amor* (*To Fail in the Principles of Love*).

Juan (the son of Luis) Vélez de Guevara (1611-75): *El mancebón de los palacios* (*The Young Man of the Palaces*) and *Los celos hacen estrellas* (*Jealousy Makes Stars*).

Fernando de Zárate (1612-after1660): *La presumida y la hermosa* (*The Beautiful, Vain Pretender*).[16]

Antonio Martínez de Meneses (1618-50): *El tercero de su afrenta* (*The Judge of His Affront*).

Sebastián Rodríguez de Villaviciosa (1618-72?): *Cuantas veo tantas quiero* (*I Love All the Girls I See*).

Diego Figueroa y Córdoba (1619-73): *La dama capitán* (*The Lady Captain*).

Francisco Antonio de Monteser (1620?-68): *El caballero de Olmedo* (a parody of Lope de Vega's play).[17]

Jerónimo de Cuéllar (1622-65): *Cada cual a su negocio (Each One Minds His Own Business)*.

Fernando de Avellaneda (1622-75): *Nuestra Señora del Pilar (Our Lady of the Pillar)*.

José Figueroa y Córdoba (1625-78): *Muchos aciertos de un yerro (Many Good Guesses of an Error)*.

Manuel León y Merchante (1631-80): *No hay amor con fingir (There Is No Love with Lying)*.

Agustín de Salazar y Torres (1642-75): *La segunda Celestina (The Second Celestina)* and *El encanto es la hermosura y hechizo sin hechizo (Enchantment Is Beauty and Glamour without Magic)*.

FRANCISCO ANTONIO DE BANCES CANDAMO

The decadent period of the once highly prolific Spanish theater closed with Francisco Antonio de Bances Candamo (1662-1704), who became popular after Calderón's death in 1681. After a successful teaching career at the University of Seville, he established himself as a dramatist in Madrid. After writing *Por su rey y por su dama (For His King and His Lady*, 1685), which premiered in the theater at the Buen Retiro, he was named the official poet and dramatist in the court of Carlos II in 1687.

By 1670, Spanish theater was in such a state of decadence that nearly all of the acting troupes had been disbanded. Thus, for the festivity of Carlos's marriage to María Luisa de Orleáns in 1679, Bances Candamo was unable to organize three troupes of actors to assist him. Clergymen and religious fanatics were harshly attacking the theater, and it was only under the king's protection that the dramatist escaped direct confrontation with the Church. During this time Bances Candamo, a wholehearted admirer of Calderón, wrote a defense of contemporary drama, *Theatro de los theatros de los passados y presentes siglos (Theater of the Theaters of the Past and Present Centuries*, 1689-90). The first of its two parts is a general commentary on Spanish drama, and the second refutes the Jesuit Ignacio Camargo's criticism of the *comedia*.

Ironically, the same favorites that defended Bances Candamo led to his departure from the court. After much jealousy had been stirred up among the courtiers, the poet was finally forced into a duel and was gravely wounded by an opponent who objected to the satirical content in his *El esclavo en grillas de oro* (*The Slave in Golden Shackles*, 1692). Bances resigned as court poet in 1693 and spent the rest of his life in various governmental positions.[18]

In addition to being a lyric poet, Bances Candamo wrote twenty-two plays.[19] Most of them were written to be performed in the theater at the Buen Retiro. They possess a stilted style that is often full of obscurities and Gongorisms, but some scattered passages in his plays contain concise language that is not typical of his work.

His dramatic pieces deal with national, classical, and foreign history and with religion. His best-known play, *La piedra filosofal* (*The Philosophical Stone*), is the most original continuation of Calderón's *La vida es sueño*. In it, traces of Góngora's poetic technique and Calderón's system of plot structure can be found. Bances Candamo's protagonist, Hispalo, like Calderón's Segismundo, meditates on reality and fiction, but Hispalo chooses to live in a world of fantasy.

Outstanding among Bances Candamo's other historical plays are *El español más amante y desgraciado Macías* (*The Most Unhappy Lover*, *Macías*), concerning the life of an unhappy troubadour; *Quien es quien premia el amor* (*The One Who Rewards Love*), a story about Queen Christina of Sweden; and *El esclavo en grillos de oro*.

This last play, treating an episode in the life of the Roman Emperor Trajan, resembles Corneille's *Cinna*. Discontented with Trajan's government, Camilo conspires against him. Upon being discovered, he is condemned to death by the senate, but instead of carrying out the punishment, the emperor appoints Camilo as a partner to help him govern. Obliged to renounce all pleasures in order to dedicate everything to his new position, Camilo suffers ill fortune, ingratitude, and conspiracies. After Camilo finally implores Trajan to free him from his high position, the emperor is satisfied and pardons him. The main plot concerns Camilo's efforts to become the emperor, his ascension, and the ensuing developments. A secondary plot revolves around the romantic loves between Camilo and Sirena, and Adriano and Octavia. The theme of blind avarice and its consequences is coupled with a motif dealing with personal liberty. Ambition can only be realized if its seeker is willing to accept the responsibility that goes with it.

The character of Camilo is well drawn. From an arrogant, avaricious nobleman, he gradually turns into an admirable young man who is humble enough to realize his mistake. His love for Sirena serves as a foil to extricate him from his situation. The intelligent, loyal Sirena is a model of womanhood. In the character of Adriano is seen a study of a young man schooled in the art of politics and war. Trajan is portrayed as an excellent and just emperor whose lesson to Camilo is reminiscent of that which Patronio gives to the count in *Conde Lucanor*. No doubt the playwright was alluding to the situation and character of Carlos II by placing Trajan in a Spanish milieu and giving him the attributes of a Spanish king. The play's numerous comments on the difficulty of running a government and the emperor's need to be beyond reproach make reference to the Spanish court and monarch of the late seventeenth century.

This post-Calderonian play abounds in excesses, but the baroque complications, such as flowery language, the use of a chorus, and elaborate scenery, were undoubtedly well received by the court audience. Throughout the first two acts a chorus, in the tradition of Greek tragedy, appears to give voice to warnings and to recapitulate the action. Adding to the confusion are seventeen characters who, with the chorus, fill the stage to the utmost. Musical instruments are used to announce almost every player's arrival. Bances Candamo knew how to please the courtly audience, construct a plot, and develop a play for the tastes of his day.

Possessing also a theological background, Bances Candamo wrote three *autos sacramentales*, the best being *El primer duelo del Mundo* (*The First Duel of the World*). The complex plots and erudite character of these works, however, detract from their poetic qualities.

CONCLUSION

The playwrights in the Calderonian cycle can be distinguished from Lope de Vega's contemporaries by their greater dramatic artistry. Those in the Lopean school wrote their lyrical pieces more quickly, making use of their inventive ability to treat various themes from the old ballads and chronicles. Borrowing subjects from national and foreign history and adapting plots from the Italian *novelle* and classical and Renaissance drama, the Lopeans successfully established the new *comedia*. The Calderonians, on the other hand, who had to satisfy more sophisticated audiences, approached neoclassical stylistic and thematic tendencies in their plays, enriching them with ingenious scenic effects and embellishing them with contrived language. While using the same subjects as their predecessors, the Calderonians compensated for their lack of dramatic invention by constructing their plots more ingeniously and adding extravagant elements to the plays they plagiarized.

The two most gifted of Calderón's followers, Rojas Zorrilla and Moreto, turned away from heroic subjects and transcendental ideas toward social criticism, especially about the rights of women, in their caricatural *comedias de figurón* and their plays of character and of manners. As a great stylist, Rojas built his plots carefully and revealed a strict moral posture, but he occasionally fell into the verbal excesses of Gongorism. The highly delineated satire through which Moreto conveyed his social message is evident in his drawing room comedies, religious plays, and comical *entremeses*, which also display skillful versification, well drawn plots, and lively dialogues.

Among the more than fifty secondary and lesser Calderonian playwrights, Cubillo de Aragón stands out for his witty mastery of theatrical effects; Diamante for the exuberant baroque style of his plays on national customs and history; Hurtado de Mendoza, for his comedies of manners and courtly dramas; Coello as a skillful adapter of older plays and a collaborator with numerous other dramatists; Leiva Ramírez and Solís de Rivadeneyra for their plays of intrigue: Cáncer for his witty improvisations which are remarkable for their wordplay and Quevedevesque burlesque satire: Hoz y Mota for his adaptations of several Spanish novels and plays; and Matos Fragoso for his *refundiciones* of several older well-known *comedias*. The Calderonian cycle closed with the lyric poet Bances Candamo, whose treatise in defense of contemporary drama and satirical historical plays could not prevent the decline of the *comedia*, which had nearly exhausted itself.

Chapter VI

The *Comedia* since 1700

THE POLITICAL and economic decline of Spain in the seventeenth century resulted from the exhaustion of the entire nation. Worn out by the long succession of wars it had waged in many parts of the globe, the nation finally lost its collective ideal of military conquest in the name of faith. The driving force that had moved the whole nation disappeared. Finding no substitute for their idealistic motivation, the Spaniards entered a period of disorientation. The withdrawal from active life and consequent isolation from the rest of Europe had an unfavorable impact on the growth of Spanish arts and, in particular, on the development of Spanish literature, which went into a long period of decadence.

Although the last Spanish Habsburgs favored and protected the theater, and the number of theaters increased, theatrical interest declined rapidly during the reign of Carlos II. Several reasons can be cited: the newer works contained decadent excesses in baroque style; there was a lack of new great dramatists and original plays; and new growth in intellectual life turned attention to scholarship and to the essay as its literary form.

After 1700, when Carlos II, the last Spanish Habsburg, died and the throne was occupied by the Bourbon family, neoclassicism and French aesthetic tendencies dominated Spain for the next century. A division occurred with regard to dramatic form, due to the French aestheticians. Nonetheless, the *comedia* did not entirely disappear from the Spanish stage. It continued to be popular with the masses through *refundiciones* until the second half of the eighteenth century, when neoclassical theater, which was patronized by the upper classes, finally took over.

In the struggle between the two aesthetic currents—the national and the neoclassical—some Spaniards refused entirely to accept the Gallic artistic tendencies. Among these few were Antonio de Zamora and José de Cañizares, who responded to the popular taste with imitations of Calderonian art.

Antonio de Zamora (1664-1728) adapted many famous plays by earlier playwrights.[1] He achieved success with two *comedias de figurón*, *Don Domingo de Don Blas* and *Don Bruno de Calahorra*, and a burlesque play, *El hechizado por fuerza* (*The Student Bewitched by Force*). In the latter work a silly student is tricked into marrying a lady who has convinced him that he will die if he should refuse. Zamora's most famous play, *No hay plazo que no se cumpla ni deuda que se pague y Convidado de piedra* (*There Is No Term That Is Kept or Debt That Is Not Paid and the Stone Guest*), was a reworking of Tirso's *El burlador de Sevilla* (*The Trickster of Seville*).

José de Cañizares (1676-1750) prolonged the life of the *comedia* into the eighteenth century and achieved his greatest success with *comedias de figurón*.[2] His *El dómine Lucas* (*The Pedant Lucas*) and *El honor da entendimiento o el más bobo sabe más* (*Honor Gives Understanding or the Greatest Simpleton Knows Most*) are satires on mania of the nobility. Among his eighty works are plays of intrigue and historical and magical dramas.

Although the great age of the *comedia* was dead by the end of the seventeenth century, some Spanish dramatists in later eras sporadically returned to certain genres that the *comedia* had popularized, and to its dramatic devices and historical-legendary subjects.

In 1778 Vicente García de la Huerta (1734-87) scored a major success with his tragedy *Raquel*, which treats the same subjects as Lope de Vega's *La judía de Toledo*. Likewise, Dionisio Solís (1774-1834) and Luciano Francisco Comella (1751-1812) adapted numerous older plays and wrote other somewhat inferior dramas in the same style, which nonetheless satisfied Spanish audiences. Ramón de la Cruz (1731-94) adapted certain principles in Italian opera to the old zarzuela and improved the genre of the *entremés* with his *sainetes* (one-act farces). One of these is *Inesilla de la Pinto* (*Sweet Inez with a Beauty Spot*), which satirizes the tragic heroine, Inez de Castro, in the earlier *comedias*. His numerous colorful productions suffered little despite the predominance of the neoclassical school in Spain. Cándido M. Trigueros (1736-1801) reworked *La Estrella de Sevilla* in his own *Sancho Ortiz de las Roelas* (1800) and revised several other plays by Lope.

After the fall of the neoclassical school, Spanish Romantic writers, many of whom lived in exile because of Ferdinand VII's dictatorial measures, continued to be drawn to the romantic and traditional subjects that the *comedia* had used so well. One of these writers, the Duke of Rivas (1791-1865), who based his ballad about the Princes of Lara, *El moro expósito* (*The Abandoned Moor*, 1829-34), on Matos Fragoso's *El traidor contra su sangre* and published his most Romantic drama, *Don Alvaro* (1835), in Paris, attempted to restore the tradition of the Golden Age drama after he returned to Spain. While the plays in his middle period, *La morisca de Alajuar* (*The Moorish Girl of Alajuar*), *Solaces de un prisionero* (*Consolations of a Prisoner*), and *El crisol de su lealtad* (*The Crucible of Loyalty*), reflect more moderation, they contain Romantic elements since they recall traditional subjects. The Duke continued to draw upon the *comedia* in a later period, showing somewhat grotesque tendencies and reactionary manifestations against the rebellious Romantic movement in *El desengaño en un sueño* (*Disillusionment in a Dream*, 1842), which is reminiscent of Calderón's *La vida es sueño*.

Another Spanish Romantic, Juan Eugenio Hartzenbusch (1806-80), also drew upon medieval legend and three earlier comedies by Rey de Artieda, Tirso de Molina, and Pérez de Montalbán when he wrote *Los amantes de Teruel* (1837). Hartzenbusch also showed interest in Calderón's dramas of honor and Rojas's cloak-and-sword plays, which he imitated respectively in *Vida por honra* (*Life for Honor*, 1855) and *El amo criado* (*The Master Valet*, 1841).

There were other Spanish Romantics who drew upon the *comedia*. The *comedias de figurón* that had been established by Rojas Zorrilla were restored by Bretón de los Herreros (1796-1873), who wrote *Marcela o ¿a cuál de los tres?* (*Marcella or Which One of the Three?*, 1831) and *La escuela de matrimonio* (*The School of Marriage*, 1852). José Zorrilla (1817-93) reflected the influence of Tirso's *El burlador de Sevilla* in *Don Juan Tenorio* (1844). His *Zapatero y el rey* (*The Cobbler and the King*, 1840) is a powerful evocation of Pedro the Cruel. Manuel

Tamayo y Baus's technique of the play-within-a-play, as seen in *Un drama nuevo* (*A New Drama*, 1867), especially evokes Calderón's *El pintor de su deshonra*. And Adelardo López de Ayala (1828-79) wrote *Un hombre de estado* (*A Statesman*, 1851) and *Rioja* (1854) in Calderonian style. So too did José Echegaray (1832-1916), whose *Mancha que limpia* (*The Stain that Cleanses*, 1895) recalls the barbarous code of honor.

A revival of the *sainete* took place in the second half of the nineteenth century when the cafes of Madrid, which were seeking to draw patrons, staged these short one-act plays and other skits that imitated the old traditional forms. These became so popular that several theaters sprang up featuring hourly performances of these short plays. Among the authors of this new genre, which became known as *género chico*, were Francisco Javier de Burgos (1778-1849), Ricardo de la Vega (1839-1910), Tomás Luceño (1844-1931), and Carlos Arniches (1866-1943).

The historical subjects, popular themes, and love and vengeance that had characterized the *comedia* continued to influence Spanish plays into the twentieth century. The popular old historical legend of Inez de Castro, which had been dramatized several times during the Golden Age and again by de la Cruz and Luciano Francisco Comella (1751-1812) in the late eighteenth century, was again recast by Alejandro Casona in *Corona de amor y muerte* (*The Crown of Love and Death*, 1955). It was also reworked in France by Henry de Montherlant (1896-1972) in his *La Reine morte* (*The Dead Queen*) in 1942. Evidence of continued interest in the heroes of the great Spanish past can be seen in the plays of Eduardo Marquina, such as *Las hijas del Cid* (*The Daughters of the Cid*, 1908) and *En Flandes se ha puesto el sol* (*In Flanders the Sun Has Set*, 1910). Among other modern Spanish dramas that especially show fascination for the old themes are *La malquerida* (*The Passion Flower*, 1913) by Jacinto Benavente (1866-1954), and several plays by Federico García Lorca (1898-1936): *Bodas de sangre* (*Blood Wedding*, 1933), *Yerma* (*Wilderness*, 1934), and *La casa de Bernarda Alba* (*The House of Bernarda Alba*, 1936).

The influence of the *comedia* was felt not only in Spanish-speaking countries, such as Mexico, where its greatest follower was Sor Juana Inés de la Cruz (1651-95), who wrote *Los empeños de una casa* (*The Obliga-

tions of a House), but elsewhere in Europe. In France, where only pedantic tragedy and complicated tragicomedy had been known, elements of the colorful, imaginative *comedia* were discovered and introduced. While the French were less interested in the historical and religious *comedias*, they were attracted to the Spanish plays of manners and of high intrigue, since French playwrights had found inspiration also from the Italian *novelle*.[3]

Among the early French playwrights who were influenced by the Spaniards was Alexandre Hardy (1569?-1632), whose *Cornélie* (after 1613) and *Force du sang* (*Kinship's Powerful Call*, after 1613), are based on Cervantes' examplary novels. Georges de Scudéry (1601-67) also followed Cervantes' novel in his *L'Amant libéral* (1636); and in his *L'Amour caché par l'amour* (*Love Concealed by Love*), Scudéry used Lope de Vega's *La selva sin amor*. Jean de Rotrou (1609-50) also imitated Lope's plays in *La Bague de l'oubli* (*The Ring of Oblivion*), *Les Occasions perdues* (*Lost Occasions*, 1633), *L'Heureuse Constance* (*Happy Constance*, 1635), and *Laure Persecutée* (*Laura Pursued*, 1636).

The ingenious ideas, plots, and rhetoric of the *comedia* gave the French playwrights not only the form and modes of expression for their dramas but also some Spanish subjects. Pierre Corneille (1606-84) was indebted to Guillén de Castro when he wrote the first French tragedy on a modern subject, *Le Cid* (1636), since he borrowed heavily from *Las mocedades del Cid* and translated many of its passages directly into French. The French play nonetheless has greater psychological depth.[4] Corneille was also the first playwright to model a work on Alarcón's comedy of manners *La verdad sospechosa*. The French dramatist's *Le Menteur* (1643) was followed by *Il Bugiardo* (1750) by Carlo Goldoni (1707-93) and by *The Liar* (1764) by Samuel Foote (1720-77).

Paul Scarron (1610-60) drew upon several Spanish plays for his works. He adapted Rojas's *Donde hay agravio no hay celos* and *No hay amigo para amigo* in his burlesques *Jodolet ou le Maître vallet* (*Jodolet or the Master Valet*, 1654) and *Le Jodolet duelliste* (1646). (Molière used the same Spanish plays later in his *Les Précieuses ridicules* [*The Affected Young Ladies*, 1659], as did William D'Avenant in *The Man's the Master* [1669].) Scarron made use of the Quixotic character in Castillo Solórzano's *comedia de figurón*, *El marqués del Cigarral*, in his *Don Japhet d'Arménie* (*Don Japhet of Armenia*, 1653), and he imitated

Antonio de Solís y Rivadeneyra's *El amor al uso* in his *L'Amour à la mode* (*Love According to Fashion*).

While the influence of the *comedia* on the works of Moliére (1622-73), the greatest French writer of comedies, is more subtle, since he was acquainted with it only indirectly through the works of Rotrou and Scarron, certain evidence points to the fact that he was drawn to Spanish plays of manners and of high intrigue. While most of his works conceal direct influence, a few are more specific. For example, it is clear that Mendoza's *El marido hace mujer* is the antecedent of the French master's *L'École des maris* (*The School for Husbands*, 1661). One also finds that the social satire in Lope de Vega's *El acero de Madrid* and *La dama boba* antedate Molière's *L'École des femmes* (*The School for Wives*, 1662), *Le Médecin malgré lui* (*The Doctor in Spite of Himself*, 1666), and *Les Femmes savantes* (*The Bluestockings*, 1672). Moreover, Molière adapted Moreto's *El desdén con el desdén* for his *La Princesse d'Élide* (1664). Other later playwrights used Moreto's play; Carlo Gozzi drew from it in writing his *Principessa filosofa* (1772), as too did Marivaux and Lesage.

After Molière, some French dramatists continued to be drawn to the old Spanish plays. Thomas Corneille (1625-1709) borrowed directly from Calderón, Rojas Zorrilla, Moreto, Solís y Rivadeneyra, and Coello in eight of the nine comedies he wrote between 1647 and 1650. The most interesting of these, Corneille's *Le Conte d'Essex* (*The Earl of Essex*, 1678), gives another version of the historical tragedy around which Coello invented the plot for his play in 1633. In France in 1639 and in 1672, Gauthier de Costes and Claudio Boyer had already treated this subject in plays of their own, and the topic was again reworked by the English in 1740, 1749, and 1753 by James Ralph, Henry Brooke, and Henry James, respectively.

In the eighteenth century some of the French plays of customs that show the strongest influence from the Spanish plays of manners and high intrigue are *Turcaret* (1709) by Alain René Lesage (1668-1747), *Le Jeu de l'amour et du hasard* (*The Capricious Game of Love*, 1730) by Pierre Carlet de Marivaux (1688-1763), and *Le Barbier de Séville* (1775) and *Le Mariage de Figaro* (1784) by Pierre de Beaumarchais (1732-99).

Since the *comedia* introduced more dramatic independence from classical rules than had been practiced in France and Italy, and since some of its works introduced subjects with profound undertones, Romantic writers and artists found inspiration in and developed some of the old Spanish characters and themes. Among them was the Don Carlos that Jiménez de Enciso, Pérez de Montalbán, and Vélez de Guevara had realistically portrayed. In the tragedy *Don Carlos* (1787) by Schiller (1759-1805), in Núñez de Arce's *El haz de leña (The Bundle of Firewood*, 1872), and in other literary treatments of the story, the prince emerges as a cosmopolitan dreamer who loves his stepmother and wants to free Spain from the absolutism of his father, a flaw which ironically destroys the young man.[5] Mira's *El esclavo del demonio* and Calderón's *El mágico prodigioso* are some of the early Spanish sources that contributed to the Faustian theme, which was brought to its height by Goethe (1749-1832). The Austrian dramatist Franz Grillparzer (1791-1872) reworked Lope's *La judía de Toledo* into a Romantic tragedy, *Die Jüdin von Toledo* (1848?-52?). In France, Prosper Merimée (1803-70) recast several *comedias* in his *Clara Gazul* (1825), *La Famille de Carvajal* (1828), and others, while Victor Hugo (1805-85) did the same in *Hernani* (1830) and *Ruy Blas* (1838). Casimir Delavigne (1793-1843) also wrote melodramatic plays on popular Spanish characters, such as *Don Juan d'Autriche (Don Juan of Austria*, 1835) and *La fille du Cid (The Daughter of the Cid*, 1839).

Among the most popular *comedias* translated in the Romantic period into English, French, German, Italian, and Polish were *La Estrella de Sevilla* and Calderón's *La vida es sueño, El alcalde de Zalamea* and *El príncipe constante.* The last play, dealing with the fifteenth-century Fernando of Portugal who sacrificed his life for his country and religion, especially attracted the Polish Romantic poet Juliusz Slowacki (1809-49), whose adaptation of it, *Ksiaze Niezlomny (The Inflexible Prince)*, aroused among the partitioned Polish nation common feelings of patriotism. The plot of *La Estrella de Sevilla* was recast again in France during World War II by Albert Ollivier, who recaptured its spirit of patriotism as an example for his countrymen during the German occupation.

The most influential figure to rise out of the Spanish *comedia* has been Don Juan. Since Tirso's presentation of him in *El burlador de Sevilla*, his personification as a seducer and socio-moral rebel has been interpreted by dramatists, poets, novelists, musicians, painters, sculptors, movie producers, and critics for over three and a half centuries. In contrast to Tirso's portrayal of him as daring and rude, the cynical, worldly nobleman in Molière's *Dom Juan* (1665) was imitated by Carlo Goldoni (1707-93) in his *Don Giovanni* (1736), while Da Ponte (the librettist of Mozart's 1787 opera) treated him partly as a ruffian. In subsequent centuries his complex character has been measured against every philosophical and psychological trend. In the Romantic period when he was regarded as a selfish demon, Goethe gave him a Faustian image; Alexandre Dumas (1803-70), in *Don Juan de Maraña* (1837), presented him as a fallen angel; and José Zorrilla portrayed him as a libertine whose soul is finally saved by the intercession of a woman's love. Finally, influenced by the psychoanalysts, the version by Edmond Rostand (1868-1918), *La Dernière nuit de Don Juan* (*The Last Night of Don Juan*, 1921), makes of him an insatiable lover, and George Bernard Shaw's *Man and Superman* (1901-03) finds in him the force of life.[6]

This discussion provides only a brief outline of the impact of the *comedia* on Western drama. A much larger study on this subject could and should be made.

THE CRITICS OF THE *COMEDIA*

For almost four centuries since its birth, the *comedia* has also drawn the attention of critics, who have interpreted its vital qualities in accordance with the perceptions of each new generation. At first the Spanish Golden Age commentators (López Pinciano and Ignacio Camargo) and dramatists (Lope de Vega, Tirso, and Bances Candamo) defended their own views of contemporary Spanish dramatic art. Whereas the neoclassicists, such as Luzán and Leandro Fernández de Moratín, voiced negative appraisals of Golden Age drama, the later Romantic critics, including Alberto Lista, Mariano J. de Larra, and Juan E. Hartzenbusch, approached the plays subjectively and impulsively.

With the rise of realism at the end of the nineteenth century, critics who worked then and into the first half of the twentieth century took a positivistic approach to historical scholarship in their histories and critical editions of sixteenth- and seventeenth-century dramatic works. Before the turn of the century Adolf von Schack's methodical history appeared, and Ramón de Mesonero Romanos's three volumes containing the dramatic works of the poets of the Spanish Golden Age, together with Manuel Cañete's work on the theater of the sixteenth century and Pedro Muñoz Peña's book about Tirso's theater, were published.

At the turn of the twentieth century Marcelino Menéndez y Pelayo established himself as the foremost critic of the *comedia* with his fifteen-volume edition of Lope de Vega's works (1890-1903); editions of the works of Alonso de la Vega, Timoneda, and Pérez de Oliva and his contemporaries; and a four-volume study of the theater of Lope de Vega. Emilio Cotarelo y Mori followed soon afterward with equally ambitious works—volumes on the works of Encina, Lope de Rueda, Tirso de Molina, Enciso, Coello y Ochoa, Diamante and his contemporaries, Mira de Amescua, and thirteen volumes on Lope de Vega. Among his other publications are two volumes of one-act plays dating from the sixteenth century through the middle of the seventeenth, and a book on the life and work of Calderón. Standard classical editions of most of the other Spanish Golden Age playwrights were published in the first half of the twentieth century by Américo Castro, Eduardo Juliá Martínez, Rudolph Schevill, and other scholars.

The same positivistic concerns during the first half of the twentieth century are evidenced by the statistical analysis of the versification of Lope's plays that Sylvanus G. Morley and C. Bruerton compiled in order to establish their chronology. During the same decades H.W. Hilborn and R.L. Kennedy assembled similar chronologies for the plays of Calderón and Tirso de Molina. Also, numerous biographies and other historically-oriented books, starting with Rennert's *Life of Lope de Vega* and his account of the theatrical personages of the Spanish Golden Age, and Jerome A. Moore's compilation of the ballads in Lope de Vega's chronicle-legend plays, indicate the scholars' predilection for history.

Various other schools and individuals have concentrated on related interests into the middle of the twentieth century and later in such areas as: the Don Juan and Don Carlos themes (Gendarme de Bévotte and F.W.C. Lieder), the problem of honor (Américo Castro), dramatic theory in Spain (H.J. Chaytor and Ramón Menéndez Pidal), the *auto sacramental* (W. Sturdevant. A.A. Parker, Marcel Bataillon, and Bruce W. Wardropper), the relation of the *comedia* to classical tragedy (Joaquín de Entrambasaguas, E.S. Morby, and Raymond L. Grismer), and structure and form (Joaquín Casalduero and M. Bataillon).

In the past three decades the study of the *comedia* has been further freed from the positivistic approach, and a vigorous dialogue between several groups of critics and scholars has ensued.[7] Some have attempted to study the evolutionary development of the *comedia* and its historical and structural characteristics by understanding it in terms both of its own time and of what it has to tell us today. Calling the *comedia* unique as a historical phenomenon, Arnold Reichenberger has stated that it reflects within the themes of honor, faith, and love the secular and religious ideologies of the fixed Spanish society. He contends that the *comedia's* "macro-structure," which progresses from "order disturbed to order restored," expressed the collective sentiment of the Spanish people.[8] Eric Bentley responded by stating that the pattern Reichenberger suggested does not restrict itself only to the Spanish *comedia* but is universal.[9]

The British Hispanists,[10] developing in the tradition of literary critics more than of scholars, have developed and adhered to a thematic-structural method of interpretation which was proposed by one of their leading members. According to Alexander A. Parker, five principles determine the structure of the plot of a *comedia*: (1) Dramatic action is more important than character delineation. In accordance with Aristotelian theory, Parker states that, since the dramatist's chief concern must be the plot, he has no time to elaborate his characters. If he does, it is incidental; the audience and the actors are the ones to fill in the details. (2) The theme, which must be true to human nature, is more important than the action or incidents in the plot. Although the theme and action do not necessarily have to be identical, they must be related through an analogy. (3) Therefore, dramatic unity exists in the theme, not in the action. (4) The moral intent of the theme requires that poetic justice be served implicitly or explicitly in the play's conclusion; this is the first useful criterion to apply in detecting the theme. (5) The dramatic causality within the plot helps to identify the moral purpose.[11]

Parker defended his analytical method, after R.D.J. Pring-Mill suggested that it is more applicable to the plays of Calderón than to those of Lope's generation, by acknowledging that, although Calderón's more perfectly structured plays came at the end of a process of historical development, the constructive potential or germ was present in the successful earlier plays. Likewise, he responded to remarks that the fourth principle permits excessive judicial criticism of the characters by stating that "poetry corrects the injustices of real life, by not allowing evil men to triumph or virtuous men to suffer."[12]

Numerous North American and other international critics, many of them members of the *Comediantes*,[13] have either added new dimensions to Parker's principles or have partially rejected them; others have applied other modern approaches to the study of the *comedia*. Bruce W. Wardropper, for example, has advanced Parker's ideas by stressing the importance of poetry as the means for translating the language into action.[14] From another viewpoint, Everett W. Hesse took his cue for a psychological analysis of the characters in the *comedia* from Parker's first principle that permits the audience or reader to fill in the details about a character.[15] James A. Parr found Parker's first three principles helpful—even highly ingenious—but denounced the last two, since they turn the critic into a moralist. Basing his comments on the seminal, academic approach that Northrop Frye advocated in the 1960s,[16] Parr declared that the critic should not illegitimately and subjectively look for the author's intent, trace chains of causality, discover where the guilt is, and judge whether the punishment is justified. Rather, he should discover what the text says, find modern relevance in it, and give more attention to form, structure, imagery, irony, language, and human values.[17] Since Parr wrote his plea for a more intrinsic approach in literary scholarship on the *comedia*, critics have moved in that direction.

Another group of new critics have advanced the ideas expressed in the 1940s by Karl Vossler, who pointed to features in Lope's plays which reveal that the dramatist regarded life as "something half-real and ambiguous." Vossler called the relationship of experience with poetic fiction the "dramatic view of the world."[18] While looking for a more philosophical meaning for imagination in the more serious Golden Age dramas, Lionel Abel called attention to the fictitious world a dramatist initiates, which is deliberately continued by a character. After review-ing numerous works form Sophocles to Brecht, he observed that two basic metaphors, which are transposed into action, predominate in drama—life is a dream, and the world is a stage. Abel made a distinc-tion between classical tragedy, which staged predetermined and dra-matically conscious heroes, and Spanish baroque drama, in which the characters express their awareness that they are being programmed, rebel against it, and exercise their free will to change their destiny. Since these characteristics are especially abundant in the poetic theater of Calderón and in certain other *comedias* of the Spanish Golden Age, Abel con-cluded that some of them should be called metadramas.

In order to illustrate his theory, Abel called attention to the play-within-a-play in Calderón's *Life Is a Dream*. The predicted outcome foretelling King Basilio's degradation at the hands of his son is averted because the monarch sets in motion, with his own invention, another set of circumstances to replace those which had previously been deter-mined by fate. Thus, since the tragic conclusion does not occur and since the king's plan fails, the tragedy has been replaced by a meta-theatre.[19]

Numerous critics have applied Abel's new dimension to the study of the *comedia*, while developing further the concept that characters on stage assume the role of the playwright in other serious plays and comedies of manners.[20] While some find evidence of the meta-theatrical technique in the mere playing of another role by a character, others contend that the playing of a new role should be something more than just a dramatic vehicle. The true test lies in the character's forma-tion of his conscience when he realizes that before being captured by the author, he has already been dramatized—from myths, legends, history, religious ideas, or social conditions.

As has already been discussed, the execution of a character's imagina-tion within a metadramatic structure is more explicitly manifested in Calderón's honor plays. Studying the role-playing qualities of characters who express an awareness of their own actions within a play, these critics contend that a character's conscious ability to assume an identity other than that which was expected of him and to achieve a desired dénoue-ment stems from classical theatrical tradition, such as can be found in Plautus's *Amphitryon*. This was not a strange concept in seventeenth-century Spain because, theologically, life on earth was regarded as a state between birth and death; only when he dies does man awaken to eternal reality. Thus, "metatheater" is founded on the view that "life has already been theatricalized . . . therefore, illusion and unreality are linked to life."[21] A few other critics, however, find the term inappropriate because of the theocentric character of the Spaniards in the seventeenth century.[22]

The most recent approaches to the *comedia* in semiotics (which actualizes the potentially unlimited number of relationships that signs have within a work[23]), stylistics and imagery,[24] and cultural anthropology continue to add to the efforts of scholarship. From this brief account, one may conclude that some approaches to the study of the *comedia* are more applicable to certain plays than to others; nonetheless, each has contributed to a collective body of criticism. Therefore the intent of this discussion has not been so much to advocate any one approach as to note and cite the valuable contributions that many of the critics have made.

CONCLUSION

The Spanish Golden Age *comedia* represents the largest combined body of plays ever written in a specific period of time in any nation in the world. Its modern heterogeneous character is comparable in magnitude to classical tragedy and comedy, to Shakespearean drama, and to French neoclassical theater. This history has attempted to trace the many aspects of the great legacy that Spain has given to the world. The vitality of Spanish Golden Age drama as it developed in the seventeenth century influenced later literatures, and as long as man cultivates dramatic art, the *comedia* will continue to be studied.

NOTES

Only critical studies are listed in these notes. For editions of plays, biographies of the playwrights, bibliographies, anthologies, and general historical studies, see the Selected Bibliography.

I. BIRTH AND DEVELOPMENT OF SPANISH NATIONAL DRAMA

1. The theory was set forth by Leandro Fernández de Moratín in "Orígenes del teatro español," in *Obras de Leandro Fernández de Moratín*, BAE, 2nd ed., 2: 145-306 (Madrid: Rivadeneyra, 1848). Among the critics in the first group are Edmund K. Chambers, Karl Young, Richard B. Donovan, Fernando Lázaro Carreter, Norman D. Shergold, and James P. Wickersham Crawford. (See Selected Bibliography, pages 234-35, for their works.) Humberto López Morales, in *Tradición y creación en los orígenes del teatro castellano* (Madrid: Ediciones Alcalá, 1968), at one time supported the liturgical theory but changed his view more recently in works cited in note 2. Among the Latinists are W. Leonard Grant and Gustave Cohen.

2. Adopting the stance of Narciso Díaz de Escobar and Francisco de P. Lasso de la Vega (in *Historia del teatro español* [Barcelona: Montaner y Simón, 1924], pp. 58-62), and some other dramatic historians, are the following: John Lihani, *Lucas Fernández* (New York: Twayne, 1973), pp. 50-54, 118, 158; O.B. Hardison, Jr., *Christian Rite and Christian Drama in the Middle Ages* (Baltimore: Johns Hopkins Press, 1965); Mary Marguerite Butler, R.S.M., *Hrotsvitha: The Theatricality of Her Plays* (New York: Philosophical Library, 1960); Humberto López Morales: "Nuevo examen del teatro medieval," *Segismundo* 4 (1968): 113-24; and idem, "Nueva hipótesis sobre el teatro medieval castellano," *Revista de Estudios Hispánicos* (Puerto Rico), 2 (1972): 7-20.

3. Butler, *Hrotsvitha*, p. 178.

4. See Raymond L. Grismer, *The Influence of Plautus before Lope de Vega* (New York: Hispanic Institute, 1944), pp. 81-100; and Lihani, *Lucas Fernández*, pp. 50-51.

5. See López Morales, *Tradición y creación*, p. 43; and Adolfo Bonilla y San Martín, *Las Bacantes, o del origen del teatro* (Madrid: Rivadeneyra, 1921), pp. 47-52.

6. See Hardison, *Christian Rite*, p. 178.

7. This play is discussed in Guillermo Díaz Plaja, "*El auto de los Reyes Magos*," *Estudios escénicos*, no. 4 (1959): 99-126; Bruce W. Wardropper, "The Dramatic Texture of the *Auto de los Reyes Magos*," *Modern Language Notes*, no. 70 (1955): 46-50; and Winifred Sturdevant, *The Misterio de los Reyes Magos: Its Position in the Development of the Medieval Legend of the Three Kings*, Johns Hopkins Studies in Romance Literatures and Languages, 10 (Baltimore, 1927).

8. For these works see Fernando Lázaro Carreter, *Teatro Medieval* (Madrid: Castalia, 1965), pp. 58-62; Stanislav Zimic, "El teatro religioso de Gómez Manrique (1412-1491)," *Boletín de la Real Academia Española* 57 (1977): 353-400; James P. Wickersham Crawford, *The Spanish Pastoral Drama* (Philadelphia: Univ. of Pennsylvania Dept. of Romanic Languages, 1915), p. 11; idem, *Spanish Drama before Lope de Vega*, 3rd ed. (Philadelphia: Univ. of Pennsylvania Press, 1967), pp. 5-6.

9. Cf. Crawford, *Spanish Drama before Lope*, p. 4; Lázaro Carreter, *Teatro Medieval*, pp. 48-58.

10. Much information about the origin and development of *autos sacramentales* can be found in the following works: Alexander A. Parker, "Notes on the Religious Drama in Medieval Spain and the Origins of the *Auto Sacramental*," *Modern Language Review*, 30 (1935): 170-82; Bruce W. Wardropper, *Introducción al teatro religioso del Siglo de Oro: La evolución del auto sacramental, 1500-1648* (Madrid: *Revista de Occidente*, 1953); and Jean-Louis Flecniakoska, *La formation de l' "auto" religieux en Espagne avant Calderón (1550-1635)* (Montpellier: Déhan. 1961).

11. For a fuller discussion of the dialogues, see Lázaro Carreter, *Teatro Medieval*, pp. 66-90; and Bonilla y San Martín, *Las Bacantes*, pp. 53-95.

12. See Lázaro Carreter, *Teatro Medieval*, pp. 63-65; Lihani, *Lucas Fernández*, p. 58.

13. See Charlotte Stern, "The Early Spanish Drama: From Medieval Ritual to Renaissance Art," *Renaissance Drama*, n.s. 6 (1973): 179, 187-89; Othón Arroniz, *La influencia italiana en el nacimiento de la comedia española* (Madrid: Gredos, 1969), pp. 310-11.

14. Francisco Vindel, *El arte tipográfico en España durante el siglo XV* (Madrid: Dirección General de Relaciones Culturales, 1951), 7: xxv-xxvi, 291-96.

15. For further study see Stephen Gilman, *The Art of "La Celestina"* (Madison: Univ. of Wisconsin Press, 1956); Alan D. Deyermond, *The Petrarchan Sources of "La Celestina"* (Oxford: Oxford Univ. Press, 1961); Marcel Bataillon, *La Célestina selon Fernando de Rojas* (Paris: Didier, 1961); Dorothy C. Clarke, *Allegory, Decalogue and Deadly Sins in "La Celestina"* (Berkeley: Univ. of California Press, 1968); Ciriaco Morón Arroyo, *Sentido y forma de "La Celestina"* (Madrid: Ediciones Cátedra, 1974); and Mack Singleton, "Morality and Tragedy in *Celestina*," *Studies in Honor of Lloyd A. Kasten* (Madison: Hispanic Seminary of Medieval Studies, 1975), pp. 249-59.

16. Richard W. Tyler, "Celestina in the *Comedia*," *Celestinesca* 5 (1981): 13-21.

17. Although López Morales (*Tradición y creación*, 42-140) attempted to deny all previous theories, claiming that Spanish drama evolved exclusively from church ritual, and heralded Juan del Encina as the "founder" of drama in Spain, he later (in "Nuevo examen del teatro medieval") recognized the rich theatrical background of many centuries out of which Spanish drama grew. For additional study on Encina, see two articles by Charlotte Stern: "Juan del Encina's Carnival Eclogues and the Spanish Drama of the Renaissance," *Renaissance Drama* 8 (1965): 181-95; and "Early Spanish Drama," pp. 189-91; Henry W. Sullivan, *Juan del Encina* (Boston: Twayne, 1976); and J. Richard Andrews, *Juan del Encina: Prometheus in Search of Prestige*, University of California Publications in Modern Philology, no. 53 (1959).

18. For the use of the *sayagués* dialect, see John Lihani, *El lenguaje de Lucas Fernández* (Bogota: Instituto Caro y Cuervo, 1973); and Paul Teyssier, *La langue de Gil Vicente* (Paris: Klinksieck, 1959).

19. Sturgis E. Leavitt, *An Introduction to Golden Age Drama in Spain* (Madrid: Castalia, 1971), p. 15. For the style in Lucas Fernández's works see two books by John Lihani: *El lenguaje de Lucas Fernández*, and *Lucas Fernández* (New York: Twayne, 1973); A. Hermenegildo, *Renacimiento, teatro y sociedad: vida y obra de Lucas Fernández* (Madrid: Cincel, 1975); and Anthony Van Beysterveldt, "Estudio comparativo del teatro profano

de Lucas Fernández y el de Juan del Encina," *Revista Canadiense de Estudios Hispánicos* 3 (1979): 161-82.

20. For interpretations of his works see Joseph E. Gillet, *Torres Naharro and the Spanish Drama of the Sixteenth Century* (Madrid: Imprenta Vda. e hijos Jaime Ratés, 1930); Stern, "Early Spanish Drama," pp. 194-98; Robert L. Hathaway, *Love in the Early Spanish Theatre* (Madrid: Plaza Mayor, 1975), pp. 101-20; Stanislav Zimic, *El pensamiento humanístico y satírico de Torres Naharro*, 2 vols. (Santander: Sociedad Menéndez Pelayo, 1978); and John Lihani, *Bartolomé de Torres Naharro* (Boston: Twayne, 1979).

21. For Gil Vicente's style see Hope Hamilton Faria, *The Farces of Gil Vicente: A Study in the Stylistics of Satire* (Madrid: Playor, 1976); Stephen Reckert, *Gil Vicente, espíritu y letra* (Madrid: Gredos, 1977); Thomas R. Hart, "Gil Vicente's *Auto de la sibila Casandra*," *Hispanic Review* 26 (1958): 35-51; Leo Spitzer, "The Artistic Unity of Gil Vicente's *Auto de sibila Casandra*," *Hispanic Review* 27 (1959): 56-77; Aubrey F.G. Bell, *Gil Vicente* (Oxford: Clarendon Press, 1927); and Jack H. Parker, *Gil Vicente* (New York: Twayne, 1967).

22. See José M. Regueiro, "Juan de Timoneda y la tradición dramática española," Ph.D. diss., Univ. of Pennsylvania, 1972; and John J. Reynolds, *Juan de Timoneda* (Boston: Twayne, 1975).

23. See Bruce W. Wardropper, "The Search for a Dramatic Formula for the *auto sacramental*," *PMLA* 65 (1950): 1196-1211.

24. A unique collection of ninety-six of these one-act plays, *Códice de autos viejos*, has been preserved in the Biblioteca Nacional; it was edited by Léo Rouanet under the title *Colección de autos, farsas y coloquios del siglo XVI*, and was published in four volumes by the Biblioteca Hispánica in 1901. All but three of these plays are in verse form, and it appears that they were intended for performance in the church. Many of them were written anonymously.

25. Crawford, *Spanish Drama before Lope*, p. 141.

26. Ibid., pp. 155-58. Also see John J. Reynolds, *Juan de Timoneda* (Boston: Twayne, 1975); and Marcel Bataillon, "Essai d'explication de l'auto sacramental," *Bulletin Hispanique* 42 (1940): 193-212.

27. See Marcelino Menéndez y Pelayo, "El maestro Fernán Pérez de Oliva," in *Obras completas de Marcelino Menéndez y Pelayo*, ed. Enrique Sánchez Reyes (Santander: Aldus, 1941), 2: 37-58; and C. George Peale, "The Tragedies of *el Maestro* Fernán Pérez de Oliva," *Kentucky Romance Quarterly* 22 (1975): 415-28.

28. John G. Weiger, *Cristóbal Virués* (Boston: Twayne, 1978), pp. 27-31. See also Weiger, *The Valencian Dramatists of Spain's Golden Age* (Boston: Twayne, 1976), Chapt. 3; and his *Hacia la comedia: De los valencianos a Lope* (Madrid: Cupsa, 1978).

29. See Cecilia Vennard Sargent, *A Study of the Dramatic Works of Cristóbal de Virués* (New York: Hispanic Institute, 1930).

30. Weiger, *Cristóbal Virués*, pp. 83-85.

31. Ibid., pp. 87-88.

32. See Weiger, *Valencian Dramatists*, pp. 21-30; and Eduardo Juliá Martínez, *Poetas dramáticos valencianos* (Madrid: Tip. de la *Revista de Archivos, Bibliotecas y Museos*, 1929), 1: i-cxxxv, 1-24.

33. For more detailed study on Cueva see Marcel Bataillon, "Simples réflexions sur Juan de la Cueva," *Bulletin Hispanique* 37 (1935): 329-36; Edwin S. Morby, "The Influence of Senecan Tragedy in the Plays of Juan de la Cueva," *Studies in Philology* 34 (1937): 383-91; N.D. Shergold, "Juan de la Cueva and the Early Theaters of Seville," *Bulletin of Hispanic Studies* 32 (1955): 1-7; Bruce W. Wardropper, "Juan de la Cueva y el drama histórico," *Nueva Revista de Filología Hispánica* 9 (1955): 149-56; Anthony

Watson, *Juan de la Cueva and the Portuguese Succession* (London: Támesis, 1971); and
Richard F. Glenn, *Juan de la Cueva* (New York: Twayne, 1973).

34. Juan de la Cueva, *El infamador, Los siete Infantes de Lara y El exemplar poético*,
ed. Francisco A. de Icaza (Madrid: Espasa-Calpe, 1924), pp. 26-29.

35. See Hugo A. Rennert, *"Marco Antonio y Cleopatra*: A Tragedy by Diego López
de Castro," *Revue Hispanique* 19 (1908): 184-86.

36. Crawford, *Spanish Drama before Lope*, pp. 176-78; Alfredo Hermenegildo, *Los
trágicos españoles del siglo XVI* (Madrid: Fundación Universitaria Española, 1961), pp.
334-70.

37. Joaquín Casalduero, *Sentido y forma del teatro de Cervantes* (Madrid: Gredos,
1966), pp. 20-21. See also Manuel Durán, *Cervantes* (Boston: Twayne, 1974); Frederick
A. de Armas, "Classical Tragedy and Cervantes' *La Numancia*," *Neophilologus* 58 (1974):
34-40; Edward H. Friedman, *"La Numancia* within Structural Patterns of Sixteenth-
Century Spanish Tragedy," *Neophilologus* 61 (1977): 74-89; and Cesáreo Bandera, *Mimesis
conflictiva: ficción literaria y violencia en Cervantes y Calderón* (Madrid: Gredos, 1975).

38. Miguel de Cervantes, *Obras completas*, ed. Angel Valbuena Prat (Madrid: Aguilar,
1970), pp. 16-18.

39. For a useful comparison of these plays see Edward H. Friedman, "Double Vision:
Self and Society in *El laberinto de amor* and *La entretenida*," *Cervantes and the
Renaissance*, ed. Michael D. McGaha (Easton, Pa.: Juan de la Cuesta, 1980), pp. 157-66.

40. See Casalduero, *Sentido y forma*, pp. 21-30.

41. Although they come from the same root, this term is not to be confused with the
wagons called *entremeses* in fourteenth-century Valencia when the Corpus Christi Day
procession first took place. The term "entremés" is more widely applied to a one-act
farcical play, which was often presented between the acts of a longer play. The term probably derived from the French word "entremets" (between the courses). The use of *entremeses* in Spanish tradition began with Rueda's *pasos* and was cultivated by Cervantes,
Quiñones de Benavente, Calderón, and others.

42. Crawford, *Spanish Drama before Lope*, pp. 186-87; Hermenegildo, *Los trágicos
españoles*, pp. 391-98.

43. Eduardo Juliá Martínez, "Renacimiento y barroco," *Historia general de las literaturas
hispánicas*, ed. Guillermo Díaz-Plaja (Barcelona: Barna, 1953), 3: 165-66.

44. An important source on the actors and conditions in sixteenth-century Spanish
theater is Agustín de Rojas Villandrando, *El viaje entretenido* (1603), ed. Jean-Pierre
Ressot (Madrid: Castalia, 1972). Like Lope de Rueda, Rojas Villandrando was an actor,
director, and playwright.

45. Richard F. Glenn, *Juan de la Cueva* (New York: Twayne, 1973), pp. 45-46; N.D.
Shergold, *A History of the Spanish Stage from Medieval Times until the End of the Seventeenth Century* (Oxford: Clarendon Press, 1967), pp. 191-96.

46. Shergold, *History of the Spanish Stage*, pp. 177-79; Othón Arroniz, *Teatros y
escenarios del Siglo de Oro* (Madrid: Gredos, 1977), pp. 22-23.

47. For the historical development of the Spanish stage during the first half of the
Golden Age, see Hugo A. Rennert in *The Spanish Stage in the Time of Lope de Vega*
(New York: Hispanic Society of America, 1909), pp. 62-73.

48. John J. Allen, *El Corral del Príncipe (1583-1744)* (Gainesville: Univ. Presses of
Florida, 1983); and his article, "Toward a Conjectural Model of the *Corral del Príncipe*,"
in *Studies in Honor of John Esten Keller*, ed. Joseph R. Jones (Newark: Juan de la Cuesta,
1980), pp. 255-71. For further information on theatrical life during the Spanish Golden
Age, see José Deleito y Piñuela, *También se divierte el pueblo* (Madrid: Espasa-Calpe,
1966), pp. 198-226, 269-70; José Antonio Maravall, *Teatro y literatura en la sociedad*

barroca (Madrid: Seminarios y Ediciones, 1972); Juan M. Rozas, *El Siglo de Oro: El teatro en tiempos de Lope de Vega* (Madrid: UNED, 1976); and José María Díez Borque, *Sociedad y teatro en la España de Lope de Vega* (Barcelona: Bosch Casa, 1978).

49. Emilio Cotarelo y Mori, *Bibliografía de las controversias sobre la licitud del teatro en España* (Madrid: Tip. de la *Revista de Archivos, Bibliotecas y Museos*, 1904), pp. 354, 356. Also see Rennert, *Spanish Stage*, pp. 73-211, 247; and Ronald E. Surtz, *The Birth of a Theater: Dramatic Convention in the Spanish Theater from Juan del Encina to Lope de Vega* (Madrid: Castalia, 1979).

50. See Hugo A. Rennert, "Spanish Actors and Actresses between 1560 and 1680," *Revue Hispanique* 16 (1907): 334-538.

II. LOPE DE VEGA AND THE FORMATION OF THE *COMEDIA*

1. According to Crawford (*Spanish Drama before Lope*, p. 188) and Bataillon ("Simples réflexions sur Juan de la Cueva," p. 335), the end of the first period of Spanish dramatic history came in 1587, when Lope de Vega had already written five plays. Rennert states that the new period started two years earlier in about 1585, when Lope began to write for the stage ("Spanish Actors and Actresses," p. 334).

2. Translated from Ricardo de Turia's *Apologético de las comedias españolas* (1616), as cited in Juliá Martínez, *Poetas dramáticos valencianos*, 1: 623.

3. Pinciano, outstanding among Spanish Aristotelian commentators, insisted on the classical conception of dramatic art but failed to distinguish between Aristotle's explanation of catharsis and Horace's principle that art should please. See Margaret Wilson, *Spanish Drama of the Golden Age* (Oxford: Pergamon Press, 1969), pp. 27-28.

4. Concerning these critics of Lope de Vega, see Joaquín de Entrambasaguas, "Una guerra literaria del Siglo de Oro: Lope de Vega y los preceptistas aristotélicos," *Estudios sobre Lope de Vega* (Madrid: C.S.I.C., 1932), pp. 63-580.

5. See Edwin S. Morby, "Some Observations on *tragedia* and *tragicomedia* in Lope," *Hispanic Review* 11 (1943): 185-209; Raymond R. MacCurdy, "The Problem of Spanish Golden Age Tragedy," *South Atlantic Bulletin* 38 (1973): 3-14; Arnold G. Reichenberger, "Thoughts about Tragedy in the Spanish Theater of the Golden Age," *Hispanófila Especial* 1 (1974): 37-44; and Gail Bradbury, "Tragedy and Tragicomedy in the Theatre of Lope de Vega," *Bulletin of Hispanic Studies* 58 (1981): 103-11.

6. The three dramatic unites were actually first defined in the sixteenth century. The first among modern critics to mention the unity of time was Giraldi Cinthio in 1543; Bernardo Segni fixed the twenty-four-hour rule in 1549. After the unity of action was more clearly defined, the limitation of place was advocated by Vicenzo Maggi in 1550. Lodovico Castelvetro was the first to insist on the use of all three unities in 1570, and he called them inviolable dramatic rules. See Joel Elias Spingarn, *A History of Literary Criticism in the Renaissance*, 2nd ed. (New York: Columbia Univ. Press, 1908), pp. 60-101; and Anthony J. Cascardi, "Lope de Vega, Juan de la Cueva, Giraldi Cinthio, and Spanish Poetics," *Revista Hispánica Moderna* 39 (1976-77): 150-55.

7. Marcelino Menéndez y Pelayo, *Calderón y su teatro* (Madrid: Tip. de la *Revista de Archivos, Bibliotecas y Museos*, 1910), pp. 23-24. Also see Margarete Newels, *Los géneros dramáticos en las poéticas del Siglo de Oro: Investigación preliminar al estudio de la teoría dramática en el Siglo de Oro* (London: Támesis, 1974); and Federico Sánchez Escribano and Alberto Porqueras Mayo, *Preceptiva dramática española del Renacimiento y el Barroco* (Madrid: Gredos, 1965).

8. This short treatise was first published by Alonso Pérez in Lope's *Rimas humanas*, Parte II (Madrid: Imprenta del Reino, 1634); it was reprinted in *Obras sueltas de Lope*

de Vega, in *BAE* 33 (Madrid: Rivadeneyra, 1856): 230-32; and by Henry John Chaytor in *Dramatic Theory in Spain* (Cambridge: Cambridge Univ. Press, 1925), pp. 14-29. Also see Ramón Menéndez Pidal, "Lope de Vega: *El arte nuevo y la nueva biografía*," *Revista de Filología Española* 22 (1935): 337-98.

9. See Sylvanus Griswold Morley, *Studies in Spanish Dramatic Versification of the Siglo de Oro*, Univ. of California Publications, no. 7 (1918): 131-73; Diego Marín, *Poesía española* (New York: Las Americas, 1962), pp. 9-27; and Tomás Navarro Tomás, *Métrica española* (Syracuse: Syracuse Univ. Press, 1956).

10. For discussions on the various character-types in the *comedia*, see Ernest Hall Templin, "The Mother in the *comedia* of Lope," *Hispanic Review* 3 (1935): 219-44; Bonnie B. Busse, "The *gracioso* in the Spanish Golden Age Dramas," M.A. thesis, Univ. of Nebraska, 1950; Charles D. Ley, *El gracioso en el teatro de la Península: Siglos XVI-XVII* (Madrid: *Revista de Occidente*, 1954); Edwin J. Webber, "On the Ancestry of the *Gracioso*," *Renaissance Drama* 5 (1974): 171-90; F. William Forbes, "The *gracioso*: Toward a Functional Re-Evaluation," *Hispania* 61 (1978): 78-83; Barbara Kinter, *Die Figur des Gracioso im spanischen Theater des 17. Jahrhunderts* (Munich: Fink, 1978); Oleh Mazur, "The Wild Man in the Spanish Renaissance and Golden Age Theatre," Ph.D. diss., Univ. of Pennsylvania, 1966; and José A. Madrigal, "La función del hombre salvaje en el teatro de Lope, Tirso y Calderón," Ph.D. diss. Univ. of Kentucky, 1973.

11. See John Lihani, "La técnica de racapitulación auténtica en el teatro del siglo XVI," in *Actas del I Congreso Internacional sobre Lope de Vega*, ed. Manual Criado de Val (Madrid: EDI-6, 1981), pp. 303-9; and Diego Marín, *La intriga secundaria en el teatro de Lope de Vega* (Mexico: Andrea, 1958).

12. Two critics who have pointed to the reflection of seventeenth-century life in Lope's plays are Gerald E. Wade, "Spain's Golden Age Culture and the *Comedia*," *Hispania* 61 (1978): 832-50; and José Deleito y Piñuela, *Sólo Madrid es Corte* (Madrid: Espasa-Calpe, 1968). Cyril A. Jones has observed that since the seventeenth-century moralists occasionally called the *comedia* immoral, its concept of life was not always in accordance with the ethics of that time; however, he agreed that this popular means of entertainment mirrored the social rules and system of honor of its time. See his "Honor in the Spanish Golden Age Drama," *Bulletin of Hispanic Studies*, 25 (1958): 199-210.

13. Charles A. Aubrun, "Las mil y ochocientas comedias de Lope," *Actas del I Congreso Internacional sobre Lope de Vega*, ed. Manuel Criado de Val (Madrid: EDI-6, 1981), pp. 473-77.

14. Silvanus Griswold Morley and Courtney Bruerton, *The Chronology of Lope de Vega's Comedias* (New York: MLA, 1940; rev. ed. by Morley, New York: Kraus, 1966).

15. The dates given in parentheses for the composition of this and subsequent plays are taken from Morley's 1968 revised Spanish edition.

16. The autograph manuscript of *Fuenteovejuna* has been lost; nevertheless, its authorship has never been disputed, since Lope de Vega mentions it in the second edition of *El peregrino en su patria* (*The Pilgrim in His Homeland*). It was printed in Parte XII of Lope's edition in 1619. For study of this play see Joaquín Casalduero, "*Fuenteovejuna*," *Revista de Filología Hispánica* 5 (1943): 21-44; Geoffrey W. Ribbans, "The Meaning and Structure of Lope's *Fuenteovejuna*," *Bulletin of Hispanic Studies* 31 (1954): 150-70; Leo Spitzer, "A Central Theme and Its Structural Equivalent in Lope's *Fuenteovejuna*," *Hispanic Review* 33 (1955): 274-92; J.B. Hall, "Theme and Structure in Lope's *Fuenteovejuna*," *Forum for Modern Language Studies* 10 (1974): 57-66; and Javier Herrero, "The New Monarchy: Structural Reinterpretation of *Fuenteovejuna*," *Revista Hispánica Moderna* 36 (1970-71): 173-85.

17. For sources and levels within the structure of *Fuenteovejuna*, see Claude E. Anibal,

"The Historical Elements of Lope de Vega's *Fuenteovejuna*," *PMLA* 49 (1934): 657-718; and William C. McCrary, "*Fuenteovejuna*: Its Platonic Vision and Execution," *Studies in Philology* 58 (1961): 179-92.

18. Kathleen Gouldson, "The Spanish Peasant in the Drama of Lope de Vega," *Bulletin of Spanish Studies* 19, nos. 73-74 (1942): 13.

19. See José A Madrigal, "*Fuenteovejuna* y los conceptos de metateatro y psicodrama: un ensayo sobre la formación de la conciencia en al protagonista," *Bulletin of the Comediantes* 31 (1979): 15-23.

20. See Angel J. Valbuena Briones, "Una perspectiva semiótica: *Fuente Ovejuna* de Lope de Vega," *Arbor* 412 (1980): 453-64.

21. Larson, *The Honor Plays of Lope de Vega* (Cambridge: Harvard Univ. Press, 1977), pp. 68-70.

22. For further study of this play, see Edward M. Wilson, "Images et structure dans *Peribáñez*," *Bulletin Hispanique* 51 (1949): 125-59; Loren L. Zeller, "The Dramatic Function of Comic Relief in Lope de Vega's 'Tragicomedia,' *Peribáñez*," *Philological Quarterly* 57 (1978): 337-57; and Nöel Salomon, *Recherches sur le thème paysan dans la "Comedia" au temps de Lope de Vega* (Bordeaux: Feretet fils, 1965).

23. Silvanus Griswold Morley, in his article "The Use of Verse-Forms by Tirso de Molina," *Bulletin Hispanique* 7 (1905): 387-408, strongly affirms that Tirso was not the author of *El rey don Pedro en Madrid*.

24. For a historical account of the life of Peter the Cruel, see Prosper Mérimée, *Histoire de Don Pèdre Ier, roi de Castille* (Paris: Charpentier, 1848); Frances Exum, "Lope's King Pedro: The Divine Right of Resistance," *Hispania* 57 (1974): 428-33; and William C. McCrary, "Theater and History: El rey don Pedro en Madrid," *Crítica Hispánica* 1 (1979): 145-67.

25. The authorship of *La Estrella* has been a topic of considerable research and debate for more than half a century. This question may never be resolved. The group of critics claiming that Lope wrote the play suggest that the two earliest known printed texts, which are not identical, may have been derived independently from an earlier printed text no longer extant. One text having 3,029 lines and entitled *La Estrella de Sevilla. Comedia famosa de Lope. Representóla Avendaño*, had been detached from a volume (folios 99-120) of various plays; its only copy was preserved in the library of Raymond Foulché-Delbosc in Paris. The other, a single edition of 2,503 lines, appears to have been printed in the mid-seventeenth century from a manuscript that belonged to a theatrical company. The other group of critics ascribe the play to a lesser known southern Spanish playwright, possibly Andrés de Claramonte. See Raymond Foulché-Delbosc, "The Author of *La Estrella de Sevilla*," *Revue Hispanique* 48 (1920): 497-678; Aubrey Bell, "The Author of *La Estrella de Sevilla*," *Revue Hispanique* 59 (1923): 296-300; idem, "The Authorship of *La Estrella de Sevilla*," *Modern Language Review* 26 (1931): 97-98; Sturgis E. Leavitt, *La Estrella de Sevilla and Claramonte* (Cambridge: Harvard Univ. Press, 1931); and Frederick A. de Armas, "The Apples of Colchis: Key to an interpretation of *La Estrella de Sevilla*," *Forum for Modern Languages Studies* 15 (1979): 1-13.

26. See two works by Américo Castro: "Algunas observaciones acerca del honor en los siglos XVI y XVII," *Revista de Filología Española* 3 (1916): 1-50; and *De la edad conflictiva* (Madrid: Taurus, 1961). For further studies on honor, see Donald Stuart, "Honor in the Spanish Drama," *Romanic Review* 1 (1910): 247-58; Jones, "Honor in the Spanish Golden Age Drama"; Peter Podol, "Non-Conventional Treatment of the Honor Theme in the Theater of the Golden Age," *Revista de Estudios Hispánicos* 7 (1973): 447-67; and José A. Madrigal, *Bibliografía sobre el pundonor: Teatro del Siglo de Oro* (Miami: Ediciones Universal, 1977). For fuller discussion of Spanish honor, see chapter 4.

27. This play, which was published in Parte XXVII, *extravagante* (Barcelona, 1633), and the following play, *El alcalde de Zalamea*, which appeared as a single *suelta* (Copias MS, Parma), are attributed to Lope. Morley and Bruerton (*Chronology*, pp. 509, 411) give no dates for their composition.

28. The first volume of Bandellos' stories was published in Lucca in 1554 and was translated into Spanish in 1603 under the title *Historia de la Marquesa de la Ferrera*. This particular *novella* is the forty-fourth in the first volume.

29. Modern interpretations of this most Calderonian of Lope's plays are found in two articles by Gerald E. Wade: "Lope de Vega's *El castigo sin venganza*: Its Composition and Presentation," *Kentucky Romance Quarterly* 23 (1976): 357-64; and "Spain's Golden Age Culture." See also Davis M. Gitlitz, "Ironía e imágenes en *El castigo sin venganza*," *Revista de Estudios Hispánicos* 14 (1980): 19-41; and William C. McCrary, "The *Duque* and the *Comedia*: Drama and Imitation in Lope's *Castigo sin venganza*," *Bulletin of Hispanic Philology* 2 (1978): 203-22.

30. Jerome A. Moore, *The Romancero in the Chronicle-Legend Plays of Lope de Vega* (Philadelphia: Univ. of Pennsylvania Press, 1940), p. 126.

31. See William C. McCrary, *The Goldfinch and the Hawk: A Study of Lope de Vega's Tragedy* (Chapel Hill: Univ. of North Carolina Studies, 1966); C. Alan Soons, "Towards an Interpretation of *El caballero de Olmedo*," *Romanische Forschungen* 73 (1961): 160-68; Albert S. Gérard, "Baroque Unity and the Dualities of *El caballero de Olmedo*," *Romantic Review* 56 (1965): 92-106; and Thomas Austin O'Connor, "The Knight of Olmedo and Oedipus: Perspectives on a Spanish Tragedy," *Hispanic Review* 48 (1980): 391-413.

32. The dramatist's historical source for this play most likely was Pedro Mexía's *Historia imperial y cesarea*, 1547 (rpt. Madrid: M. Sánchez, Acosta de G. de León, 1655), pp. 515-19.

33. Lope may have used more historical sources than Mexía's *Historia* for this play. The entire plot with all its details can be found in the third volume of Antonious Bonfinius's *Rerum Vngaricarum Decades* (Basilea: Ex Officina Oporiniana, 1568, pp. 446-536), a history of Hungary that was commissioned by King Mathias Corvin and completed in 1495. See Maria Strzalkowa, "La question des sources de la tragicomédia de Lope de Vega *El rey sin reino*," *Archivum neophilologicum* (Cracow: Akademia Umiejetnośći), 3, 2 (1950): 1-26.

34. See Marcelino Menéndez y Pelayo, ed., *Obras de Lope de Vega*, Real Academia Española (Madrid: Rivadeneyra, 1890-1913), vol. 13; rpt. in BAE 158 (Madrid: Atlas, 1965): 325.

35. Although Barrezo Barrezi appears as the compiler and publisher of this account— *Relacione della segnalata e come miracolosa conquista del paterno imperio, consegvita del serenissimo Giovine Demetrio, Gran Duca de Moscovia* (Venice, 1605)—Antonio Possevino was the real author. This work was translated into Spanish by Juan Mosquera and published in Villadolid by Andrés de Merchán in 1606. See Gertrud V. Poehl, "La fuente de *El gran duque de Moscovia* de Lope de Vega," *Revista de Filología Española* 19 (1932): 47-48.

36. According to Marcel Bataillon, this play is a synthesis of a Spanish short story which was derived from an earlier French one, *Le charbonnier et le roy*, and a Spanish legend about a Juan Labrador. See Bataillon's *"El villano en su rincón," Bulletin Hispanic* 51 (1949): 5-38; and 52 (1950): 397. Other sources for this play are discussed in Marcel Bataillon, *Varia lección de clásicos españoles* (Madrid: Gredos, 1964), pp. 329-74; Joaquín Casalduero, "Sentido y forma de *El villano en su rincón*," *Revista de la Universidad de Madrid* 11 (1962): 547-64; and John E. Varey, "Towards an Interpretation of Lope de Vega's *El villano en su rincón*," *Studies in Spanish Literature of the Golden*

Age, ed. Roy O. Jones (London: Támesis, 1973), pp. 315-37.

37. Alva V. Ebersole, "Metateatro, Lope y *Argel fingido y renegado de amor,*" *Perspectivas de la comedia,* vol. 2 (Valencia: Soler, 1979): 151-57.

38. It is thought to be the forty-fifth novel in Bandello's first volume (see note 28). Comments on this play are found in *El perro del hortelano y El castigo sin venganza de Lope de Vega,* ed. A. David Kossoff (Madrid: Castalia, 1970), pp. 28-50; and Bruce W. Wardropper's "Comic Illusion: Lope de Vega's *El perro del hortelano,*" *Kentucky Romance Quarterly* 14 (1967): 101-11.

39. For Lope's mythological plays see Marcelino Menéndez y Pelayo, *Estudios sobre el teatro de Lope de Vega,* ed. Adolfo Bonilla y San Martín, vol. 2 (Madrid: Victoriano Suárez, 1921): 142-271.

40. The particular story is from Canto I: vv. 416-557.

41. Regarding Lope's hagiographic plays and those of other playwrights, see Gordon Heyward Sumner, "Una bibliografía anotada de las comedias de santos del siglo diez y siete," Ph.D. diss., Florida State Univ., 1979.

42. For a study on this topic see Susan L. Fischer, "Psychological and Esthetic Implications in Role-Change in Selected Plays of Calderón," Ph.D. diss., Duke Univ., 1973.

43. See Michael D. McGaha, "Lope's Christian Irony: The Structure of *La fianza satisfecha,*" *Bulletin of the Comediantes* 30 (1978): 123-31.

44. For Lope's *autos* see Osvaldo A. Estenoz, "Retórica en los autos sacramentales de Lope de Vega," Ph.D. diss., State Univ. of New York at Buffalo, 1977; T. Maza Solano, "El auto sacramental *La Maya,* de Lope de Vega, y las fiestas populares del mismo nombre en la Montaña," *Boletín de la Biblioteca Menéndez y Pelayo* 17 (1935): 369-87; Arturo M. Cayuela, "Los autos sacramentales de Lope, reflejo de la cultura religiosa del poeta y de su tiempo," *Razón y Fe* 108 (1935): 168-90, 330-49; and J.M. Aicardo, "Autos sacramentales de Lope de Vega," *Razón y Fe* 19-23 (1907-8).

III. THE PROLIFERATION OF THE *COMEDIA*

1. See Marcelino Menéndez y Pelayo, *Antología de poetas hispano-americanos,* Real Academia Española (Madrid: Rivadeneyra, 1903), 1: 49; and John G. Weiger, *The Valencian Dramatists of Spain's Golden Age* (Boston: Twayne, 1976). Also see Angel Valbuena Prat, *Historia de la literatura española* (Barcelona: Gustavo Gili, 1964), 2: 368.

2. See Weiger, *Valencian Dramatists,* pp. 50-109; Emilio Pujol, *Tárrega: ensayo biográfico* (Valencia, 1978).

3. Rinaldo Froldi, *Lope de Vega y la formación de la comedia* (Salamanca: Anaya, 1968), pp. 10, 133; and William E. Wilson, *Guillén de Castro* (New York: Twayne, 1973), pp. 11-16.

4. These plays are discussed in Wilson, *Guillén de Castro,* pp. 62-99; and by Luciano García Lorenzo in *El teatro de Guillén de Castro* (Barcelona: Planeta, 1976).

5. For further study see Alva V. Ebersole, "La originalidad de *Los malcasados de Valencia,*" *Hispania* 55 (1972): 456-62.

6. In this collection of works, Tirso includes a rebuttal of the critics who championed the sanctity of the classical unities. Claiming that the new *comedia* deserves the place it occupies in Spain, he mentions certain advantages it has over the ancient plays. He points out the inconvenience the playwright experiences, for example, if he must observe the unity of time. "How," he asks, "could a discreet young man fall in love with a prudent young lady, solicit her, court her, and marry her in the space of twenty-four hours? His experiences of jealousy, desperation, and hope—affections without which true love has no meaning—could not possibly be conveyed between the morning and night of

the same day and in the same place." (Freely translated from Tirso de Molina, *Cigarrales de Toledo* [Madrid: Espasa-Calpe, 1968], pp. 80-83.)

7. There was possibly even an earlier version, now lost, before the two known ones, but the latest play which has survived was first published in *Doze comedias nuevas de Lope de Vega, y otros autores: Segunda parte . . .* (Barcelona: Jerónimo Margarit, 1630). See Albert E. Sloman, "The Two Versions of *El burlador de Sevilla*," *Bulletin of Hispanic Studies* 42 (1965): 18-33. For recent speculation that the play may have been written by Andrés de Claramonte, see Alfredo Rodríguez López-Vázquez, *Andrés de Claramonte: Autor de "El burlador de Sevilla"* (La Coruña: Gráficas Coruñesas, 1982).

8. Cf. Daniel Rodgers, "Fearful Symmetry: The Ending of *El burlador de Sevilla*," *Bulletin of Hispanic Studies* 41 (1964): 141-59.

9. For studies on this topic, see Oscar Mandel, *The Theatre of Don Juan* (Lincoln: Univ. of Nebraska Press, 1963), pp. 3-21; and Armand E. Singer, "Don Juan's Women in *El burlador de Sevilla*," *Bulletin of the Comediantes* 33 (1981): 67-71.

10. Among many studies on Don Juan, see Charles V. Aubrun, "Le Don Juan de Tirso de Molina," *Bulletin Hispanique* 59 (1957): 26-61; Benedetto Croce, "El Burlador de Sevilla," *Quaderni della Critica* 6 (1946): 70-76; Georges Gendarme de Bévotte, *La Légende de Don Juan*, 2 vols. (Paris: Hachette, 1911); Ruth Lundelius, "Tirso's View of Women in *El Burlador de Sevilla*," *Bulletin of the Comediantes* 27 (1975): 5-14; Gregorio de Marañón, *Biología de Don Juan* (Mexico City: *El Universal Ilustrado*, 1924); Dorothy Epplen Mackay, *The Double Invitation in the Legend of Don Juan* (Stanford: Stanford Univ. Press, 1943); Andrés Révész, *El anti-Tenorio* (Madrid: A. Aguado, 1944); Victor Said Armesto, *La Leyenda de Don Juan* (Madrid: Sucs. de Hernando, 1908); Armand E. Singer, *The Don Juan Theme, Versions, and Criticism* (Morgantown: West Virginia Univ. Press, 1965); Gerald E. Wade's introduction to his edition of *El burlador de Sevilla* (New York: Scribner's, 1968); John E. Varey, "Social Criticism in *El burlador de Sevilla*," *Theatre Research International* 2 (1977): 197-221; Leo Weinstein, *The Metamorphoses of Don Juan* (Stanford: Stanford Univ. Press, 1959); Jean Rousset, *Le Mythe de Don Juan* (Paris: Arman Colin, 1978); and Alva V. Ebersole, *Disquisiciones sobre "El burlador de Sevilla"* (Salamanca: Almar, 1980).

11. For these viewpoints see Gerald E. Wade, "The Character of Tirso's *El burlador de Sevilla*: A Psychoanalytical Study," *Bulletin of the Comediantes* 31 (1979): 33-42; and Ion T. Agheana and Henry Sullivan, "The Unholy Martyr: Don Juan's Misuse of Intelligence," *Romanische Forschungen* 81 (1969): 311-25.

12. The dates of this and subsequently mentioned plays by Tirso have been taken from Blanca de los Ríos's editions of his plays; and from Ruth L. Kennedy, "Studies for the Chronology of Tirso's Theater," *Hispanic Review* 11 (1943): 17-46.

13. Various more distant sources have been traced to Oriental folkloric tales, to a Spanish folk tale (*Del hermitaño y el carnicero* [The Hermit and the Butcher], the third story in Don Juan Manuel's *El conde Lucanor*), and to an account of the life of San Pafnucio. Also see Ramón Menéndez Pidal, "*El condenado por desconfiado* de Tirso de Molina," *Estudios literarios*, 3rd ed. (Buenos Aires: Espasa-Calpe, 1942), pp. 11-71.

14. For more detailed interpretations of this play see Alexander A. Parker, "Santos y bandidos en el teatro español del Siglo de Oro," *Arbor* 13 (1949): 395-416; Karl Vossler, "Alrededor de *El condenado por desconfiado*," *Revista Cubana* 14 (1940): 19-37; Julio Cejador y Frauca, "*El condenado por desconfiado*," *Revue Hispanique* 57 (1923), 127-59; and Robert Ter Horst, "The Sacred and the Profane in the Plays of Tirso de Molina: A Preliminary Sketch for Ruth Lee Kennedy," *Bulletin of the Comediantes* 32 (1980): 99-107.

15. See Nancy Lou Kennington, "A Structural Analysis of the Extant Trilogies of Tirso de Molina," Ph.D. diss., Univ. of North Carolina, 1966.

16. The biblical source for this play is I Kings 16:29 to II Kings 9:20. For further study, see Carolyn F. Smith, "Dialectics of Tragicomedy in Tirso's *La mujer que manda en casa*," *Perspectivas de la comedia*, ed. Alva V. Ebersole (Valencia: Soler, 1978), pp. 111-18.

17. Frederick H. Fornoff, *Tirso's Christmas Tragedy, "La vida y muerte de Herodes:"* *A Study of Ritual Form in Drama* (Chapel Hill: Univ. of North Carolina Dept. of Romance Languages, 1977).

18. See Everett W. Hesse, "The Incest Motif in Tirso's *La venganza de Tamar*," *Hispania* 47 (1964): 268-76.

19. See Ruth Lee Kennedy, "*La prudencia en la mujer* and the Ambient That Brought It Forth," *PMLA* 63 (1948): 1131-90.

20. For more discussion of this play see Sandra L. Brown, "The Hero's Tragic Fall in *La adversa fortuna de don Alvaro de Luna*," *Hispanófila* 1 (1974): 63-69; and two works by Raymond R. MacCurdy: "Tragic *Hamartia* in *La próspera y adversa fortuna de don Alvaro de Luna*," *Hispania* 47 (1964): 82-90; and *Tragic Fall: Don Alvaro de Luna and Other Favorites in Spanish Golden Age Drama*, North Carolina Studies in Romance Languages and Literatures (Chapel Hill, 1978).

21. For these plays and their characters, see Angela B. Dellepiane de Martino, "Ficción e historia en la *Trilogía de los Pizarros* de Tirso," *Filología* 4 (1952-53): 49-168; Mazur, "Wild Man"; and Madrigal,"La función del hombre salvaje" (see chapt. 2, note 10, above).

22. See Helmut Hatzfelt, "The Styletype of Tirso de Molina's *Don Gil de las calzas verdes*: The Problem of the Moderate Baroque," *Neohelicon* 7 (1979): 29-41; and Everett W. Hesse, "Tirso and the Drama of Sexuality and Imagination," *Iberomania* 11 (1980): 54-64.

23. See Ricardo Doménech's introduction to his edition of Tirso's *Don Gil de las calzas verdes* (Madrid: Taurus, 1969).

24. See José Alsina, "Heroínas clásicas: *Marta la piadosa*," in "El teatro," *Blanco y Negro*, no. 1920 (March 4, 1928).

25. The structure of this play is based on three intrigues: the *indiano* imposter, the seduced woman in pursuit of the seducer, and the gentleman who loves the village maid. See Jean Le Martinel and Gilbert Zonana, eds., introduction to Tirso's *La villana de Vallecas* (Paris: Ediciones Hispano-Americanas, 1964).

26. For the symbolic meaning in this play, see Premraj R.K. Halkhoree, "Satire and Symbolism in the Structure of Tirso de Molina's *Por el sótano y el torno*," *Forum for Modern Languages Studies* 4 (1968): 374-86.

27. Everett W. Hesse, *New Perspectives on Comedia Criticism* (Potomac, Md.: Porrúa Turanzas, 1980), p. 64.

28. For a discussion of this play-within-a-play, see Henry W. Sullivan, *Tirso de Molina and the Drama of the Counter Reformation* (Amsterdam: Rodopi, 1976), pp. 135-38.

29. Eleázar Huerta, "Tirso, *El vergonzoso*," *Atenea* 139 (1948): 371-86.

30. José M. Castro y Calvo, *El arte y la experiencia en la obra de Tirso de Molina* (Barcelona: Ariel, 1953).

31. See Sturgis E. Leavitt, "Juan Ruiz de Alarcón en el mundo del teatro en España," *Hispanófila* 60 (1977): 1-12.

32. See Susan Staves, "Liars and Lying in Alarcón, Corneille and Steele," *Revue de Littérature Comparée* 46 (1972): 514-27.

33. See José Martel and Hymen Alpern's introduction to *La verdad sospechosa* in their edition of *Diez comedias del Siglo de Oro*, 2nd ed., rev. by Leonard Mades (New York: Harper and Row, 1968), p. 514 .

34. See Mary A.L. Vetterling, "La magia en las comedias de Juan Ruiz de Alarcón," *Cuadernos Americanos* 39 (1980): 230-47.

35. Clotilde Evelia Quirarte, *Personajes de Juan Ruiz de Alarcón* (Mexico: El libro español, 1939), p. 57.

36. For example, see James A. Casteñeda, *Mira de Amescua* (Boston: Twayne, 1977), p. 170.

37. Adolf Friedrich von Schack, *Historia de la literatura y del arte dramático en España* (Madrid: M. Tello, 1887), 3: 291-92.

38. Alison Weber, "*Hamartia* in *Reinar después de morir*," *Bulletin of the Comediantes* 28 (1976): 89-95.

39. Some works on this subject are María del Pilar Oñate, *El feminismo en la literatura española* (Madrid: Espasa-Calpe, 1938); Carmen Bravo Villasante, *La mujer vestida de hombre en el teatro español: Siglos XVI-XVII* (Madrid: *Revista de Occidente*, 1955); and Malveena McKendrick, *Woman and Society in the Spanish Drama of the Golden Age* (London: Cambridge Univ. Press, 1974).

40. Marcelino Menéndez y Pelayo, ed., *Antología de poetas*, 13: 165, n. 2.

41. Edward Nagy, *Villanos, hampones, y soldados, en tres comedias de Luis Vélez de Guevara* (Valladolid: Severino Cuesta, 1979).

42. Schack, *Historia de la literatura*, 3: 302-3. Also see Angel Valbuena Briones, "Ante el centenario de Vélez de Guevara: Sus comedias novelescas y una relación con Calderón," *Arbor* 398 (1979): 176-87.

43. Schack, *Historia de la literatura*, 3: 305.

44. See Rudolph Schevill, "The *comedias* of Diego Ximénez de Enciso," *PMLA* 18 (1903): 194-210; Emilio Cotarelo y Mori, "Don Diego Jiménez de Enciso y su teatro," *Boletín de la Real Academia Española* 1 (1914): 209-48; and Schack, *Historia de la literatura*, 3: 329-67.

45. See Alfredo Rodríguez López-Vázquez, *Andrés de Claramonte, Autor de "El burlador de Sevilla"* (La Coruña: Gráficas Coruñesas, 1982), pp. 9-13.

46. See page 55, above, concerning the contested authorship of this play.

47. A discussion of this play is presented on pp. 56-58, above. Concerning the debate over its authorship, see chapter 2, note 25.

48. See this chapter, note 8, above.

49. These works are discussed by Eugenio Asensio in *Itinerario del entremés* (Madrid: Gredos, 1965), pp. 124-76; and by Hannah E. Bergman in *Luis Quiñones de Benavente y sus entremeses* (Madrid: Castalia, 1965).

50. Hannah E. Bergman, *Luis Quiñones de Benavente* (New York: Twayne, 1972), pp. 17-18, 137.

51. These works, together with his plays and interludes, are discussed by Armando Cotarelo y Valledor in *El teatro de Quevedo* (Madrid: Aguirre, 1945); and by Asensio in *Itinerario del entremés*, pp. 177-245.

52. See Karl Gregg, "Del Poyo's *Judás* and Tirso's *Don Juan*," *Symposium* 29 (1975): 345-60.

53. See Vern G. Williamsen, *The Minor Dramatists of Seventeenth-Century Spain* (Boston: Twayne, 1982), pp. 26-35.

54. See Louise Fothergill-Payne, *La alegoría en los autos y farsas anteriores a Calderón* (London: Támesis, 1977); and Ricardo Arias, *The Spanish Sacramental Plays* (Boston: Twayne, 1980), pp. 111-21.

IV. CALDERÓN: THE APOGEE OF THE *COMEDIA*

1. See Angel J. Valbuena Briones, *Calderón y la comedia nueva* (Madrid: Espasa-Calpe, 1976); and Richard W. Tyler and Sergio D. Elizondo, *The Characters, Plots and Settings*

of Calderón's Comedias (Lincoln: Univ. of Nebraska Society of Spanish and Spanish-American Studies, 1981).

2. The dates for this and subsequently mentioned Calderonian plays are taken from Harry W. Hilborn, *A Chronology of the Plays of D. Pedro Calderón de la Barca* (Toronto: Univ. of Toronto Press, 1938). Also see Shirley B. Whitaker, "The First Performance of Calderón's *El sitio de Bredá*," *Renaissance Quarterly* 31 (1978): 515-31.

3. The early volumes of Calderón's plays were published during his lifetime either by his brother, José, or by a friend, Juan de Vera Tassis y Villarroel in five *partes* (each having twelve plays) in 1636, 1637, 1664, 1672, and 1677. After the dramatist's death, Vera Tassis published an additional four *partes*, bringing the total to nine volumes that included 108 plays; however, some of these are not authentic. A tenth *parte* was planned but was never published because of the death of Vera Tassis. Some other plays by Calderón are scattered in single editions and others have been lost.

4. See James E. Maraniss, *On Calderón* (Columbia: Univ. of Missouri Press, 1978), pp. 5-6.

5. This play is fully discussed by Everett W. Hesse in *Calderón de la Barca* (New York: Twayne, 1967), pp. 49-53.

6. Robert Ter Horst, "From Comedy to Tragedy: Calderón and the New Tragedy," *Modern Language Notes* 42 (1977): 191.

7. See Henryk Ziomek, "Historic Implications and Dramatic Influences in Calderón's *Life Is a Dream*," *Polish Review* 20 (1975): 111-28.

8. For a semiotic approach to the meanings behind the ideas of "Life" (which as an antonym of death projects the ideas of reality, free will, light, and goodness) and of "Dream" (which is associated with visionary imagination, darkness, evil, stupor, fate, and illusion), see Angel J. Valbuena Briones, "Una aplicación de la crítica semiótica al análisis sintagmático de *La vida es sueño*," *Arbor* 428 (1981): 374-75.

9. Lope de Vega, *El galán de la Membrilla* in *Obras escogidas*, ed. Federico Carlos Sáinz de Robles, 4th ed., 3 (Madrid: Aguilar, 1967): 876; and *El castigo sin venganza* in *Obras escogidas*, 1 (Madrid: Aguilar, 1964): 936. In writing these verses Lope de Vega may, in turn, have been inspired by a short anonymous poem whose quatrain is as follows: "Soñaba yo que tenía / alegre mi corazón / mas a le fe, madre mía, / que los sueños, sueños son" ("I dreamed that my heart was rejoicing, but regretfully, my dear mother, dreams remain dreams"). Found in Pedro de Padilla, *Thesoro de varias poesías* (Madrid, 1580), f. 466. See also Georges Güntert, "El gracioso en Calderón: Disparate e ingenio," *Cuadernos Hispanoamericanos* 324 (1977): 440-53.

10. See Arturo Farinelli, *La vita è un sogno* (Torino: Fratelli Bocca, 1916), pp. 283-85; and Everett W. Hesse's edition of Calderón's *La vida es sueño* (New York: Scribner's, 1961), pp. 4-6.

11. See Albert E. Sloman, "The Structure of Calderón's *La vida es sueño*," *Modern Language Review* 48 (1953): 293-300.

12. For another perspective on Segismundo's character, see José A. Madrigal, "La metamorfosis de Segismundo desde una perspectiva simbólica," *Studies in Foreign Languages and Literatures* (Richmond: Eastern Kentucky Univ., 1977): 353-58.

13. This topic is discussed by Thomas A. O'Connor, "*La vida es sueño*: A View from Metatheater," *Kentucky Romance Quarterly* 25 (1978): 13-26; and Everett W. Hesse in *Interpretando la comedia* (Madrid: Porrúa Turanzas, 1977), pp. 115-30.

14. On Spanish honor as interpreted by Calderón, see Francisco de Ayala, "Sobre el punto de honor castellano," *Revista de Occidente* 5 (August 1963): 151-74; George Tyler Northup, ed., *Three Plays by Calderón* (New York: D.C. Heath, 1926), pp. xvi-xvii; Frank P. Casa, "Honor and the Wife-Killers of Calderón," *Bulletin of the Comediantes*

29 (1977): 6-23; Edwin Honig, "Calderón's Strange Mercy Play," in *Critical Essays on the Theatre of Calderón*, ed. Bruce W. Wardropper (New York: New York Univ. Press, 1965), pp. 167-92; Everett W. Hesse, *La comedia y sus intérpretes* (Madrid: Castalia, 1972), pp. 148-53; Peter N. Dunn, "Honour and the Christian Background in Calderón," *Bulletin of Hispanic Studies* 37 (1960): 75-105; and Carolyn F. Smith, "Imagination and Ritual in the Honor Tragedies of Calderón," Ph.D. diss., Univ. of Kentucky, 1972.

15. See Cyril A. Jones, introduction to *El médico de su honra* (Oxford: Clarendon, 1961); Raymond R. MacCurdy, "Critical Review of *El médico de su honra* as Tragedy," *Bulletin of the Comediantes* 31 (1979): 3-14; Frances Exum, " '¿Yo a un vasallo . . . ?': Prince Henry's Role in Calderón's *El médico de su honra*," *Bulletin of the Comediantes* 29 (1977): 1-6; and William R. Blue, " '¿Qué es esto que miro?': converging Sign Systems in *El médico de su honra*," *Bulletin of the Comediantes* 30 (1978): 83-96.

16. See the interpretation of Bruce W. Wardropper, "The Dramatization of Figurative Language in the Spanish Theatre," *Yale French Studies* 47 (1972): 189-98; and idem, "La imaginación en el metateatro calderoniano," *Actas del Tercer Congreso Internacional de Hispanistas* (Mexico: El Colegio de México, 1970), pp. 928-30.

17. For a study of this play, see Alexander A. Parker, "The Spanish Drama of the Golden Age: A Method of Analysis and Interpretation," *The Great Playwrights*, ed. Eric Bentley (Garden City, N.Y.: Doubleday, 1970) 1: 682-83, and note 5.

18. Clark Colahan, "Art and Imagination in Calderón's *El pintor de su deshonra*," *Bulletin of the Comediantes* 33 (1981): 73-80.

19. Peter N. Dunn, "Patrimonio del alma," *Bulletin of Hispanic Studies* 41 (1964): 18-85.

20. For a discussion of the social implications of Pedro Crespo's role in this drama, see Geörgy Luckács, *The Historical Novel*, trans. Hannah and Stanley Mitchell (Boston: Beacon, 1963), pp. 153-54.

21. See Angel J. Valbuena Briones, ed., *Obras completas de Don Pedro Calderón de la Barca*, 5th ed. (1966), 1: 712; and idem, *Perspectiva crítica de los dramas de Calderón* (Madrid: Rialp, 1965), pp. 232-35.

22. See Albert E. Sloman, *The Dramatic Craftsmanship of Calderón: His Use of Earlier Plays* (Oxford: Dolphin, 1958), pp. 59-93.

23. Valbuena Briones, ed., *Obras completas de Calderón* 1: 69-70.

24. For additional studies on this play see Hesse, *Calderón de la Barca*, pp. 64-70; and Gwynne Edwards, "Calderón's *Los cabellos de Absalón*: A Reappraisal," *Bulletin of Hispanic Studies* 48 (1971): 218-38.

25. Susan L. Fischer, "Calderón's *Los cabellos de Absalón*: A Metatheater of Unbridled Passion," *Bulletin of the Comediantes* 28 (1976): 103-13.

26. For a thorough discussion of this play, see Sloman, *Dramatic Craftsmanship*, pp. 159-87.

27. Cf. Edward M. Wilson and W.J. Entwistle, "Calderón's *Príncipe constante*: Two Appreciations," *Modern Language Review* 34 (1939): 207-22; Arnold G. Reichenberger, "Calderón's *El príncipe constante*, a Tragedy?" *Modern Language Notes* 75 (1960): 670; Robert Sloane, "Action and Role in *El príncipe constante*," *Modern Language Notes* 85 (1970): 167-83; Stephen Lipmann, "'Metatheater' and the Criticism of the *Comedia*," *Modern Language Notes* 91 (1976): 231-46; and José A. Madrigal, "*Fuenteovejuna* y los conceptos de metateatro y psicodrama," *Bulletin of the Comediantes* 31 (1979): 15-23.

28. For more on this significant play, see George R. Shivers, "La unidad dramática en *La cisma de Inglaterra* de Pedro Calderón de la Barca," in *Perspectivas de la comedia*, ed. Alva V. Ebersole (Valencia: Soler, 1978), pp. 133-43; Alexander A. Parker, "Henry VIII in Shakespeare and Calderón: An Appreciation of *La cisma de Ingalaterra*," *Modern*

Language Review 43 (1948):327-52; and Susan L. Fischer, "Reader-Response Criticism and the *Comedia*: Creation of Meaning in Calderón's *La cisma de Ingalaterra*," *Bulletin of the Comediantes* 31 (1979): 109-25.

29. Sources that discuss the role of the Devil in this and other Calderonian plays are Valbuena Briones, ed., *Obras completas de Calderón*, 1: 603-5; Angel L. Cilveti, *El demonio en el teatro de Calderón* (Valencia: Albatros, 1976); and A.A. Parker, *The Theology of the Devil in the Drama of Calderón* (London: Blackfriars, 1958). For the "metatheatrical" aspects of the characters' roles, see A. Roger Moore, "Metatheater and Magic in *El mágico prodigioso*," *Bulletin of the Comediantes* 33 (1981): 130-32.

30. The manuscript of *El gran duque de Gandía* was found in Czechoslovakia in 1957, and an edition of it has been prepared by Václav Cerný.

31. Ramón Silva provides a good study of these plays in "The Religious Drama of Calderón," *Bulletin of Spanish Studies* 15 (1938): 172-95.

32. Honig, "Calderón's Strange Mercy Play," p. 169.

33. See Northup, *Three Plays by Calderón*, p. xxxvi.

34. Gerald Brenan, *The Literature of the Spanish People* (Cambridge: Cambridge Univ. Press, 1951), pp. 277, 293. For additional study of these plays, see William R. Blue, "Romance in Calderón's Last Plays"; and Susan L. Fischer, "Calderón's *El mayor encanto, amor*, and the Mode of Romance," both in *Studies in Honor of Everett W. Hesse* (Lincoln: Univ. of Nebraska Society of Spanish and Spanish-American Studies, 1981), pp. 23-24, 99-112.

35. Information on Calderón's zarzuelas has been drawn from Emilio Cotarelo y Mori, *Historia de la zarzuela* (Madrid: Tip. de la *Revista de Archivos, Bibliotecas y Museos*, 1934), pp. 43-60; Gilbert Chase, *The Music of Spain* (New York: W.M. Norton, 1941), pp. 96-105; and Paul Henry Lang, *Music in Western Civilization* (New York: W.M. Norton, 1941), pp. 422, 676.

36. For further study see Ludwig Pfandl, "El auto sacramental," *Historia de la literatura española en la edad de oro*, trans. Jorge Rubió Balaguer (Barcelona: Gustavo Gili, 1952), pp. 467-87; Eugenio Frutos, *La filosofía de Calderón en sus autos sacramentales* (Zaragoza: Institución Fernando el Católico, 1981); and Nicolas Shumway, "Calderón and the Protestant Reformation: A View from the *Autos Sacramentales*," *Hispanic Review* 49 (1981): 329-48.

37. See Geoffrey M. Voght, "Calderón's *El cubo de la Almudena* and Comedy in the *Autos sacramentales*," in *Critical Perspectives on Calderón de la Barca*, ed. Frederick A. de Armas, David M. Gitlitz, and José A. Madrigal (Lincoln, Neb.: Society of Spanish and Spanish-American Studies, 1981), pp. 141-60; and Alice M. Pollin, "Calderón de la Barca and Music: Theory and Examples in the *Autos* (1675-1681)," *Hispanic Review* 41 (1973): 362-70.

38. Valbuena Prat, ed., *Obras completas*, 3: 32-37. Also see Sister M. Francis de Sales McGarry, *The Allegorical and Metaphorical Language in the "Autos sacramentales" of Calderón* (Washington: Catholic Univ. of America,1937); Alexander A. Parker, *The Allegorical Drama of Calderón* (Oxford: Dolphin, 1943); and Ricardo Arias, *The Spanish Sacramental Plays* (Boston: Twayne, 1980), pp. 128-46.

39. Lipmann, "'Metatheater' and the Criticism of the *Comedia*."

40. For a fuller interpretation of this *auto*, see Robert W. Felkel, "*El gran teatro de mundo* of Pedro Calderón de la Barca and the Centrality of Grace," *Bulletin of the Comediantes* 31 (1979): 127-34.

41. For the *autos* taken from the New Testament, see Donald T. Dietz, *The "auto sacramental" and the Parables in Spanish Golden Age Literature* (Chapel Hill: Univ. of North Carolina Department of Romance Languages, 1973).

42. Northup, *Three Plays by Calderón*, pp. xl-xli.

43. For this topic, see Manuel Durán and Roberto González Echevarría, eds., *Calderón y la crítica: Historia y antología*, 2 vols. (Madrid: Gredos, 1976).

V. THE DECLINE: CALDERÓN'S CONTEMPORARIES AND IMITATORS

1. For further study see Raymond R. MacCurdy, *Francisco de Rojas Zorrilla* (New York: Twayne, 1968), pp. 34-134.

2. William M. Whitby, "Appearance and Reality in *Del rey abajo, ninguno*," *Hispania* 42 (1959): 186-91; also see Margaret A. Van Antwerp, "'El fénix es': The Symbolic Structure of *Del rey abajo, ninguno*," *Hispanic Review* 47 (1979): 441-54; and Cristina González, "Sobre *Del Rey abajo, ninguno*," *Bulletin of the Comediantes* 32 (1980): 49-53.

3. Raymond R. MacCurdy, "Women and Sexual Love in the Plays of Rojas Zorrilla: Tradition and Innovation," *Hispania* 62 (1979): 255-65.

4. Edwin B. Place, "Notes on the Grotesque: The *comedia de figurón* at Home and Abroad," *PMLA* 54 (1939): 412-21.

5. Information on Moreto's work has been obtained from Ruth Lee Kennedy, *The Dramatic Art of Moreto*, Smith College Studies in Modern Languages, 13 (Northampton, Mass., 1932); Frank P. Casa, *The Dramatic Craftsmanship of Moreto* (Cambridge: Harvard Univ. Press, 1966); Jack H. Parker, "Some Aspects of Moreto's *Teatro menor*," *Philological Quarterly* 5 (1972): 205-17; Anthony van Beysterveldt, "La inversión del amor cortés en Moreto," *Cuadernos Hispanoamericanos* 283 (1974): 88-114; and Frances Exum, "Moreto's Playmakers: The Rôles of Four *Graciosos* and Their Plays-within-the Play," *Bulletin of Hispanic Studies* 55 (1978): 311-20.

6. James A. Casteñeda, *Agustín Moreto* (New York: Twayne, 1974), p. 46.

7. Cf. Roger Moore, "Ornamental and Organic Conceits in Moreto's *El lego del Carmen*," *Bulletin of the Comediantes* 31 (1979): 135-43.

8. Angel Valbuena Prat, ed., *Alvaro Cubillo de Aragón*, in Clásicos Olvidados, 3 (Madrid: Blass, 1928), p. 5; Shirley B. Whitaker, *The Dramatic Works of Alvaro Cubillo de Aragón* (Chapel Hill: Univ. of North Carolina Press, 1975); and John H. Seekamp, "The Dramatic Craftsmanship of Alvaro Cubillo de Aragón and the Sources for Some of His Plays," Ph.D. diss., Rutgers Univ., 1974.

9. See Emilio Cotarelo y Mori, "Don Juan Bautista Diamante y sus comedias," *Boletín de la Real Academia Española* 3 (1916): 272-97, 454-97; and Narciso Díaz de Escovar, "Poetas dramáticos del siglo XVII: Juan Bautista Diamante," *Boletín de la Real Academia de la Historia* 90 (1927): 216-26.

10. See Gareth Alban Davies, "A Chronology of Antonio de Mendoza's Plays," *Bulletin of Hispanic Studies* 48 (1971): 97-110; and idem, *A Court Poet: Antonio de Mendoza, 1586-1644* (Oxford: Dolphin, 1971).

11. See Angel Valbuena Prat, *Literatura dramática española* (Barcelona: Labor, 1930), pp. 269-70; and Donald E. Schmiedel, "Coello's Debt to Góngora," *Bulletin of the Comediantes* 25 (1973): 34-40.

12. See Schack, *Historia de la literatura*, 5: 217; Adolfo de Castro, ed., *Poetas líricos de los siglos XVI y XVII*, in *BAE*, 42 (1854; rpt. Madrid: Atlas, 1951): lxix-lxxii; Narciso Díaz de Escovar, "Don Jerónimo de Cáncer y Velasco," *Revista Contemporánea* 121 (1901): 399-409; and Luciano García Lorenzo, "La comedia burlesca en el siglo XVII: *Las mocedades del Cid*, de Jerónimo de Cáncer," *Segismundo* 13 (1977): 131-46.

13. See Narciso Díaz de Escovar, "Poetas dramáticos del siglo XVII: Juan Claudio de la Hoz y Mota," *Boletin de la Real Academia de la Historia* 89 (1926): 351-57.

14. See Ramón de Mesonero Romanos, "Teatro de Matos Fragoso," *Semanario Pin-*

toresco Español 16 (1852): 114-18; and Elsa Leonor Di Santo, "Noticias sobre la vida de Juan de Matos Fragoso," *Segismundo* 14 (1978-80): 217-32.

15. See Glen F. Dille, "Antonio Enríquez Gómez's Honor Tragedy, *A lo que obliga el honor,*" *Bulletin of the Comediantes* 30 (1978): 97-111; and I.S. Révah, "Un pamplet contre l'inquisition d'Antonio Enríquez Gómez: la seconde partie de la *Política angélica,*" *Revue des Etudes Juives* 131 (1962): 81-168.

16. For this dramatist, see David M. Gitlitz, "La angustia de ser negro: tema de un drama de Fernando de Zárate," *Segismundo* 2 (1975): 65-85.

17. See Robert Moune, "*El caballero de Olmedo* de F.A. de Monteser: comedia burlesca y parodia," in *Risa y sociedad en el teatro español del Siglo de Oro* (Paris: Centre Nat. de la Recherche Scientifique, 1980), pp. 83-93.

18. See Wickersham Shaffer Jack, "Bances Candamo and the Calderonian Decadents," *PMLA* 44 (1929): 1079-89.

19. Mesonero Romanos, "Teatro de Bances Candamo," *Semanario Pintoresco Español* 18 (1853): 82-84.

VI.   THE *COMEDIA* SINCE 1700

1. Arnhilda B. González-Quevedo, "Antonio de Zamora: su vida y sus obras," *Hispanófila* 5 (1976): 36-46.

2. See Alva V. Ebersole, *José de Cañizares, dramaturgo olvidado del siglo XVIII* (Madrid: Insula, 1974); and Kim L. Johns, "José de Cañizares: Traditionalist and Innovator," Ph.D. diss., Univ. of North Carolina, 1976.

3. Ernest Martinenche, *La comédie espagnole en France* (Paris: Hachette, 1900), p. 79.

4. Jacob B. Segall, *Corneille and the Spanish Drama* (New York: AMS Press, 1966); John M. Mendicoa, "Los paralelos estructurales y estilísticos en la técnica dramática de Guillén de Castro," Ph.D. diss., Catholic Univ. of America, 1973.

5. Frederick W.C. Lieder, "The Don Carlos Theme," *Harvard Studies and Notes in Philology and Literature*, no.12 (Cambridge: Harvard Univ. Press, 1930), p. 3.

6. For further study see Tirso de Molina, *El burlador de Sevilla y convidado de piedra*, ed. Gerald E. Wade (New York: Scribner's, 1969), pp. 17-26; and Leo Weinstein, *The Metamorphoses of Don Juan* (Stanford: Stanford Univ. Press, 1959).

7. For analyses of many of the critical approaches, see Bruce W. Wardropper, "On the Fourth Centenary of Lope de Vega's Birth," *Drama Survey* 2 (1962): 121-26; James A. Parr, "An Essay on Critical Method, Applied to the *Comedia,*" *Hispania* 57 (1974): 434-44; and Eduardo Forastieri Braschi, *Aproximación estructural al teatro de Lope de Vega* (Madrid: Hispanova, 1976).

8. See two articles by Arnold Reichenberger with the same title, "The Uniqueness of the *Comedia,*" in *Hispanic Review* 27 (1959): 303-16; and 38 (1970): 164-73.

9. Eric Bentley, "The Universality of the *Comedia,*" *Hispanic Review* 38 (1970): 147-62.

10. The British Hispanists have included William James Entwistle, Edward M. Wilson, Ivy V. McClelland, Alexander A. Parker, Norman D. Shergold, John E. Varey, Geoffrey W. Ribbans, Cyril A. Jones, Bruce W. Wardropper, Peter N. Dunn, and Albert E. Sloman. Other internationals who have identified themselves with the British school are Joaquín Casalduero, Diego Marín, Charles Aubrun, Alan S. Trueblood, Raymond R. MacCurdy, William M. Whitby, Frank P. Casa, and Alva V. Ebersole.

11. Alexander A. Parker, "The Approach to the Spanish Drama of the Golden Age" (London: Hispanic and Luso-Brazilian Councils; rpt. in *Tulane Dramatic Review* [1959], 42-59); and idem, "Spanish Drama of the Golden Age," pp. 679-707.

12. Parker, "Spanish Drama," pp. 680, 686.

13. The Comediantes, with a membership of over two hundred, meet annually when the Modern Language Association convenes, and promotes the publication of the *Bulletin of the Comediantes*, which was founded by Everett W. Hesse in 1949.

14. Bruce W. Wardropper, "The Implicit Craft of the Spanish *Comedia*," *Studies in Spanish Literature of the Golden Age*, ed. R.O. Jones (London: Támesis, 1973), pp. 339-56.

15. Everett W. Hesse discusses and applies his psychological approach in his books: *Análisis e interpretación de la comedia* (Valencia: Castalia, 1968); *La comedia y sus intérpretes; Interpretando la comedia; New Perspectives on Comedia Criticism*; and *Essays on Spanish Letters of the Golden Age* (Potomac, Md.: Porrúa Turanzas, 1981).

16. Northrop Frye, "Literary Criticism," in *The Aims and Methods of Scholarship in Modern Languages and Literature*, ed. James Thorpe (New York: MLA, 1963), pp. 57-69.

17. See Parr, "Essay on Critical Method."

18. Karl Vossler, *Lope de Vega y su tiempo*, trans. Ramón Gómez de la Serna, 2nd ed. (Madrid: Revista de Occidente, 1940), pp. 244-320.

19. Lionel Abel, *Metatheatre: A New View of Dramatic Form* (New York: Hill and Wang, 1963), p. 72.

20. See Alan S. Trueblood, "Rôle-Playing and the Sense of Illusion in Lope de Vega," *Hispanic Review* 37 (1964): 305-18; Wardropper, "La imaginación en el metateatro calderoniano," pp. 923-30; Sloane, "Action and Role in *El príncipe constante*," pp. 167-83; Fischer, "Psychological and Esthetic Implications of Role-Change"; idem, "Lope's *Lo fingido verdadero* and the Dramatization of the Theatrical Experience," *Revista Hispánica Moderna* 29 (1976-77): 156-66; Lipmann, "'Metatheater' and the Criticism of the *Comedia*," pp. 231-46; Hesse, *Interpretando la comedia*, pp. 115-30; McCrary, "The *Duque* and the *Comedia*"; Frances Exum, "Moreto's Playmakers: The Rôles of Four *Graciosos* and Their Plays-within-the-Play," *Bulletin of Hispanic Studies* 55 (1978): 311-20; Madrigal, "*Fuenteovejuna* y los conceptos de metateatro"; and Ebersole, "Metateatro, Lope y *Argel fingido*."

21. Lipmann, "'Metatheater' and Criticism," p. 232.

22. See three articles by Thomas Austin O'Connor: "Is the Spanish *Comedia* a Metatheater?" *Hispanic Review* 43 (1975): 275-89, and Arnold G. Reichenberger's postscript, pp. 289-91; "Metatheater and the *Comedia*: A Further Comment," *Modern Language Notes* 92, 1-2 (1977): 336-38; and "*La vida es sueño*: A View from Metatheater," *Kentucky Romance Quarterly* 25 (1978):13-26.

23. See José M. Díez Borque, "Aproximación semiológica a la escena del teatro del Siglo de Oro español," in *Semiología del teatro* (Barcelona: Planeta, 1975), pp. 49-92; and Daniel Laferrière, "What Is Semiotics?" *Semiotic Scene: Bulletin of the Semiotic Society of America* 1 (1977): 2-4. A.J. Valbuena Briones and William R. Blue have used semiotics in their interpretations of the plays of Lope de Vega and Calderón (see above, chapter 2, note 20; and chapter 4, notes 8 and 15).

24. For examples of this approach, see Wilson, "Images et structure dans *Peribáñez*"; and Spitzer, "A Central Theme and Its Structural Equivalent in Lope's *Fuenteovejuna*" (see chapter 2, note 22); Hatzfeld, "The Styletype of Tirso de Molina's *Don Gil de las calzas verdes*" (see chapter 3, note 22); John G. Weiger, "On the Application of Stylostatistics to the Analysis of the *Comedia*," *Bulletin of the Comediantes* 32 (1980): 63-73; and John B. Wooldridge, "A *Comedia* Stylistic Device for Examples and Comparisons," *Perspectivas de la comedia: II*, ed. Alva V. Ebersole (Valencia: Soler, 1979), pp. 49-60.

Selected Bibliography

Since most secondary sources for this book are cited in the notes, this bibliography lists primary sources for the Spanish Golden Age playwrights, together with pertinent biographies and bibliographies. After a list of anthologies and collections of works, the playwrights are grouped in accordance with the major sections of the book, and arranged chronologically. General historical and critical studies not always cited in the notes conclude this bibliography.

ANTHOLOGIES AND COLLECTIONS OF WORKS

Antología de poetas hispano-americanos. Ed. Marcelino Menéndez y Pelayo. Vol. 1. Real Academia Española. Madrid: Rivadeneyra, 1903.

Autos sacramentales desde sus orígenes hasta fines del siglo XVII. Ed. Eduardo González Pedroso. Madrid: Rivadeneyra, 1952.

Colección de autos, farsas y coloquios del siglo XVI. Ed. Léo Rouanet. 4 vols. Madrid: Biblioteca Hispánica, 1901.

Colección de entremeses, loas, bailes, jácaras y mojigangas desde fines del siglo XVI a mediados del XVIII. Ed. Emilio Cotarelo y Mori. In *NBAE,* Vols. 17 and 18. Madrid: Bailly-Baillière, 1911.

Diez comedias del siglo de oro. Ed. José Martel and Hymen Alpern. 2nd ed., rev. by Leonard Mades. New York: Harper and Row, 1968.

Dramáticos contemporáneos a Lope de Vega. Ed. Ramón de Mesonero Romanos. *Parte I.* In *BAE,* vol. 43. Madrid: Rivadeneyra, 1857.

Dramáticos contemporáneos de Lope de Vega. Ed. Ramón de Mesonero Romanos. *Parte II.* In *BAE,* vol. 45. Madrid: Rivadeneyra, 1857; rpt. Madrid: Atlas, 1951.

Dramáticos posteriores a Lope de Vega. Ed. Ramón de Mesonero Romanos. In *BAE,* vols. 47 and 49. Madrid: Rivadeneyra, 1858-59.

Obras dramáticas del siglo XVI. Ed. Gabriel Ochoa. Madrid, 1914.

Poetas dramáticos valencianos. Ed. Eduardo Juliá Martínez. 2 vols. Madrid: Tip. de la *Revista de Archivos, Bibliotecas y Museos,* 1929.

Poetas líricos de los siglos XVI y XVII. Ed. Adolfo de Castro. In *BAE*, vol. 42. Madrid: Rivadeneyra, 1854; rpt. Madrid: Atlas, 1951.

Spanish Drama of the Golden Age. Ed. Raymond R. MacCurdy. New York: Appleton-Century-Crofts, 1971.

Teatro español del Siglo de Oro. Ed. Bruce W. Wardropper. New York: Scribner's, 1970.

THE PRE-LOPEAN PLAYWRIGHTS

EDITIONS OF PLAYS

Bermúdez, Jerónimo. *Primeras tragedias españolas.* Ed. Mitchell D. Triwedi. Chapel Hill: Univ. of North Carolina Department of Romance Languages, 1975.

Cervantes, Miguel de. *Obras completas.* Ed. Angel Valbuena Prat. Madrid: Aguilar, 1970.

"Una comedia latina de la Edad Media: el *Liber Panphili.*" Ed. Adolfo Bonilla y San Martín. *Boletín de la Real Academia de la Historia* 70 (1917): 395-467.

Cueva, Juan de la. *Comedias y tragedias de Juan de la Cueva.* 2 vols. Ed. Francisco A. de Icaza. La Sociedad de Bibliófilos Españoles. Madrid: "Imprenta Ibérica" E. Maestre, 1917.

_____. *El infamador, Los siete infantes de Lara y El exemplar poético.* Ed. Francisco A. de Icaza. Madrid: Espasa-Calpe, 1924.

Encina, Juan del. *Obras completas.* Ed. Ana María Rambaldo. 3 vols. Clásicos Castellanos. Madrid: Espasa-Calpe, 1978.

Fernández, Lucas. *Teatro selecto clásico.* ed. Alfredo Hermenegildo. Madrid: Escelicer, 1972.

Horozco, Sebastián de. *Representaciones.* Ed. Fernando González Ollé. Madrid: Castalia, 1979.

López de Castro, Diego. *Marco Antonio y Cleopatra.* Ed. Hugo A. Rennert. *Revue Hispanique* 19 (1908): 184-237.

Pérez de Oliva, Fernán. "Hernán Pérez de Oliva: *Teatro.*" Ed. William Atkinson, *Revue Hispanique* 69 (1927): 521-659.

_____. *Teatro.* Ed. C. George Peale, Córdoba: Real Academia de Córdoba, 1976.

Rojas, Fernando de. *La Celestina.* Ed. Bruno M. Damiani. Madrid: Cátedra, 1980.

Rueda, Lope de. *Obras de Lope de Rueda.* Ed. Emilio Cotarelo y Mori. 2 vols. Real Academia Española. Madrid: Hernando, 1908.

_____. *Teatro completo.* Ed. Angeles Cardona de Gibert. Barcelona: Bruguera, 1976.

_____. *Teatro de Lope de Rueda.* Ed. J. Moreno Villa. Clásicos Castellanos. Vol. 59. Madrid: Espasa-Calpe, 1924.

Sánchez de Badajoz, Diego. *Farsas*. Ed. José M. Díez Borque. Madrid: Cátedra, 1978.

Timoneda, Juan de. *Obras*. Ed. Eduardo Juliá Martínez. Madrid: Sociedad de Bibliófilos Españoles, 1947-48.

————. *Obras completas de Juan de Timoneda*. Ed. Marcelino Menéndez y Pelayo. Sociedad de Bibliófilos Valencianos. Valencia: Est. Tip. Doménech, 1911. Vol. 1.

Torres Naharro, Bartolomé de. *Comedias*. Ed. Dean William McPheeters. Madrid: Castalia, 1973.

————. *Teatro selecto de Torres Naharro*. Ed. Humberto López Morales. Madrid: Escelicer, 1970.

Vega, Alonso de la. *Tres comedias de Alonso de la Vega*. Ed. Marcelino Menéndez y Pelayo. Dresden: Gedruckt für die Gesellschaft für romanische Literatur, 1905.

Vicente, Gil. *A Critical Edition with Introduction and Notes of Gil Vicente's "Floresta de Engaños."* Ed. Constantine C. Stathatos. Chapel Hill: Univ. of North Carolina Press, 1972.

————. *"Édition critique de l'auto de Inés Pereira."* Ed. I.S. Révah. In *Recherches sur les oeuvres de Gil Vicente*. Lisbon: Institut Français au Portugal, 1955.

————. *Gil Vicente: Farces and Festival plays*. Ed. Thomas R. Hart. Eugene: Univ. of Oregon, 1972.

————. *Obras completas*. Ed. Marques Braga. Lisbon: Livraria Sá da Costa, 1953-59.

————. *Obras dramáticas castellanas*. Ed. Thomas R. Hart. Madrid: Espasa-Calpe, 1968.

BIOGRAPHIES

Hermenegildo, Alfredo. *Renacimiento, teatro y sociedad: vida y obra de Lucas Fernández*. Madrid: Cincel, 1975.

López Prudencio, José. *Diego Sánchez de Badajoz: estudio crítico, biográfico y bibliográfico*. Madrid: Tip de la *Revista de Archivos, Bibliotecas y Museos*, 1915.

BIBLIOGRAPHIES

Abrams, Fred. "Lope de Rueda: Una bibliografía analítica en el cuarto centenario de su muerte." *Duquesne Hispanic Review* 4 (1965): 39-55.

Bibliografía vicentina. Ed L. de Castro e Azevedo. Lisbon: Biblioteca Nacional, 1942.

Cardona de Gilbert, Angeles, ed. *Fernando de Rojas: "La Celestina."* Barcelona: Bruguera, 1975.

Castro E. Azevedo, L., ed. *Bibliografía vicentina*. Lisbon: Biblioteca Nacional, 1942.

Rodríguez Moñino, Antonio. "El teatro de Torres Naharro (1517-1936): Indicaciones bibliográficas." *Revista de Filología Española* 24 (1937): 37-82.

Schizzano Mandel, Adrienne. *"La Celestina" Studies: A Thematic Survey and Bibliography, 1824-1970*. Metuchen, N.J.: Scarecrow Press, 1971.

Stathatos, Constantine C. "French Contributions to the Study of Gil Vicente: A Bibliography (1942-1975)." *Luso-Brasilian Review* 15 (1978): 105-16.

Tuson, Vicente. *Lope de Rueda: bibliografía crítica. Cuadernos Bibliográficos* 16. Madrid: C.S.I.C., 1965.

LOPE DE VEGA

EDITIONS OF PLAYS

El castigo sin venganza. Ed. Cyril A. Jones. London: Pergamon Press, 1969.

Doze comedias nuevas de Lope de Vega, y otros autores. Segunda parte . . . . Barcelona: Jerónimo Margarit, 1630.

An Edition with Notes and Introduction of Lope de Vega's "La prueba de los amigos." Ed. Henryk Ziomek. Athens: Univ. of Georgia Press, 1973.

Obras de Lope de Vega. Ed. Emilio Cotarelo y Mori. 13 vols. Real Academia Española. Madrid: Tip. de la *Revista de Archivos, Bibliotecas y Museos*, 1916-30.

Obras de Lope de Vega. Ed. Marcelino Menéndez y Pelayo. 15 vols. Real Academia Española. Madrid: Rivadeneyra, 1890-1913; rpt. in *BAE*, vols. 157-59, 177-78, 186-88, 190-91, 195-98, 211-15, 223-25, 233-34, 246, and 248-50. Madrid: Atlas, 1936-72.

Obras escogidas: Teatro. Ed. Federico Carlos Sáinz de Robles. 4th ed. Vols. 1 and 3. Madrid: Aguilar, 1964, 1967.

A Paleographic Edition of Lope de Vega's Autograph Play "La nueua victoria de D. Gonzalo Cordoua." Ed. Henryk Ziomek. New York: Hispanic Institute, 1962.

El perro del hortelano y el Castigo sin venganza. Ed A. David Kossoff. Madrid: Castalia, 1970.

BIOGRAPHIES

Alberto de la Barrera y Leirado, Cayetano. "Nueva Biografía de Lope de Vega." *Obras completas de Lope de Vega*. Madrid: Real Academia Española, 1890. Vol. 1.

Astrana Marín, Luis. *Vida azarosa de Lope de Vega*. Barcelona: Juventud, 1941.

Baeza, José. *Lope de Vega*. Barcelona: Aralucé, 1962.

Entrambasaguas, Joaquín de. *Vida de Lope de Vega*. Madrid: Labor, 1942.

_____. *Vivir y crear de Lope de Vega*. Madrid: Aldus, 1946.

González de Amezúa y Mayo, Agustín. *Lope de Vega en sus cartas*. Madrid: Real Academia Española, 1935-43.
Hayes, Francis C. *Lope de Vega*. New York: Twayne, 1967.
Laplane, Gabriel. *Lope de Vega*. Paris: Hachette, 1936.
Lázaro Carreter, Fernando. *Lope de Vega*. Madrid: Anaya, 1966.
Montalván, Juan Pérez de. *Fama posthuma a la vida y muerte del Doctor Frey Lope Félix*. Madrid: Imprenta del Reino, 1636.
Rennert, Hugo A. *The Life of Lope de Vega*. Glasgow: Gowans and Gray, 1904.
Sáinz de Robles, Federico C. *Lope de Vega*. Madrid: Espasa-Calpe, 1962.
Vossler, Karl. *Lope de Vega y su tiempo*. Trans. Ramón Gómez de la Serna. 2nd ed. Madrid: *Revista de Occidente*, 1933.
Vosters, Simón A. *Lope de Vega y la tradición occidental*. 2 vols. Madrid: Castalia, 1977.
Zamora Vicente, Alonso. *Lope de Vega, su vida y su obra*. Madrid: Gredos, 1961.

BIBLIOGRAPHIES
Brown, Robert B. *Bibliografía de las comedias históricas, tradicionales y lengendarias de Lope de Vega*. México: Academia, 1958.
Grismer, Raymond L. *Bibliography of Lope de Vega*. 2 vols. Minneapolis: Burgess-Beckwith, 1965.
Parker, Jack H., and Arthur M. Fox, eds. *Lope de Vega Studies, 1937-62: A Critical Survey and Annotated Bibliography*. Toronto: Univ. of Toronto Press, 1964.
Pérez y Pérez, M.C. *Bibliografía del teatro de Lope de Vega*. Madrid: C.S.I.C., 1973.
Simon Díaz, José, and Juana de José Prados. *Ensayo de una bibliografía de las obras y artículos sobre la vida y escritos de Lope de Vega*. Madrid: Centro de Estudios sobre Lope de Vega, 1955.

THE LOPEAN CYCLE (EXCEPT TIRSO DE MOLINA)

EDITIONS OF PLAYS
Belmonte Bermúdez, Luis. *El sastre del Campillo*. Ed Frederick A. de Armas. Chapel Hill: Univ. of North Carolina Dept. of Romance Languages, 1975.
Castro, Guillén de. *Las hazañas del Cid*. Ed. John G. Weiger. Barcelona: Puvill, 1980.
_____. *Los malcasados de Valencia*. Ed. Luciano García Lorenzo. Madrid: Castalia, 1976.
_____. *Las mocedades del Cid*. Ed. Luciano García Lorenzo. Madrid: Cátedra, 1978.
_____. *Obras*. 5 vols. Ed. Eduardo Juliá Martínez. Madrid: Imp. de la *Revista de Archivos, Bibliotecas y Museos*, 1925.

Godínez, Felipe. *La traición contra su dueño*. Ed. Thomas C. Turner. Madrid: Castalia, 1975.

Mira de Amescua, Antonio. *A Critical Edition of Mira de Amescua's "La fe de Hungría" and "El monte de la piedad."* Ed. James C. Maloney. New Orleans: Tulane Univ., 1975.

————. *Teatro de Mira de Amescua*. Ed. Angel Valbuena Prat. Clásicos Castellanos. Madrid: Espasa-Calpe, 1926.

Monroy y Silva, Cristóbal. *Dos comedias inéditas de Don Cristóbal de Monroy y Silva*. Ed. Manuel R. Bem Barroca. Madrid: Castalia, 1976.

Ruiz de Alarcón, Juan. *Obras completas*. Ed. Alva V. Ebersole. 2 vols. Valencia: Castalia, 1966.

————. *La verdad sospechosa*. Ed. Alva V. Ebersole. Madrid: Cátedra, 1976.

Valdivieso, José de. *Teatro completo*. Ed. Ricardo Arias and Robert V. Piluso. Madrid: Isla, 1977.

Vélez de Guevara, Luis. *El amor en vizcaíno, los celos en francés y El príncipe viñador*. Ed. Henryk Ziomek. Zaragoza: Ebro, 1975.

————. *Autos*. Ed. Angel Lacalle. Madrid: Hernando, 1931.

————. *La creación del mundo*. Ed. Henryk Ziomek and Robert W. Linker. Athens: Univ. of Georgia Press, 1974.

————. *The Dramatic Works of Luis Vélez de Guevara*. Ed. Forrest E. Spenser and Rudoph Schevill. Publications in Modern Philology. Berkeley: Univ. of California Press, 1937.

————. *Más pesa el rey que la sangre, y Blasón de los Guzmanes*. Ed. Henryk Ziomek. Zaragoza: Ebro, 1976.

BIOGRAPHIES

Bacon, George William. *The Life and Dramatic Works of Dr. Juan Pérez de Montalván. Revue Hispanique* 26 (1912): 1-474.

Castro Leal, Antonio. *Juan Ruiz de Alarcón, su vida y su obra*. Mexico: Ediciones *Cuadernos Americanos*, 1943.

Cotarelo y Mori, Emilio. *Mira de Amescua y su teatro*. Madrid: Tip. de la *Revista de Archivos, Bibliotecas y Museos*, 1931.

García Soriano, Justo. "Damián Salucio del Poyo." *Boletín de la Real Academia Española* 13 (1926): 269-82, 474-506.

Gregg, Karl C. "A Brief Biography of Antonio Mira de Amescua." *Bulletin of the Comediantes* 26 (1974): 14-22.

Jiménez Rueda, Julio. *Juan Ruiz de Alarcón y su tiempo*. Mexico: Porrúa, 1939.

Kincaid, William A. "The Life and Works of Luis de Belmonte Bermúdez," *Revue Hispanique* 74 (1928): 1-240.

Menéndez Onrubia, Carmen. "Hacia la biografía de un iluminado judío: Felipe Godínez (1585-1659)." *Segismundo* 13 (1977): 89-130.

Parker, Jack H., Juan Pérez de Montalván. New York: Twayne, 1975.

Parr, James A., ed. *Critical Essays on the Life and Work of Juan Ruiz de Alarcón*. Madrid: Dos Continentes, 1972.

Poesse, Walter. *Juan Ruiz de Alarcón*. New York: Twayne, 1972.

Profeti, María G. *Montalbán*. Pisa: Pisa U.P., 1970.

Pujol, Emilio. *Tárrega: ensayo biográfico*. Valencia, 1978.

BIBLIOGRAPHIES

Abreu Gómez, Ermilio. *Ruiz de Alarcón: Bibliografía crítica*. Mexico: Botas, 1939.

Hauer, Mary G. Luis Vélez de Guevara: *A Critical Bibliography*. Chapel Hill: Univ. of North Carolina Studies in Romance Languages and Literatures, 1975.

Poesse, Wlater. *Ensayo de una bibliografía de Juan Ruiz de Alarcón y Mendoza*. Valencia: Castalia, 1964.

Profeti, Maria Gracia. *Per una bibliografía di J. Pérez de Montalbán*. Verona: Universita degli studi di Padova, 1976.

TIRSO DE MOLINA

EDITIONS OF PLAYS

El burlador de Sevilla y convidado de piedra. Ed. Gerald E. Wade. New York: Scribner's, 1968.

Cigarrales de Toledo. Madrid: Espasa-Calpe, 1968.

Comedias escogidas de Fray Gabriel Téllez. Ed. Juan E. Hartzenbusch. In *BAE*, vol. 5. Madrid: Rivadeneyra, 1848.

Comedias de Tirso de Molina. Ed. Emilio Cotarelo y Mori. In *NBAE*, vols. 4 and 9. Madrid: Bailly-Baillière, 1906-7.

El condenado por desconfiado. Ed Daniel Rogers. Toronto: Pergamon, 1974.

Don Gil de las calzas verdes. Ed Ricardo Doménech. Madrid: Taurus, 1969.

Obras. Ed María del Pilar Palomo. In *BAE*, vols. 236-39, 242, 243. Madrid: Ediciones Atlas, 1970-71.

Obras dramáticas completas. Ed. Blanca de los Ríos. 3 vols. Madrid: Aguilar, 1946, 1952, 1959.

Villana de Vallecas. Ed. Jean Le Martinel and Gilbert Zonana. Paris: Ediciones Hispano-Americanas, 1964.

BIOGRAPHIES

Castro, Américo. *Tirso de Molina*. Madrid: Espasa-Calpe, 1932.

Muñoz Peña, Pedro. *El teatro del maestro Tirso de Molina*. Valladolid: Hijos de Rodríguez, 1889.

Penedo Rey, Fray Manuel, ed. *Historia general de la Orden de Nuestra Señora de las Mercedes*. 2 vols. Madrid: Provincia de la Merced de Castilla, Colección *Revista Estudios*. 1973-74.

Sanz y Díaz, José. *Tirso de Molina*. Madrid: Compañía Bibliográfica Española, 1964.
Vossler, Karl. *Lecciones sobre Tirso de Molina*. Madrid: Taurus, 1965.
Wilson, Margaret. *Tirso de Molina*. Boston: Twayne, 1977.

BIBLIOGRAPHIES
Hesse, Everett W. "Catálogo Bibliográfico de Tirso de Molina (1648-1948), incluyendo una sección sobre la influencia del tema de Don Juan," *Estudios* 5 (1949): 781-889.
Williamsen, Vern G., et al. *An Annotated Analytical Bibliography of Tirso de Molina Studies, 1627-1977*. Columbia: Univ. of Missouri Press, 1979.

CALDERÓN DE LA BARCA, PEDRO

EDITIONS OF PLAYS
Calderón de la Barca: Autos sacramentales. Ed. Angel Valbuena Prat. 2 vols. Clásicos Castellanos. Madrid: Espasa-Calpe, 1967.
Celos aun del aire matan. Ed. Matthew D.Stroud. San Antonio: Trinity Univ. Press, 1981.
Comedias. A facsimile edition. 19 vols. Ed. Don W. Cruikshank and J.E. Varey. London: Gregg International, 1973.
Las comedias de D. Pedro Calderón de la Barca. 4 vols. Ed. Juan Jorge Keil. Leipzig: Ernest Fleischer, 1827-30.
Comedias de don Pedro Calderón de la Barca. 4 vols. Ed. Juan E. Hartzen-busch. In *BAE*, vols. 7, 9, 12, 14. Madrid: Rivadeneyra, 1849-52.
Eight Dramas of Calderón. Trans. Edward Fitzgerald. London: Macmillan, 1906.
Four Plays. Trans. Edwin Honig. New York: Hill and Wang, 1961.
Four Comedies. Trans. Kenneth Muir. Lexington: Univ. Press of Kentucky, 1980.
El gran duque de Gandía. Ed. Václav Cerný. Prague: L'Académie Tchécoslo-vaque des Sciences, 1963.
El médico de su honra. Ed. Cyril A. Jones. Oxford: Clarendon Press, 1961.
Obras completas de Calderón de la Barca. Vol. 1: *Dramas*. Ed. Luis Astrana Marín. Madrid: Aguilar, 1932. 5th ed. Ed. A. Valbuena Briones, 1966. Vol. II: *Comedias*. Ed. Angel Valbuena Briones. Madrid: Aguilar, 1956. Vol. 3: *Autos Sacramentales*. Ed. Angel Valbuena Prat. Madrid: Aguilar, 1952.
Six Plays. Trans. Denis Florence Mac-Carthy. New York: Las Americas, 1961.
Three Plays by Calderón. Ed. George Tyler Northup. New York: D.C. Heath, 1926.
La vida es sueño. Ed. Everett W. Hesse. New York: Scribner's, 1961.

BIOGRAPHIES

Cotarelo y Mori, Emilio. *Ensayo sobre la vida y obras de Calderón*. Madrid: Tip. de la *Revista de Archivos, Bibliotecas y Museos*, 1924.

Frutos Cortés, Eugenio. *Calderón de la Barca*. Madrid: Labor, 1949.

Menéndez y Pelayo, Marcelino. *Calderón y su teatro*. Madrid: Tip. de la *Revista de Archivos, Bibliotecas y Museos*, 1910.

Valbuena Prat, Angel. *Calderón, su personalidad, su arte dramático, su estilo y sus obras*. Barcelona: Juventud, 1941.

BIBLIOGRAPHIES

Parker, Jack H., and Arthur M. Fox, eds. *Calderón de la Barca Studies, 1951-69: A Critical Survey and Annotated Bibliography*. Toronto: Univ. of Toronto Press, 1971.

Reichenberg, Kurt, and Roswitha Reichenberg. *Bibliographisches Handbuch der Calderón-Forschung: (Manual bibliográfico calderoniano)*. Kassel: Thiele and Schwartz, 1979.

THE CALDERONIAN CYCLE

EDITIONS OF WORKS

Bancas Candamo, Francisco. *Autos sacramentales de Bances Candamo*. Ed. José Pérez Filiú. Madrid: C.S.I.C., 1975.

––––––. *Theatro de los theatros de los passados y presentes siglos*. Ed. Duncan Moir. London: Támesis, 1970.

Cubillo de Aragón, Alvaro. *Alvaro Cubillo de Aragón*. In Clásicos Olvidados, vol. 3. Ed. Angel Valbuena Prat. Madrid: Blass, 1928.

Rojas Zorrilla, Francisco. *Obras*. Ed. Raymond R. MacCurdy. In Clásicos Castellanos. Madrid: Espasa-Calpe, 1961.

Rosete Niño, Pedro. *Comedia famosa de Píramo y Tisbe*. Ed. Pedro Correa Rodríguez. Pamplona: Universidad, 1977.

Vélez de Guevara, Juan. *Los celos hacen estrellas*. Ed. John E. Varey and N.D. Shergold. London: Támesis, 1970.

BIOGRAPHIES

"Dramáticos españoles del siglo XVII: Don Antonio Coello y Ochoa." Ed. Emilio Cotarelo y Mori. *Boletín de la Real Academia Española* 5 (1918): 550-600.

Mathías, Julio. *Un dramaturgo del siglo XVII: Francisco de Leiva*. Madrid: Nacional, 1970.

BIBLIOGRAPHY

MacCurdy, Raymond R. *Francisco de Rojas Zorrilla: bibliografía crítica. Cuadernos Bibliográficos* 18. Madrid: C.S.I.C., 1965.

Selected Bibliography 227

GENERAL HISTORICAL STUDIES

Bleiberg, Germán, and Julián Marías, eds. *Diccionario de literatura española*. Madrid: *Revista de Occidente*, 1964.
Brenan, Gerald. *The Literature of the Spanish People*. Cambridge: Cambridge Univ. Press, 1951.
Cañete, Manuel. *Teatro español del siglo XVI*. Madrid: M. Tello, 1885.
Chambers, Edmund K. *The Mediaeval Stage*. London: Oxford Univ. Press, 1903.
Cohen, Gustave. *Études d'Histoire de Théâtre en France au Moyen-Age et à la Renaissance*. 7th ed. Paris: Gallimard, 1956.
Crawford, James P. Wickersham. *Spanish Drama before Lope de Vega*. 3rd ed. Philadelphia: Univ. of Pennsylvania Press, 1967.
———. *The Spanish Pastoral Drama*. Philadelphia: Univ. of Pennsylvania Department of Romanic Languages, 1915.
Díaz de Escovar, Narciso, and Francisco de P. Lasso de la Vega. *Historia del teatro español*. Barcelona: Montaner y Simón, 1924.
Díaz-Plaja, Guillermo, ed. *Historia general de las literaturas hispánicas*. Vol. 3. Barcelona: Barna, 1953.
Donovan, Richard B. *The Liturgical Drama in Medieval Spain*. Toronto: Pontifical Institute of Medieval Studies, 1958.
Grant, W. Leonard. *Neo-Latin Literature and the Pastoral*. Chapel Hill: Univ. of North Carolina Press, 1965.
Hardison, O.B., Jr., *Christian Rite and Christian Drama in the Middle Ages*. Baltimore: Johns Hopkins Press, 1965.
Hathaway, Robert L. *Love in the Early Spanish Theatre*. Madrid: Plaza Mayor, 1975.
Hermenegildo, Alfredo. *La tragedia en el renacimiento español*. Barcelona: Planeta, 1973.
———. *Los trágicos españoles del siglo XVI*. Madrid: Fundación Universitaria Española, 1961.
Jack, Wickersham Shaffer. "The Early *Entremés* in Spain: The Rise of a Dramatic Form." Ph.D. diss., Univ. of Pennsylvania, 1923.
Lázaro Carreter, Fernando. *Teatro medieval*. Madrid: Castalia, 1965.
Leavitt, Sturgis E. *An Introduction to Golden Age Drama in Spain*. Madrid: Castalia, 1971.
López Morales, Humberto. *Tradición y creación en los orígenes del teatro castellano*. Madrid: Ediciones Alcalá, 1968.
Moratín, Leandro Fernández de. "Orígenes del teatro español." *Obras de Leandro Fernández de Moratín*. In *BAE*, 2nd ed., 2: 145-306. Madrid: Rivadeneyra, 1848.
Pfandl, Ludwig. *Historia de la literatura española en la edad de oro*. Trans. Jorge Rubió Balaguer. Barcelona: Gustavo Gili, 1952.

Schack, Adolf Friedrich von. *Historia de la literatura y del arte dramático en España*. Trans. Eduardo de Mier. Madrid: M. Tello, 1885-1887. Vols. 1-5.

Shergold, Norman D. *A History of the Spanish Stage from Medieval Times until the End of the Seventeenth Century*. Oxford: Clarendon Press, 1967.

Spingarn, Joel Elías. *A History of Literary Criticism in the Renaissance*. 2nd ed. New York: Columbia Univ. Press, 1908.

Stern, Charlotte. "The Early Spanish Drama: From Medieval Ritual to Renaissance Art." *Renaissance Drama*, n.s. 6 (1973): 177-201.

Valbuena Prat, Angel. *Historia de la literatura española*. 3 vols. Barcelona: Gustavo Gili, 1964.

_____. *Historia del teatro español*. Barcelona: Noguer, 1956.

_____. *Literatura dramática española*. Barcelona: Labor, 1930.

Varey, John E., and N.D. Shergold. *Teatros y comedias en Madrid, 1600-99*. 4 vols. London: Támesis, 1971-79.

Wardropper, Bruce W. *Introducción al teatro religioso del Siglo de Oro: La evolución del auto sacramental, 1500-1648*. Madrid: *Revista de Occidente*, 1953.

Wilson, Edward M., and Duncan Moir. *A Literary History of Spain: The Golden Age of Drama, 1492-1700*. New York: Barnes and Noble, 1971.

Wilson, Margaret. *Spanish Drama of the Golden Age*. Oxford: Pergamon Press, 1969.

Young, Karl. *The Drama of the Medieval Church*. 2 vols. Oxford: Clarendon Press, 1933.

GENERAL BIBLIOGRAPHIES

Barrera y Leirado, Cayetano Alberto de la. *Catálogo bibliográfico del teatro antiguo español, desde sus orígenes hasta mediados del siglo XVIII*. Madrid: Rivadeneyra, 1860. Facsimile editions, Madrid: Gredos, 1969; London: Támesis, 1969.

Cotarelo y Mori, Emilio. *Bibliografía de las controversias sobre la solicitud del teatro en España*. Madrid: Tip. de la *Revista de Archivos, Bibliotecas y Museos*, 1904.

McCready, Warren T. *Bibliografía temática de estudios sobre el teatro español antiguo*. Toronto: Univ. of Toronto Press, 1966.

Madrigal, José A. *Bibliografía sobre el pundonor: Teatro del Siglo de Oro*. Miami: Ediciones Universal, 1977.

Sumner, Gordon Heyward. "Una bibliografía anotada de las comedias de santos del siglo diez y siete." Ph.D. diss. Florida State Univ., 1979.

Williamsen, Vern G., and John J. Reynolds. "Bibliography of Publications on the *Comedia*." *Bulletin of the Comediantes*, Yearly Fall issues.

Index